After the Caliphate

For my girls, Fiona and Maya

After the Caliphate

The Islamic State and the Future of the Terrorist Diaspora

Colin P. Clarke

polity

First published in 2019 by Polity Press
Reprinted 2010 (twice)

Polity Press
65 Bridge Street
Cambridge CB2 1UR, UK

Polity Press
101 Station Landing
Suite 300
Medford, MA 02155, USA

ISBN-13: 978-1-5095-3387-9
ISBN-13: 978-1-5095-3388-6 (pb)

A catalogue record for this book is available from the British Library.

Library of Congress Cataloging-in-Publication Data
Names: Clarke, Colin P., author.
Title: After the Caliphate : the Islamic State & the future of the terrorist
  diaspora / Colin P. Clarke.
Description: Medford, MA : Polity Press, [2019] | Includes bibliographical
  references and index.
Identifiers: LCCN 2018044631 (print) | LCCN 2018046064 (ebook) | ISBN
  9781509533893 (Epub) | ISBN 9781509533879 (hardback) | ISBN 9781509533886
  (pbk.)
Subjects: LCSH: IS (Organization) | Terrorism--Religious aspects--Islam. |
  Terrorism--Prevention.
Classification: LCC HV6433.I722 (ebook) | LCC HV6433.I722 C624 2019 (print) |
  DDC 363.325--dc23
LC record available at https://lccn.loc.gov/2018044631

Typeset in 10 on 16.5 Utopia Std by
Servis Filmsetting Ltd, Stockport, Cheshire
Printed and bound in the United States by LSC Communications

For further information on Polity, visit our website: politybooks.com

Contents

Acknowledgments

I am grateful to many people for contributing to this study and for their enduring support, without which this effort would not have been possible. I owe so much to the University of Pittsburgh's Graduate School of Public and International Affairs (GSPIA), especially to Phil Williams, who is both a mentor and a friend. At the RAND Corporation, I would like to thank my friends and colleagues Chad Serena, Christopher Paul, Patrick Johnston, Brian Michael Jenkins, Seth Jones, Andy Liepman, and Howard Shatz, among others, for intellectually stimulating conversations over the years. Also, special thanks are due to Valerie Nelson, who helped me with the dozens of op-eds that originally motivated me to write this book. Her help, but more importantly her sense of humor and wit, were indispensable to me while I was writing. At Carnegie Mellon University, I thank Kiron Skinner and my wonderful colleagues, as well as my students, with whom I've spent countless hours speaking about the subjects covered in this book.

At Polity, I would like to offer the sincerest thanks to Louise Knight, Nekane Tanaka Galdos, and their team. Polity was such a well-organized group and Louise's sense of humor helped push me through. Her patience, encouragement, and kindness brightened many of my days.

I would like to acknowledge the many named and unnamed scholars and practitioners who took time away from their busy schedules to avail me of their expertise and knowledge in this area, whether in interviews or in conversations about this subject which helped shape my thinking, including Graeme Wood, Daniel Byman, John Horgan, Bruce Hoffman, J. M. Berger, Haroro Ingram, Aaron Zelin, Daveed Gartenstein-Ross, Michael Kenney, Martha Crenshaw, Elisabeth Kendall, Fred Wehrey, Mia Bloom, Derek Henry Flood, Zack Gold, Zachary Abuza, Jason Warner, Craig Whiteside, Amir Jadoon, Hassan Hassan, Amar Amarasingam, Charlie Winter, Rukmini Callimachi, Brian Fishman, Assaf Moghadam, Tom Joscelyn, Robin Simcox, Pieter Van Ostaeyen, Louis Klareves, Jean-Marc Oppenheim, Mary Beth Altier, and Sam Mullins.

I am so thankful to Ali Soufan and my colleagues at The Soufan Center in New York City. I read about Ali and his heroism when I was a graduate student and have always admired him, even before I knew him. Especially given the topic discussed in this book, which can be dark at times, I think this world needs more heroes, and Ali is one of mine. Moreover, sometimes people you idolize from afar let you down once you meet them in person, but not Ali. For all of his success, he's an even better person, so it's surreal that I now have the opportunity to work alongside him.

Many thanks to Alastair Reed, Renske van der Veer, Bart Schuurman, Christophe Paulussen, Jos Kosters, and my colleagues at The International Centre for Counter-Terrorism – The Hague (ICCT); Michael Noonan and my colleagues at the Foreign Policy Research Institute (FPRI) in Philadelphia; and Seamus Hughes and his team at the Program on Extremism at George Washington University.

Most importantly, I would like to thank my family and friends, who mean everything to me. I've been blessed to have a tight-knit group of friends and we've done an admirable job of keeping in touch over the many years. It's amazing to watch how our lives have changed as we each raise families of our own. None of this would be possible without my parents, Phil and Maureen, who instilled in me the value of hard work, not by spelling it out explicitly, but by quietly setting the example. I love you guys. Thanks go to my brother Ryan and my sister Katie, who are my siblings but, more importantly, my friends. Lastly, I would like to thank my wife Colleen, an amazing partner and mother and the rock of our family. Her smile alone is enough to get me through my toughest days. Without her help, this book would certainly not have been possible.

Any and all mistakes contained here within are the sole responsibility of the author.

Foreword

Ali H. Soufan

Almost 18 years ago, the United States was attacked by al-Qaeda, a Salafi-jihadist terrorist organization of around 400 members, based primarily in Afghanistan and led by Osama bin Laden. The United States responded swiftly, and, along with its allies and partners, defeated that version of al-Qaeda. Today, however, a new jihadist threat has emerged around the world. It consists of many different organizations that have successfully embedded themselves in local conflicts, making them incredibly difficult to target.

In *After the Caliphate*, terrorism scholar Colin P. Clarke traces the evolution of the global jihadist movement from its earliest days all the way up to and through the collapse of the caliphate. In my career as an FBI Special Agent, I experienced firsthand the depth of commitment of some of al-Qaeda's most committed ideologues. Clarke's book goes a long way toward capturing the essence of what made al-Qaeda, and then the Islamic State (IS), so unique – an unwavering commitment to reinstating the rule of the caliphate through any means necessary. Over time, the leadership of the global jihadist movement has changed hands, from Osama bin Laden to Abu Musab al-Zarqawi to Abu Bakr al-Baghdadi. What will the future of the movement look like? Will Hamza bin Laden, Osama's son, re-emerge to lead al-Qaeda in its next chapter as the group seeks to reclaim the leadership of aspiring jihadists from Europe to the Middle East and beyond? Or will the movement splinter and fracture, leading to a decentralized and dispersed cluster of groups and lone actors tenuously linked by ideology and common cause?

During his bloody reign, the Jordanian al-Zarqawi planted the seeds for the rise of IS, exporting his draconian vision throughout the broader region. Other jihadist ideologues, including Abu Musab al-Suri, contributed significantly to the call to establish a caliphate, something al-Qaeda was never able to achieve but that IS ultimately did. Bloodshed plays into the jihadis' overall game-plan, which has always been about exploiting chaos and weaponizing sectarianism. There is a common factor linking the franchise groups and affiliates of both IS and al-Qaeda. That factor is the narrative of bin Ladenism. We must dedicate ourselves to destroying that narrative and only when we do so will we finally defeat them. But the threat is far from static and has in fact mutated from an organization that attacked the United States on September 11, 2001 into what it is today – a dystopian ideology. Bullets don't kill narratives, messages, thoughts, or beliefs. What we need is a new strategy that moves away from the myopic obsession with tactical gains and ad-hoc counterterrorism responses. Indeed, it is the legacy of our tactic-driven response to 9/11 that has facilitated the growth of bin Ladenism far beyond what Osama bin Laden could have ever imagined.

The United States in particular, and the West in general, have failed to adequately understand the worldview and belief system underpinning the global jihadist movement. In the words of Olivier Roy, a world-renowned scholar of Islam, the threat posed by IS is not about the radicalization of Islam, but, rather, about the Islamization of radicalism. Groups like al-Qaeda and IS have successfully mobilized the grievances of Muslims, especially young Muslim men, who are seeking to take control of their own destinies to provide meaning to what they see as an otherwise meaningless existence, characterized by mediocrity, isolation, tedium, and a perception of discrimination and an overall lack of opportunities to succeed in mainstream society. The global jihadist movement has filled this void by propagating a narrative that highlights the action, excitement, and camaraderie of joining the caliphate. IS excelled at tailoring its messages to myriad demographics and lowering the barriers to entry for those not well steeped in Islamic theology, culture, or practice.

Following the events of the Arab Spring, bin Laden ordered al-Qaeda to begin focusing more on issues directly related to the grassroots and local levels. The Iraq war was a primary motivation for many jihadists nearly a decade prior, when the US invasion of Iraq helped breathe new life into the ideology and narrative espoused by al-Qaeda. But the Arab Spring refocused the movement, or at least al-Qaeda, on rebuilding its network and planting the seed for future generations. Bruce Hoffman has called this deliberate strategy "quietly and patiently rebuilding." The global jihadist movement endures by taking advantage of chaos in failed states and ungoverned territories. At a more granular level, al-Qaeda has used the past few years to refocus its effort, allowing IS to suffer the brunt of the West's counterterrorism efforts while its members ingratiate themselves in parochial conflicts in Yemen, Mali, and the Philippines.

What primarily brings together jihadists in the contemporary era is no longer the shared experience of training camps, although that is one factor, but rather something far more tangible – a commitment to the jihadist narrative and the ideas and beliefs that drive the recruitment of new members and the regeneration of this global network of terrorists. If we ever hope to bring an end to the so-called Global War on Terror, it is essential to find political solutions to the conflicts in weak states where jihadist groups seek refuge and safe haven. Only by diminishing the environment that fuels radicalism and terrorism can the international community begin to make sustainable and lasting progress. This means looking beyond purely military solutions and working to ensure that those regions most beset by bin Ladenism have a vested interest in working together toward an improved future.

The cancer of bin Ladenism has metastasized across the Middle East and North Africa and beyond. The split between IS and al-Qaeda was part ideological, but also a difference between and among personalities. IS has changed from a terrorist group to a proto-state and is now reverting back to a clandestine guerrilla organization focused on subversion and the selective application of violence. Now that the caliphate has been crushed, Clarke's book is critical in helping us understand what might happen next. From the deserts of North Africa to the jungles of Southeast Asia, *After the Caliphate* is a groundbreaking work of scholarship that fills a critical void in the contemporary literature on terrorism studies and should prove a useful guide to scholars and practitioners alike.

Introduction

"Soon after buying her, the fighter brought the teenage girl a round box containing four strips of pills, one of them colored red."[1] This is a line from a story by Rukmini Callimachi of *The New York Times* from March 12, 2016. Re-read that line again, and let it sink in. The sentence describes a jihadist terrorist from the Islamic State (IS) who purchased a teenage girl, from the Yazidi religious minority in Iraq, at the equivalent of a slave auction and was forcing her to consume birth-control pills to ensure that, no matter how many times he savagely raped her, his captive would not become pregnant. This situation played itself out throughout parts of territory in Iraq and Syria under the control of IS, which declared itself a caliphate and set out to build what terrorism expert Martha Crenshaw calls a "counter-state" using any and all means necessary, including rape, murder, and torture.[2]

The brutality was not merely limited to sexual slavery. There were also beheadings and crucifixions. Some IS captives were burned alive, while others were locked in a cage and submerged in water until they drowned. Many of these actions were recorded and posted online by the group itself, to promote a level of anomic violence that would come to shape and in many ways define its brand. Just a few years ago, horrified onlookers must have wondered how we arrived at a place where a terrorist organization could conquer and control territory, systematically eliminate its rivals, and intimidate the international community from action to halt this blatant display of barbarism.

By mid-2018, the physical caliphate had all but been destroyed, its fighters killed, captured, and chased from their erstwhile strongholds in Raqqa and Mosul. But, as Graeme Wood points out, the caliphate was more than just a territory or a proto-state – it was, and indeed still is, "a phenomenon in both physical and mental space."[3] IS as an idea, as an ideology, and as a worldview is far from over. The group will eventually seek to relocate to another country and establish new franchise and affiliate groups. The purpose of this book is to analyze what happens next with the Islamic State and to determine whether or not, and to what extent, it will manage to adapt and regroup after the physical fall of the caliphate. What form will its relationship with al-Qaeda take? How might its tactics and strategy change in the future? This book will attempt to answer these questions and more, while taking stock of IS – its roots, its evolution, and its monumental setbacks – to provide some insights into what the road ahead could look like.

In many respects, the establishment of the caliphate was an anomaly. Historically, the global jihadist movement has been largely decentralized, consistently inconsistent in its ability to marshal the resources and groundswell of support necessary to achieve anything close to what IS did when it established the caliphate with a headquarters in Raqqa. From bin Laden to Khalid Sheikh Mohammed, the global jihadist movement has had its share of charismatic personalities. But for the past four decades, it rarely constituted anything close to a monolithic movement operating with a common purpose and core agenda.

The future of the movement is therefore likely to resemble its past – with peripatetic and divided groups of militants dispersing to new battlefields, from North Africa to Southeast Asia, where they will join existing civil wars, establish safe havens and sanctuaries, and seek ways of conducting spectacular attacks in the West that inspire new followers and motivate existing supporters. In this fragmented and atomized form, IS could become even more dangerous and challenging for counterterrorism forces, as its splinter groups threaten renewed and heightened violence throughout the globe. Even if foreign fighters return home in much smaller numbers than initially expected, the next five-year period could very well be characterized by a spike in attacks.

At its peak from 2014 to 2016, the caliphate briefly represented the apex of the global jihadist movement – the closest thing it has ever had to a lasting presence. But with the caliphate in ruins, it will revert to decentralized and dispersed clusters of groups and lone individuals or self-starter groups, tenuously linked by ideology and common cause, although, as history has shown, over time parochial interests tend to trump the movement's globally focused veneer.[4] In order to understand how we got to where we are today and what lies ahead, it is critical to look back to the roots of IS – both how and what it learned from its predecessors, and how it differs from other milieus within the global jihadist universe.

The opening chapter takes us from the beginnings of the global Salafi-jihadist movement following the Soviet invasion of Afghanistan in 1979 and traces its evolution through the next three decades, leading up to the events of September 11, 2001. Initially dubbed the "Arab Afghans," fighters from the Middle East, North Africa, and elsewhere flocked to Afghanistan to help repel the Soviet Red Army following Moscow's hasty invasion. These militants moved on following the Afghan conflict to form the core of al-Qaeda, growing the organization in Sudan before branching out to fight in places like Somalia, Bosnia, Algeria, and Chechnya during the 1990s. Differences over objectives and ideology led to numerous splits within the movement, as fighters

3

dispersed from al-Qaeda to join existing militant groups throughout the globe, although due to the trappings of globalization, many
were able to remain linked to the core organization from perches in
Southeast Asia, Europe, and elsewhere.

After the US invasion of Afghanistan in 2001 and an unrelenting drone campaign, al-Qaeda scattered and established franchise
operations in Yemen (al-Qaeda in the Arabian Peninsula, AQAP),
North Africa (al-Qaeda in the Islamic Maghreb, AQIM), and Iraq
(al-Qaeda in Iraq, AQI), while also maintaining ties with groups in
parts of Africa (al-Shabaab) and Asia (Abu Sayyaf Group and Jemmah
Islamiyah). Core al-Qaeda in Afghanistan and Pakistan was largely
decimated, but several of the franchise groups flourished during this
period, including AQAP and AQI, the latter of which was led by the
spiritual godfather of IS, the Jordanian Abu Musab al-Zarqawi. Over
time, AQI would morph into the Islamic State in Iraq (ISI) in the mid-
2000s, a name which the group would keep until early 2013 when it
changed officially to IS, following its falling-out with al-Qaeda. The
detailed history of the movement described in this first chapter is
critical because one potential future alternative in the post-caliphate
environment is a return to the franchising model that al-Qaeda pioneered following the onslaught against its core organization based in
South Asia.

The book then moves to explore the genesis of the Islamic State and
the structural factors and variables that contributed to its rise, including rampant sectarianism in Iraq and the political vacuum caused by
the Syrian civil war. A close look at IS infrastructure, decision-making
apparatus, and its approach to building the caliphate shows how
each informed the group's approach to conquering new territory and
implementing the pillars of a sovereign state, while also developing a
unique ability to recruit foreign fighters. This analysis is accompanied

by a strategic snapshot of IS's ideology, its long-term objectives, and a discussion of the group's capacity to plan and conduct attacks (operational capabilities) and to maintain itself as a cohesive entity (organizational capabilities). In particular, it is these organizational capabilities which will play a substantial role in determining the future of the organization, helping it transition smoothly from a territorially based insurgent organization to an underground, clandestine terrorist group. Its network-like qualities, affiliate franchise groups, and social media expertise contribute to its protean structure and ability to survive.

The Islamic State is a pioneering terrorist group in several ways, from its ability to raise and spend money to its multi-tiered approach to conducting terrorist attacks (inspired vs. directed). IS's use of social media and encryption to direct terrorist attacks overseas sets it apart from any terrorist groups of the past. As evidenced by the Paris November 2015 attacks and the Brussels March 2016 attacks, at its peak, IS sustained the ability to strike into the heart of Europe. The second chapter examines various aspects of the group's financing and its tactics, including how IS operates on the battlefield, from vehicle-borne improvised explosive devices (VBIEDs) to ambushes and hit-and-run attacks. This extends to IS's exhortation for its followers to conduct attacks in the West, including a synopsis of so-called vehicular terrorism, a tactic pioneered by IS that has emerged as a new trend in terrorism directed against the West.

Chapter 3 offers a rigorous evaluation of the Islamic State's future, based – in part – on the current trends we are witnessing. This includes a deeper discussion of the so-called free-agent jihadists or roving militants who will seek to travel to active conflict zones to link up with existing terrorist and insurgent groups, acting as a force multiplier. For most of its surviving fighters, the war is not over – many of these militants will almost certainly move on to new battlefields to continue waging jihad. As *New Yorker* columnist and Middle East expert Robin Wright recently commented, "hundreds of Jihadis are believed to be searching for new battlefields or refuge in Muslim countries."[5] The mobilization of jihadists in Iraq and Syria dwarfs similar phenomena that helped define civil wars and insurgencies in Afghanistan, Bosnia, Algeria, and Chechnya. This is an especially ominous observation since the foreign fighter networks formed during those conflicts went on to form the core of al-Qaeda.

Wherever IS fighters fleeing Iraq and Syria congregate next, it will most probably be in a weak state plagued by persistent civil conflict, sectarian tensions, and an inability of the government to maintain a monopoly on the use of force within its borders. There are several potential candidates for the next IS headquarters, including North Africa (Libya, the Sinai Peninsula in Egypt), Central Asia (Afghanistan, the Caucasus), Southeast Asia (the Philippines, Indonesia), or destinations within the Middle East, possibly including Yemen. What these destinations have in common are weak security services, existing or recent sectarian conflict, and a population considered fertile for and receptive to the Islamic State's propaganda. Moreover, recent IS propaganda has demonstrated an interest in expanding beyond already-existing affiliates, to include insinuating its fighters and garnering new recruits in countries like Myanmar, India, and the Democratic Republic of Congo (DRC).

The penultimate chapter focuses on "core IS" in Iraq and Syria and how it will seek to transition from an insurgent organization to a terrorist group. Three years after IS captured major cities and towns throughout Iraq and Syria, the anti-IS coalition has made significant progress in countering the group and retaking territory. Nevertheless, predictions of the group's ultimate demise are premature. Rather than an end to the group, what we are witnessing is more accurately a transition from an insurgent organization with a fixed headquarters to a clandestine terrorist network dispersed throughout the region and globe. The differences matter, as counterterrorism and counterinsurgency are two completely different strategies. Insurgent organizations hold and seize territory, can exercise sovereignty over a population, operate in the open as armed units, and can engage in mass mobilization, while terrorists conduct attacks with members operating in small cells – they rarely hold territory, and if they do it tends to be for a short period of time. At the time of this writing, IS leadership is more fractured, flimsy, and sporadic than at any point to date, but its intelligence service, the Emni, remains intact and is working to exploit missteps by the Islamic State's adversaries, including the Kurds, the Assad regime, and the Iraqi government, especially to the extent that these actors reinforce already-existing sectarian issues in the region.

One major inflection point is IS's ongoing competition with al-Qaeda and whether this will result in IS seeking rapprochement with the latter group or, on the contrary, intensifying its current rivalry as a way to differentiate itself and "outbid" its erstwhile collaborator. IS and al-Qaeda are competing for influence throughout the globe: in Afghanistan, Yemen, Libya, Saudi Arabia, Tunisia, Mali, Sinai, South and Southeast Asia, Syria/Iraq, Iran, the Caucasus, and Africa. As IS fighters disperse following the collapse of the caliphate, some have speculated that these fighters will reinforce existing *wilayats*, or provinces, but the collapse could have a deleterious effect upon the IS brand and thus lead to an ascendant al-Qaeda in places we might expect to see IS reinforced. Current and aspiring jihadists may view the al-Qaeda–IS relationship and competition through a zero-sum lens; the two groups "play off each other's successes and failures."[6] In some theatres, the two groups may engage in a process of outbidding, ramping up violence in the near term to prove dedication and capability. The question of "preference divergence," wherein franchises face the dilemma of investing in local interests versus diverting resources toward global objectives, now seems more relevant than at any previous point in the conflict.

What is being done to counter IS and its returnees, including the hardcore fighters and mercenaries who will remain in the region, is the focus of the final chapter. This includes finances, logistics, and support for existing militant structures throughout the region and beyond. What are the policy implications of dealing with returning foreign fighters? What can and should states do to help deal with this immense challenge? Finally, how will the counterterrorism strategy pursued by the West affect the various trajectories of the splintered IS elements?

Answering these and other questions, this chapter engages with the myriad public policy issues concomitant with returnees and the decision of how best to reintegrate these people into society, or whether to deal with them in a more punitive manner. Entire families that at one time willingly departed Europe to join the Islamic State are now trickling back home, posing significant challenges to European authorities. Not all returnees should be viewed the same, as some will be willing to reintegrate, others will be reluctant to, and still others may be incapable of doing so, traumatized by the horrors of what they witnessed (and in some cases participated in) during the conflicts in Iraq and Syria.

While causing a terrorist organization to break apart might seem like a positive outcome – indeed, this is one of the primary objectives of most counterterrorism campaigns – it often causes the emergence of new, and in some cases more violent, splinter organizations (indeed, we could already be witnessing this in parts of the Sinai Peninsula in

Egypt). Dismantling and destroying IS and similar organizations are worthy strategic goals, but policymakers must also be prepared to limit the effectiveness of splinter groups as they emerge in the aftermath of a successful campaign against the parent group. The coalition fighting IS must continue to pursue a multipronged strategy. On the one hand, splinter cells must be aggressively targeted through capture-and-kill operations to prevent further metastasizing. On the other, this approach cannot be pursued in isolation; rather, it must be coupled with efforts to promote good governance and reduce corruption in fragile states while building the partner capacity of security forces in the most affected countries.

Countering IS has become a global priority. Yet there still exists nothing close to an international consensus on what must be done to prevent a future mobilization of jihadists motivated by a desire to establish a caliphate by any and all means necessary, with death and destruction paramount to this quest. The Global Coalition to Defeat ISIS consisted of five specific lines of effort, including: providing military support to partners fighting IS; impeding the worldwide flow of foreign fighters; stopping the financing and funding of its organization; addressing humanitarian crises in the region; and exposing the true and odious nature of this barbaric group determined to enslave its enemies and conquer its neighbors. The international community has vowed "never again," but can it keep that pledge? What makes this time different? This book offers some possible responses to the threat posed by a resurgent, post-caliphate IS. But first, let's go back to the beginning – to 1979 – and the events that triggered the modern era of the global jihadist movement and everything it epitomizes.

1

The Long Road to the Caliphate

Osama bin Laden was killed on May 2, 2011, following a United States Special Operations Forces raid on his compound in Abbottabad, Pakistan. His death marked a major turning point in the US-led Global War on Terror, closing a chapter that had begun nearly a decade earlier on September 11, 2001. But the significance of bin Laden to the global jihadist movement goes back much further, and can be traced back to Afghanistan in late 1979, following the Soviet invasion of that country and the subsequent defense of the territory by Afghans and foreign fighters from throughout the Islamic world.[1] The earliest known attempt to organize foreign fighters, many of them from Arab countries, was through the establishment of al-Qaeda,[2] or "the Base," at a meeting in Peshawar, Pakistan, in 1988. Al-Qaeda itself was the outgrowth of an organization called Maktab al-Khidamat (MAK), established by a Palestinian named Abdullah Azzam.

The organization's early efforts focused on recruiting Arab fighters to join the resistance in Afghanistan, where the so-called mujahedin, or holy warriors, were fighting to expel Soviet troops from the country.[3] At this point in al-Qaeda's nascent history, the goal of establishing a caliphate was more of an abstraction than anything. The immediate necessity was merely embryonic survival. Early members of MAK, which was initially founded in 1984, included Azzam, bin Laden, and the Algerian Abdullah Anas. In the mid-1980s, bin Laden met and joined forces with Ayman al-Zawahiri, the current leader of core al-Qaeda. Zawahiri eventually merged key members of his group, Egyptian Islamic Jihad (EIJ), with al Qaeda, once it emerged as its own entity in the late 1980s, at which point MAK had become more focused on humanitarian efforts rather than actual fighting.[4]

Al-Qaeda has continued to evolve over the years. Now entering its third decade, al-Qaeda is many things – terrorist organization, global jihadist network, brand and franchise group for Salafi-jihadists throughout the world. But beyond al-Qaeda, the global jihadist movement is a collection of groups and personalities – it is far from the unitary actor so often portrayed in the media. This trope actually plays into the hands of the jihadists, distorting the magnitude of the threat and making the movement seem omnipotent, when in reality it suffers from many of the same shortcomings, vulnerabilities, principal–agent and collective action challenges as other transnational non-state actors. The establishment of the caliphate has been a unifying, if not quixotic, rallying point for jihadists. But it's been more of a battle cry, or an ideal, than an actual realization. That is, until IS was able to establish one that spanned the deserts of Syria and major cities in Iraq.

To many, Osama bin Laden and al-Qaeda represented the threat posed by jihadists to the West. But as witnessed by the emergence of the IS, the threat is, and in fact always has been, much broader than al-Qaeda. So while the killing of bin Laden was both a symbolic and tactical achievement against al-Qaeda and its allies, from a strategic standpoint, the battle continues. Even in the immediate aftermath of bin Laden's death, few serious commentators believed that his demise in any way signaled the end of the global jihadist movement. Accordingly, remarking on the event, reputed terrorism expert Brian Michael Jenkins soberly noted, "the death of bin Laden does not end al-Qaeda's global terrorist campaign."[5] Nor did it foreshadow an end to the global jihadist movement that al-Qaeda helped to spawn.

Al-Queda has always been a central node – indeed, *the* central node – in the constellation of jihadist entities throughout the globe. But the movement is much bigger than one man, more complex than one organization. This book takes as its starting point the global jihadist movement as it coalesced during the Soviet–Afghan War, and the 1980s as its logical beginning. The movement as a whole remains the unit of analysis throughout this research. To even begin to understand what the global jihadist movement is, there are several critical questions this chapter will seek to answer:

- *What are the origins of the global jihadist movement and how has it evolved over time?*
- *What is the ideology underpinning and motivating this movement?*
- *What are the goals and objectives of the movement?*
- *What strategy is the movement pursuing to achieve its goals?*
- *How is the movement structured to execute this strategy?*

Evolution over Time

"The global jihadist movement" is a rather broad term encompassing groups, organizations, and individuals, as well as hinting at a specific worldview motivated by the ideology of Salafi-jihad, which advocates a raised awareness among Muslims to reclaim their faith and use violence, when necessary, to restore Islam to its proper status as a beacon of religious, political, military, economic, and cultural guidance.[6] There is no universally accepted definition of what constitutes the global jihadist movement or how to measure its evolution over time, which provides scholars with a real challenge in terms of analysis.

This all leads to the difficulty of attempting to study the movement as a singular and consistent unit of analysis. Even al-Qaeda, certainly a more discrete entity, poses "a common analytic problem" in terms of "defining just what the group is."[7] It is part of the reason why, even years after the 9/11 attacks, prominent terrorism scholars still openly posited the question, "what is the current Al Qaeda? An organization? A movement? An ideology?"[8] To ascertain a more fundamental understanding of al-Qaeda and the global jihadist movement it helped create, it might make sense to start with the death of its leader, an event that left millions worldwide hopeful that the scourge of Salafi-jihadist terrorism would die along with the man who was, for more than a decade, the world's most sought-after man.

Al-Qaeda, perhaps correctly, is frequently analyzed as the nucleus of the global jihadist movement, conceptualized as four distinct – though not mutually exclusive – dimensions: al-Qaeda Central; al-Qaeda Affiliates and Associates; al-Qaeda Locals; and the al-Qaeda Network. Al-Qaeda Central is essentially the core of the original al-Qaeda and is comprised of the group's initial leadership, including Ayman al-Zawahiri, and is based in Pakistan. Al-Qaeda Affiliates and Associates are made up of "formally established" terrorist groups that have worked closely with al-Qaeda over the years, including the Libyan Islamic Fighting Group (LIFG), the Islamic Movement of Uzbekistan (IMU), and Jemmah Islamiyah in Indonesia. Al-Qaeda Locals are "amorphous groups of Al Qaeda adherents" with "a previous connection of some kind" to al-Qaeda, no matter how tenuous. Finally, the al-Qaeda Network consists of homegrown Islamic radicals scattered throughout the globe with no connection whatsoever with al-Qaeda or any other terrorist group, but who are prepared to conduct an attack in solidarity with the ideology of Salafi-jihad.[9]

Daniel Byman's analysis largely overlaps with Hoffman's, but instead collapses the second and third categories together, which he labels as "formal Al Qaeda affiliates or other groups that have varied relationships with the core but cooperate at least to some extent."[10] But the most satisfying analysis of the global jihadist movement is by Seth Jones, who also largely agrees with both Hoffman and Byman, but who more clearly draws a distinction between "affiliated Al Qaeda groups" and "other Salafi-jihadist groups." The former are groups that became formal branches of al-Qaeda by having their emirs swear *bay'at* – loyalty – to core al-Qaeda's leaders, which is then either officially accepted or rejected.[11] At one time, al-Qaeda affiliates included al-Qaeda in the Arabian Peninsula (AQAP), al-Qaeda in the Islamic Maghreb (AQIM), al-Shabaab in Somalia, al-Qaeda in Iraq (AQI), and Jabhat al-Nusra (JN) in Syria. More recent developments regarding the latter two groups will be discussed in more detail in forthcoming chapters. Groups that are more appropriately labeled as "other Salafi-jihadist groups" include Ansar al-Sharia Libya, the East Turkestan Islamic Movement, and Imarat Kavkaz in the Caucasus.[12] Byman refers to similar groups, namely those that might receive training from a franchise group, as Ansar Dine in Mali did from AQIM, as "affiliates, once-removed," something akin to a jihadi distant cousin.[13]

Ideological Underpinnings

It would be wholly inaccurate to attempt to portray a monolithic ideology shared by the global jihadist movement. But, writ large, the ideology of Salafi-jihadism is the overarching banner under which most of the world's violent Sunni jihadists unite. This ideology is a specific strand of militant Sunni Islamism and can be defined as groups that stress the need to return to the "pure" Islam practiced by the Salaf, or pious ancestors, and those believing that violent jihad is a personal religious duty.[14] Many trace the origins of this line of thought back to Ibn Taymiyyah, an Islamic philosopher who advocated and participated in jihad against the Crusaders and the Mongols in the late thirteenth century.[15] Still others list the most prominent influences for modern-day jihadists as the Muslim Brotherhood, or Sayyid Qutb, an Egyptian Islamist whose views had a tremendous impact upon leading al-Qaeda ideologues, including Ayman al-Zawahiri, who credited Qutb with being "the spark that ignited the Islamic revolution against the enemies of Islam at home and abroad."[16]

But Azzam found the Brothers' worldview to be slightly parochial and instead agitated for a different ideology, one based on a "territorial view of Islam" focused on the necessity of driving infidels from Muslim lands.[17] In 1984, Azzam authored a *fatwa* titled *In Defence of Muslim Lands*, which provided the ideological underpinnings of modern-day jihad, laying out the justifications for and the differences between offensive and defensive jihad.[18] Interestingly, IS focused far more on seizing, holding, and governing territory than al-Qaeda ever did.

In many ways, the dominant ideology espoused by groups like al-Qaeda, the Islamic State, and others reflects the notion that violent jihad is the only path to defending the Islamic world. As part of its brand, al-Qaeda considered itself to be *the* vanguard of Muslims everywhere – the worldwide Islamic community, or *ummah*. In declaring jihad on America, bin Laden argued that the West, and in particular the United States, was overtly hostile to Islam and the only way to respond to this aggression was with extreme force and violence – the only language that America understands. The Salafi-jihadi ideology believes in an inextricable link between the United States and Israel, commonly referred to as the Crusader–Zionist alliance, a theme also referenced in speeches by hardline Islamist groups from Lebanon to Palestine. In his speeches, bin Laden exhorted his followers to fight back and defend Islam from the United States, which has unleashed against Muslims "an ocean of oppression, injustice, slaughter and plunder."[19] Therefore, the next logical step is jihad. In essence, the core of the Salafi-jihadist ideology is individual jihad fused with collective revenge.[20]

From an intellectual standpoint, jihadi totalitarian ideology is a closed system, but it also allows for disagreements over strategy, tactics, and other critical issues.[21] In short, interpretation is not as draconian as some scholars make it out to be and debate is tolerated. Analysis of al-Qaeda's internal documents reveals a group at ease with allowing for internal disagreement and debate amongst its members and the leadership.[22] One well-known ideological divide in the broader jihadist universe dates back to the early 1980s and is between those who desire to strike "the far enemy" and those whose interests are more locally focused, preferring to target what they perceive as apostate regimes throughout the Muslim world. In any case, al-Qaeda followed a dual strategy which allowed it to pursue both objectives simultaneously.[23] But this strategic incongruence is reflected in the global jihadist movement's multifaceted nature. It is a network of networks rather than a single, coherent entity.

Primarily, and almost exclusively, the bulk of guidance on contemporary insurgency is manufactured by Salafist ideologues. Individuals like Ayman al-Zawahiri, Abu Musab al-Suri, Anwar al-Awlaki, and Abu Yahya al-Libi served among al-Qaeda's most prominent voices, proffering advice on strategy, operations, and tactics (in addition to a host of other issues including diet, grooming, and marriage).[24] These modern-day insurgency theorists were highly adept at propagating the narrative that the Muslim *ummah* is being oppressed and only through force would this oppression cease, allowing Muslims to regain their dignity and honor. And even though it has since been crushed, the establishment of the caliphate was intended to be positive affirmation that an Islamic State could be a viable entity in the contemporary era of international relations.

Goals and Objectives

What are the goals and objectives of the global jihadist movement – or, in other words, what is the movement's *raison d'être*, or reason for being? At some point, attacking the West, and the United States more specifically, ultimately superseded other goals as the primary motivation of the global jihadist movement, led by al-Qaeda. Indeed, this motivation to kill Americans on US soil became "so obsessive that it impelled the group to seek out ways to achieve this task," driving innovation in tactics, techniques, and procedures.[25] Other correlated objectives included taking over territory and developing physical sanctuaries and safe havens from which to operate, with the longer-term objective of declaring "emirates" in these territories.[26]

Some would argue that, when looking at the data on where jihadists have successfully attacked, the United States falls further down the list of al-Qaeda's primary targets. The same factors that make Europe so vulnerable to the threat posed by terrorists, and especially by foreign fighters (geography; the number of citizens who traveled to Iraq or Syria; lack of counterterrorism capabilities, including screening, watch-listing, and whole-of-government programs; poor continent-wide information-sharing and intelligence and law-enforcement coordination; and the relationship between Muslim communities and host-nation governments) present favorably for the United States. As former Director of the National Counterterrorism Center (NCTC), Nicholas Rasmussen acknowledged in Congressional testimony, compared to European counterparts, US ports of entry are under far less strain from migration, and US law enforcement agencies are not nearly as overtaxed by the sheer numbers of terrorist plots and potential suspects.[27] The greater threat to the US homeland specifically comes from individual and small autonomous cells, which are hard to detect, radicalized online, and capable of executing low-level attacks. Put simply, the data indicate that the far greater threat emanates from individuals who are already in the United States. As Brian Michael Jenkins has observed in his empirical study on the origins of America's jihadists, "American jihadists are made in the United States, not imported. Of the 178 jihadist planners and perpetrators, 86 were U.S-born citizens. The other were naturalized U.S. citizens (46) or legal permanent residents (23) – in other words, people who had long residencies in the United States before arrest."[28]

As captured in the title of this book, establishing an Islamic caliphate has long been a goal central to the movement. Perhaps one of the biggest misconceptions surrounding the differences between al-Qaeda and the Islamic State is that the latter favored establishing a caliphate while the former did not, which is inaccurate. Both organizations believe in establishing a caliphate, but they each see this happening along different timelines. For al-Qaeda, the establishment of a global caliphate, part of the "Definitive Victory" phase of its seven-stage plan, would occur no earlier than the 2020–2 timeframe, the final stage in al-Qaeda's "Twenty-year plan."[29] Al-Qaeda's goals changed over time, as the group's leadership recognized that its initial focus on a caliphate stretching from historic "Al-Andalus" to Southeast Asia first required laying the groundwork by gaining legitimacy at the local level. The manner in which al-Qaeda has pursued this goal has led it to intervene in numerous civil wars. In fact, terrorist groups do not cause civil wars, but emerge from them, since "wars are perhaps the richest soil for seeding and growing violent groups of all stripes."[30]

And while many have remarked that the Islamic State has eclipsed al-Qaeda as the pre-eminent and most successful terrorist group in the contemporary era, it is important to take note of one of al-Qaeda's overarching goals – to advance the global jihadist movement "as a whole," even if it is not al-Qaeda leading the movement, a goal which "it has made considerable strides toward" even as it has been hampered. Indeed, the byproducts of al-Qaeda's success include the proliferation of foreign fighters, the destabilization of regimes where jihadists maintain a presence, and the cultivation of anti-Western sentiment amongst pockets of the Muslim world, especially in Europe.[31] Al-Qaeda's actions have helped contribute to a self-sustaining network of jihadists and, even as "Al Qaeda declines, the broader movement it fostered remains robust, with other causes and organizations capitalizing on the ideology and networks that the group promulgated."[32]

It also remains paramount to remember the fundamentals upon which the global jihadist movement resides – namely, the pursuit of jihad. Even as al-Qaeda's goals have shifted and evolved over time, its original goal remains the most important to the movement as a whole – to "promote jihad awareness" and "prepare and equip" jihadist cadres in order to develop "a unified international Jihad movement."[33] Accordingly, as spelled out in al-Qaeda's Constitutional Charter, all other goals are subsidiary to jihad: "An Islamic Group, its only mission is to Jihad, because Jihad is one of the basic purposes for which al-Qaeda personnel come together. In addition, they perform other Islamic duties if possible. Jihad will take precedence over other duties in case of interference."[34]

On the recruitment front, the core demographic of the movement remains disenfranchised, disillusioned, marginalized youth that are vulnerable to radicalization and the message of violent religious extremism. The Islamic State has dipped into this same pool to populate its ranks, with perhaps more of an emphasis on enlisting Westerners with criminal backgrounds, especially in Europe, where terrorists and criminals now recruit from the same milieu.[35] Even well before the Islamic State was credited with inspiring lone wolf attacks in its name, al-Qaeda had always urged potential followers to conduct "DIY terrorism," or do-it-yourself attacks against soft targets in the West.[36] As the name suggests, lone wolves can be non-affiliated jihadists who simply share the same worldview and accept core tenets of a similar ideology while acting independently of any specific organization. Recruiting in diaspora communities is another favored method of encouraging supporters to launch attacks.[37] Jihadist groups have been particularly successful in rallying European-born Muslims and converts to their cause and, in the past decade, there have been plots and attacks throughout Western Europe, including several spectacular attacks in European capitals such as London, Paris, Madrid, and Berlin.

Strategic Decision-making

Al-Qaeda's leadership is tasked with making decisions that will both help to grow the organization and get it closer to achieving its primary objectives. In part, al-Qaeda relied on spectacular attacks as part of its global strategy. Throughout the 2000s, al-Qaeda's leadership believed that external operations against the West would help it achieve its goals of "integration, unity, growth, and gaining strategic leadership in the militant milieu" and therefore required its franchises to attack Western interests.[38] These attacks were designed to achieve several interrelated objectives simultaneously, including garnering widespread attention for the global jihadist cause, bringing Muslims under the banner of al-Qaeda as a vanguard movement, and driving the United States from Muslim lands, as occurred in Lebanon in 1983 and again in Somalia in the early 1990s.[39] Spectacular attacks like 9/11 were designed to invite overreaction. As Assaf Moghadam astutely notes, "wounded and humiliated governments subjected to such surprise attacks are more likely to opt for harsh and risky responses against the perpetrators, thereby running the risk of drawing the two sides into an escalating, often protracted confrontation that is costly in both human and economic terms."[40]

Another strategic objective and deliberate part of al-Qaeda's plan is to forge unity among "foreign militants" in the broader jihadist universe, as smaller groups begin to perceive al-Qaeda as the "strong horse" and unite behind it.[41] Al-Qaeda has also demonstrated a knack for pragmatism when operating in the midst of other countries' civil wars. In Yemen, Iraq, Mali, and Somalia, jihadists have functioned in an almost parasitic manner. After infiltrating the ranks of local rebel groups, militants parrot their grievances and champion parochial objectives. Al-Qaeda ingratiates its fighters within extant networks of insurgents fighting against what they deem to be oppressive regimes. This ramps up proselytization efforts and introduces a narrative that mixes local issues with that of the global jihad.[42] There exists a constant tension over striking the proper balance between local and global objectives: "Civil war, domestic and transnational terrorism, and the involvement of foreign fighters have been essential components of jihadist strategy since the 1980s."[43]

Through its participation in conflicts throughout the globe, al-Qaeda has fostered relationships and sustained alliances with other militant organizations and has been far more effective on this front than most terrorist groups historically.[44] Moreover, as al-Qaeda scholar Barak Mendelsohn declares in his book on the expansion of al-Qaeda's franchises, "Following a carefully planned strategy is particularly important for an actor with ambitious territorial aspirations that require navigating an intricate environment encompassing multiple fronts."[45] The group has expanded beyond its base in South Asia to encompass wide swaths of Africa and the Middle East. It has ensured longevity by devolving power to its local franchises.[46] The continued expansion of al-Qaeda is part of a multi-pronged strategy that also includes "bleeding wars" of attrition in Afghanistan and Iraq, as well as building an infrastructure of supporters in the West, especially in Europe.[47]

Throughout the group's evolution, its leadership has continued to play a major role in its longevity. The Amir is the overall leader of al-Qaeda and is tasked with a broad array of responsibilities, including planning on multiple levels (operational, strategic, tactical, logistical, and organizational), approving annual plans and budgets, and, just like any corporate chief executive officer, serving as the face of the organization.[48] As the founder of al-Qaeda and leader of the organization until his death at the hands of US Special Forces in May 2011, there is still debate over exactly how important bin Laden was to the movement.[49] Though bin Laden fancied himself part "lecturer-businessman" / part "activist theologian," his leadership style has been described as "soft-mannered, long-winded, project-oriented, media conscious."[50] On the other hand, his former deputy and now overall Amir of core al-Qaeda, Ayman al-Zawahiri, has been described as "a formidable figure," a "committed revolutionary," who is simultaneously "pious, bitter, and determined," and since its early days had been "the real power behind Al Qaeda."[51]

Organizational Structure

Since it would be a mistake to analyze the global jihadist movement as a monolithic entity, there is no single unified organizational structure, per se. However, scholars and analysts have discerned how groups like al-Qaeda and the Islamic State have chosen to structure their organizations, so analyzing those groups is useful in gaining a greater understanding of the infrastructure. In many ways, al-Qaeda has always been "more an idea or a concept than an organization" and "an amorphous movement tenuously held together by a loosely networked transnational constituency rather than a monolithic, international terrorist organization with either a defined or identifiable command and control apparatus."[52] In terms of its organizational structure, al-Qaeda has always been something of a paradox, "tightly supervised at the top but very loosely spread at the bottom."[53] At its peak, the group maintained an indelible or semi-permanent presence in 76 countries, "including those without discernable Muslim communities, but which were suitable for procurement, e.g. Japan, Bulgaria, Slovakia."[54]

Al-Qaeda is best described as a networked transnational constituency which, especially since the attacks of September 11, 2001, has shown itself to be a nimble, flexible, and adaptive entity, even as it has been reduced considerably by the constant barrage of American counterterrorism efforts worldwide. After all, "[f]or more than a decade, it has withstood arguably the greatest international onslaught directed against a terrorist organization in history."[55] As an organization, al-Qaeda was not averse to taking risks. Accordingly, its organizational style encouraged the adoption of innovative terrorist techniques, such as those devised by individuals outside of the group's organizational boundaries, including "independent terrorist

23

entrepreneurs" like Khalid Sheikh Mohammed, the so-called "master-mind" of the 9/11 attacks.[56]

As Rohan Gunaratna remarked in his landmark work on al-Qaeda, part of what makes the organization so unique is its "mobility and capacity for regeneration."[57] Within the broader jihadi universe, al-Qaeda existed as a central node and maintained connections, link-ages, and alliances with a diverse array of groups, including the Afghan Taliban, Chechen rebel groups, Abu Sayyaf Group (ASG) in the Philippines, and the IMU.[58] In many ways, Afghanistan, despite its geographic location outside of the Middle East and North Africa, has served as one of the, if not the, most critical hubs in the global jihad over the past four decades. It is a place that militants have continually returned to, even after other conflicts have drawn them away.

Still, there is no such thing as a permanent headquarters for the global jihadist movement. Whether in Khartoum or in Kandahar, jihad-ists are opportunistic by nature and, like a trickling stream, will always find their way to the lowest point, or the area most beyond the reach of formal governments and standing armies. After the Soviet occupation of Afghanistan drew down, Pakistan began pressuring foreign fighters to leave the region. Many jihadists fled abroad to Yemen, Sudan, and Jordan. Bin Laden was still providing support to members of EIJ, a sig-nificant contingent of whose fighters remained behind in Afghanistan and Pakistan. Another large group of EIJ fighters relocated along with Zawahiri to Sudan, where they hatched a plot to assassinate Egyptian leader Hosni Mubarak during an official state visit. The assassination attempt failed, but the plot highlighted further tension between bin Laden's focus on the "far enemy" and Zawahiri's continued obsession with Egypt and apostate regimes within the Middle East and North Africa.

The core of what had become al-Qaeda also traveled with bin Laden from Afghanistan to Sudan, which the Saudi militant viewed as having serious potential as his group's next logistical headquarters.[59] Initially, bin Laden's concerns shifted to supporting jihadists in Yemen in their battle against the Communists, although he also allegedly provided support to militants in the Philippines, Algeria, Jordan, Eritrea, Pakistan, Bosnia, Tajikistan, Lebanon, Libya, Chechnya, Somalia, and Egypt during this time.[60] After the 1995 Dayton Accords ended the Bosnian conflict, some foreign fighters made their way to Sudan, while many other battle-hardened jihadis returned to Afghanistan, bringing back newfound expertise and tradecraft which they would teach to their militant brethren in al-Qaeda training camps, where Egyptians, Chechens, Uzbeks, and Palestinians honed their skills. In terms of geopolitics, failed states usually make for poor neighbors, but can serve as welcome hosts to non-state actors, including transnational terrorist groups and violent insurgencies. Al-Qaeda's Afghan sanctuary ebbed and flowed for two decades in the lead-up to 9/11, providing somewhat hospitable terrain for the militants, while affording them with access to other jihadists.

While it started as a single, monolithic entity, al-Qaeda today is a decentralized, networked, transnational terrorist organization. Al-Qaeda also needs a healthy budget to maintain its rather substantial structural costs, in addition to the costs of conducting operations. This includes money for subsistence living for its members (as well as for those who have families), communications, travel expenses, media and propaganda, and the provision of social services to selected constituents in an effort to buoy its popular support.[61] As groups grow more networked, it can be more challenging to retain their cohesiveness. Maintaining lines of communication, agreeing on shared goals and objectives, and remaining relevant in the increasingly crowded universe of global jihad are time-consuming and expensive undertakings, especially when law enforcement and intelligence services around the world are seeking to combat this network wherever it pulses.

One of the core missions of a terrorist organization's bureaucracy is to fulfill a human resources function, to include recruiting new members. Despite the image conjured when envisioning a dark network dispersed throughout dozens of countries worldwide and forced to communicate covertly, al-Qaeda remained a highly bureaucratic organization throughout most of the 1990s and 2000s. In the lead-up to the attacks of September 11, 2001, al-Qaeda could accurately be characterized as a "unitary organization" with many of the characteristics of a "lumbering bureaucracy."[62] In al-Qaeda's training camps in Afghanistan, recruits were required to take a written exam and sign a contract before acceptance into the group. The contract detailed the moral responsibilities of would-be al-Qaeda members, as well as the stipulations of remuneration, including marital and family allowances, vacation time, and reimbursements for expenses incurred.[63] The group's organizational structure included the following components, in addition to the top leadership: the Secretary, the Command Council, the Military Committee, the Documentations Unit, the Political Committee, the Media Committee, the Administrative and Financial Committee, the Security Committee, and the Religious Committee.[64]

Campaigns and Operations

So what has the global jihadist movement looked like in action? That is, where has the movement launched attacks, conducted operations, and waged campaigns of violence to achieve its goals? Following the end of the war against the Soviets, many jihadists fled Afghanistan to join new conflicts, linking up with militants in other countries where civil wars raged. According to Fawaz Gerges, "Bin Laden tapped into a rising generation of mujahideen . . . radicalized by the Afghan war and the persecution of Muslim communities in Bosnia, Chechnya, and elsewhere."[65] Indeed, veterans of the conflicts in Afghanistan, Bosnia, and Chechnya formed the core of al-Qaeda, which was cementing its reputation as the most capable entity within the broader global jihadist movement.

Bosnia

In the early 1990s, during the brutal wars that characterized the disintegration of the Federal Republic of Yugoslavia, some areas of the Balkans featured battles that had Bosnian Muslims fighting for survival against Bosnian Serbs, who were Orthodox Christian. The plight of Bosnian Muslims led to an organized call for foreign fighters to travel to Bosnia to help, as many jihadists did, initially under the guise of a variety of charities and humanitarian services. The projected numbers vary widely, but most reliable estimates suggest that between 3,000 and 4,000 foreign fighters actually fought in Bosnia, many of whom were veterans of the war in Afghanistan, hailing from the United States, Turkey, Jordan, Iran, Syria, and elsewhere.[66]

In April 1992, Sheikh Abu Abdel Aziz Barbaros established the El Mudžahid Battalion and worked to recruit fellow jihadists to join al-Qaeda-linked militants in Bosnia.[67] Unsurprisingly, a significant effort was made to recruit volunteers from Western Europe, given the proximity to the conflict.[68] The call to jihad was endorsed by influential clerics throughout the Middle East, especially as the Serbian military ramped up its campaign of ethnic cleansing. Islamic charities, including Al-Kifah and the Benevolence International Foundation (BIF), led by bin Laden associate Enaam Arnaout, siphoned off funds to support the jihadists. When the conflict in Bosnia ended in 1995 with the signing of the Dayton Accords, hundreds of foreign fighters left Bosnia and headed elsewhere to fight, including many who went to Chechnya.[69]

Chechnya

Throughout the 1990s, Russia fought two wars against rebels in Chechnya seeking to secede and declare independence. Initially, the rebels' guiding ideology was secular-nationalist in nature, but soon morphed to Islamist-inspired after the arrival of jihadist foreign fighters in the mid-1990s. Jihadists slowly built a presence toward the end of the first Chechen war (1994–6) and factored significantly into several prominent battles against Russian soldiers.[70] Many of these foreign fighters were veterans of previous conflicts, including the Soviet–Afghan War, Tajikistan, and Bosnia.[71] Among these fighters were Sheikh Ali Fathi al-Shisani, a Jordanian-Chechen, and Ibn al-Khattab.[72] Khattab was a Saudi militant responsible for establishing training camps and indoctrinating Chechen fighters with Saudi-imported Wahhabism, not the traditional Sufism more common to Chechens, which is more moderate.[73] Khattab provided money and ideological inspiration, but also brought tangible fighting skills, leading an ambush on a Russian convoy in the mountains at Yaryshmardy in April 1996 that killed nearly 100 soldiers.[74] In addition to their ability to raise funds, jihadist foreign fighters in the Chechen theatre were especially valued for their fighting and organizational skills.[75]

There was a point in time when Chechnya was extremely important to al-Qaeda and the global jihadist movement. In 1996, al-Zawahiri was arrested trying to travel there, and spent six months in a prison in Dagestan.[76] In his book *Knights Under the Prophet's Banner*, he argued that Chechnya could become a "strategic lynchpin" for the jihadist movement with the territory forming part of a "mujahid Islamic belt" across the region, connecting to Pakistan in the east and Turkey and Iran in the south.[77] The continuity between conflicts was also important, as fighters exchanged new skills which helped enhance the global jihadist movement's ability to influence conflicts it inserted itself into anywhere, unconstrained by geography: "These conflicts were further linked by a common group of fighters who gained credibility and combat experience ultimately culminating in improved military effectiveness."[78]

Franchise Groups and Affiliates

The other important development affecting the global jihadist movement was the ebb and flow of al-Qaeda and its dispersion following the US-led invasion of Afghanistan in 2001. The same thing is currently happening with the Islamic State, as it seeks to expand in Afghanistan, the Sinai Peninsula, and Southeast Asia, to name just a few places. Accordingly, the key to understanding what comes next with the Islamic State's collapse is looking back at how al-Qaeda devolved. The group's expansion has been described as a goal in and of itself as well as part of the organization's strategy to survive and penetrate new territories.

Throughout the early to mid-2000s, al-Qaeda expanded to Saudi Arabia (2003), Iraq (2004), Algeria (2006), and Yemen (2007). It formed franchises in Somalia (2010), Syria (2012), and an affiliation in South Asia through al-Qaeda in the Indian Subcontinent (2014). Al-Qaeda's expansion occurred in two specific ways – either implementing "in-house" expansion through establishing an affiliate group on its own, as it did in Saudi Arabia and Yemen, or merging with existing jihadist groups in exchange for an official pledge of allegiance from the group to al-Qaeda. This model was on display in Iraq, with Abu Musab al-Zarquwl's group, Tawhid wal Jihad; in Algeria, with the Salafist Group for Preaching and Combat (GSPC); and in Somalia, with al-Shabaab.[79]

There are pros and cons to establishing affiliates. On the positive side, franchise groups made al-Qaeda seem ubiquitous, as AQI, AQAP, AQIM, and al-Shabaab conducted attacks in al-Qaeda's name. The method of franchising also offers "strategic reach" and allows the group to ingratiate itself into new theatres. But there are many negative aspects, too, including that an affiliate can damage the brand through its actions, as AQI did with its relentless sectarian attacks against Iraqi Shiites. Affiliates can also exploit the brand name and enjoy its benefits without doing much in return to advance the core group's mission, something Daniel Byman calls "shirking."[80] Moreover, enlisting affiliates led to a change in the strategic direction of core al-Qaeda, which had to spend more time attempting to manage the franchise groups, and in some cases "make concessions to address the narrow concerns of local groups joining its global banner."[81] Will IS face the same predicament? Or will its offshoots secure even more autonomy as the core of the group is crushed and its command-and-control capabilities systematically dismantled?

Saudi Arabia

In the spring of 2003, bin Laden stood up al-Qaeda's first franchise group, al-Qaeda in the Arabian Peninsula (the group initially referred to itself as "the mujahideen in the Arabian Peninsula") using al-Qaeda's own fighters as an example of "an in-house creation."[82] Although al-Qaeda operatives in Saudi Arabia were able to launch some successful attacks, including the Riyadh compound bombings in 2003, the militants were systematically wiped out by Saudi internal security services. For a counterterrorism force that many outside observers were probably skeptical of, "the results were impressive: many on the most wanted lists were either captured or killed in shootouts across the kingdom."[83]

The other major reason why the al-Qaeda venture in Saudi Arabia failed was due to the much greater attraction of traveling to Iraq, where aspiring jihadists could engage with and kill American soldiers. The war in Iraq, therefore, was a much higher priority for Saudi jihadists. "To potential recruits and donors, there was no doubt paramilitary warfare in Iraq represented a politically more legitimate and theologically less controversial enterprise than bombings in the streets of Riyadh," according to Thomas Hegghammer.[84] In sum, "the decision to introduce a Saudi branch proved disastrous" for al-Qaeda, although its franchise in Iraq would enjoy far more success – at least initially, before succumbing to problems resulting from its rampant sectarian agenda later on.[85]

Iraq

Al-Qaeda's Iraq franchise was its first affiliate resulting from a merger, in which Abu Musab al-Zarqawi's Jama'at al-Tawhid wal-Jihad (TWJ) and al-Qaeda joined forces. Both groups had their own motives for the merger. For al-Qaeda, the group's leadership felt compelled to expand into Iraq after the US invasion, lest it risk being marginalized at a time when jihadists were flocking to the country to fight American soldiers. Al-Qaeda lacked a domestic infrastructure in Iraq, and so had to partner with another jihadist outfit already established in the area. For Zarqawi and TWJ, the move to merge with al-Qaeda to form AQI was a pragmatic decision to gain access to core al-Qaeda's deep-pocketed donors throughout the Gulf, as well as to adopt a brand that would help attract foreign fighters.

Saudi militants in AQI provided the most money of any foreign contingent to the group, and also accounted for nearly three-quarters of all AQI's suicide bombers at the height of the insurgency in 2006 and 2007.[86] The most common nationalities of foreign fighters who traveled to fight in Iraq were, in order, Saudi, Libyan, and Syrian.[87] Moreover, since TWJ was composed primarily of militants from Jordan, Syria, Lebanon and the Palestinian territories, AQI had a significant non-Iraqi core from its inception.[88]

From the start, there were tensions between AQI's Iraqi members and foreigners.[89] These tensions extended to the leadership, including the Jordanian-born Zarqawi, who himself was constantly at odds with core al-Qaeda's leadership on a number of issues – above all, his penchant for targeting Shiites.[90] The insubordination of AQI would be a harbinger of the future, foreshadowing the rise of IS.[91] As Fishman notes, "Zarqawi and Al Qaeda were allies of convenience rather than genuine partners."[92] Zarqawi never fell in line with core al-Qaeda's agenda and consistently clashed with bin Laden and Zawahiri, successfully maintaining his autonomy and ignoring the leadership's repeated pleas to focus on the Americans rather than the Shia.

The egregious sectarianism of AQI was more than just a theological dispute – core al-Qaeda recalled what happened in Algeria, after the population turned against the Armed Islamic Group (GIA), a Salafi-jihadist group that resorted to killing fellow Muslims and even targeting neutrals who did not provide overt support to its agenda. Indeed, there was another connection between AQI and Algeria, since, amongst its foreign members, Zarqawi's group boasted many militants from the Maghreb who would help core al-Qaeda establish links with the GSPC to form al-Qaeda in the Islamic Maghreb, or AQIM.[93]

Algeria

Al-Qaeda's Algerian franchise, like AQI in Iraq, resulted from a merger and was not an organic al-Qaeda "startup." Al-Qaeda allied with the GSPC in an effort to expand its brand and its operations throughout North Africa. As with its other affiliates, there was consistent pressure from core al-Qaeda for AQIM to expand its purview to focus more on the global jihad, as opposed to purely localized objectives. Its most high-profile attack against a Western target occurred within Algeria, against the Tigantourine gas facility in In Amenas.[94] And while AQIM did conduct attacks outside of Algeria, including in Niger, Mali, and Mauritania, it never developed into the global threat core al-Qaeda had hoped it would.[95] By 2013, nearly 90 percent of AQIM activity took place within Algeria, and 80 percent of its attacks were directed against state security forces.[96] It was never able to escalate beyond this, more likely due to a lack of capability than a lack of will or desire.

Al-Qaeda was similarly disappointed by its inability to capitalize upon GSPC's European connections, especially in France, where Zawahiri and others believed they could tap into Muslim anger over that country's controversial headscarf ban.[97] GSPC also had connections in Germany, Spain, and the United Kingdom.[98] Camille Tawil, a journalist and long-time al-Qaeda watcher, speculates that the group was hoping to use GSPC's European linkages to pull off an attack similar to the 2004 Madrid train bombings.[99] This is yet another area where IS has proven to have bested al-Qaeda, evidenced by its deadly reach into Europe and its ability to direct, inspire, or launch attacks in Belgium, France, Spain, Germany, the UK, and elsewhere.

The decision to join with al-Qaeda was a far more pragmatic one for Algerian jihadists. GSPC was a failing group, so by adopting the al-Qaeda brand it hoped to bring in a fresh influx of recruits from throughout the region.[100] Moreover, leaders like Abdelmalek Droukdal had a somewhat personal reason for seeking the affiliation, as he believed it would enhance his own standing within the organization, as well as making AQIM appear to be more dangerous than it might have been otherwise.[101] Joining al-Qaeda was not popular with everyone in GSPC – rather than join AQIM, many jihadists accepted the government's amnesty, which could be one of the reasons why Algeria has been less affected by the wave of jihadist violence that swept across the region with a renewed ferocity after the emergence of IS.

Even though it never launched major attacks in the West, AQIM did pioneer innovative methods, including an intense focus on propaganda and "media jihad."[102] There was also a clear indication of tactics shared through training, as after 2007 AQIM began utilizing improvised explosive devices and coordinated suicide bombings.[103] Above all else, AQIM is perhaps best known for its ability to finance its organization through crime, especially kidnapping.[104] Al-Qaeda's North African affiliate grew so successful at funding its organization through criminal activities that it was able to begin sending money back to core al-Qaeda in something akin to a mafia soldier kicking a "tax" up to the *capo*, in a sign of respect. Ideologically, core al-Qaeda and AQIM held largely the same views, which helped attenuate unnecessary friction between the groups. Still, even with an ideological affinity, core al-Qaeda desperately needed one of its franchises to develop the capability to launch a spectacular attack in the West. Its next franchise group in Yemen would evolve to fill this role.

Yemen

Al-Qaeda's Yemen franchise occurred as an in-house expansion, with the establishment of "The al-Qaeda Organization of Jihad in the South of the Arabian Peninsula," which became "The al-Qaeda Organization in the Land of Yemen" and eventually gave way to al-Qaeda in the Arabian Peninsula (AQAP) when al-Qaeda's Saudi and Yemeni networks merged in early 2009.[105] In 2013, AQAP leader Nasir al-Wuhayshi was elevated to the position of al-Qaeda's general manager by its leader, Ayman al-Zawahiri, a nod to the importance of AQAP amongst the orbit of al-Qaeda affiliates. Accordingly, AQAP used its leaders' ties to core al-Qaeda leadership as a recruiting pitch to persuade aspiring jihadists to join its ranks.

Of all the affiliates, AQAP emerged to become the most operationally capable. When core al-Qaeda went years without being able to pull off a spectacular attack against the West, AQAP managed several "near misses" against US airliners, including the notorious underwear bomber plot and another plot against cargo planes with explosive-laden printer cartridges onboard. AQAP was considered such a high-level threat that former CIA Director David Petraeus once referred to the group's master bombmaker, Ibrahim Hassan al-Asiri, as "the world's most dangerous man."[106] Al-Asiri was killed in a drone strike in Yemen in August 2018.

Another important success by AQAP has been the continued evolution of jihadist propaganda and media outreach.[107] A major part of this success was due to the emergence of American-born radical cleric Anwar al-Awlaki, who before his death had developed a global following among jihadists, especially those from the West who were drawn to his cult of personality, including Nidal Hasan, a US Army psychiatrist who communicated with Awlaki through email for over a year before going on a shooting rampage at Fort Hood, Texas, in November 2009, where he killed 13 people.[108] Awlaki's influence continues to live on today on the Internet, years after his death.[109]

AQAP was also the most adept of all the franchises at effectively balancing local versus global objectives.[110] "AQAP has been far more sensitive to local grievances and tribal identities, In part because al-Qaeda has learned and transmitted lessons about respecting nationalism to its affiliate," notes Byman.[111] In Yemen, jihadists have maintained good relations with the local tribes and been flexible with the imposition of *sharia*, jettisoning the more draconian rules more common to the Islamic State. Yet, even while focusing on issues most pressing to Yemeni tribesmen, AQAP still managed to play a role in the Charlie Hebdo attacks in Paris, France, in January 2015.[112] The group also maintains an increasingly close relationship with Al-Shabaab in Somalia and has served before as an interlocutor between other franchises, including Shabaab, AQIM, and JN.[113]

Somalia

Harakat al-Shabaab al-Mujahidiin (a.k.a. Shabaab, or "The Youth") is a radical fundamentalist faction that split off from the Islamic Courts Union (ICU) in Somalia, which itself was the outgrowth of al-Itihaad al-Islamiya (AIAI).[114] Many of al-Shabaab's founders fought in Afghanistan during the anti-Soviet jihad in the 1980s.[115] When the United States deployed to Somalia in the early 1990s to provide humanitarian assistance, bin Laden used this event as an opportunity to position al-Qaeda militants in East Africa, a move that would facilitate al-Qaeda's bombing of the US embassies in Nairobi, Kenya, and Dar es Salaam, Tanzania, several years later, in 1998.[116] Al-Shabaab formally coalesced around 2005, when a network of Afghan veterans of Somali origin, ex-AIAI militants, and al-Qaeda remnants throughout the Horn of Africa joined forces.[117]

Approximately a year after its founding, al-Shabaab was able to network and recruit among Somali clans to grow its organization following Ethiopia's invasion of Somalia in late 2006.[118] The Ethiopian incursion breathed new life into what was at the time a rather fledgling organization, although one imbued with an experienced jihadist pedigree. The fighting between Shabaab and Ethiopian forces became known as the "dirty war," with both sides eschewing previously recognized norms regarding the use of violence. Shabaab introduced suicide bombing to Somalia for the first time, while the Ethiopians responded by using white phosphorous bombs to clear out entire neighborhoods.[119] Atrocities committed by Ethiopian forces led to the mobilization of foreign fighters, including members of the Somali diaspora living in the United States, as more than 40 Americans traveled to Somalia to join al-Shabaab.[120]

Even though many foreign fighters were motivated by Somali nationalism, defending Somalis from Christian Ethiopia also dovetailed with al-Qaeda's narrative. In 2010, al-Qaeda and Shabaab formally merged, as the Somali terror group's leader Ahmed Godane declared his group's intention to operate with a more "global mindset."[121] Al-Qaeda had considered Somalia as a place to seek safe haven back in the early 1990s, but decided against it due to terrain considered inhospitable for a terrorist group as well as issues related to the country's complex clan dynamics.[122] Furthermore, al-Qaeda was cognizant of the population's hostility toward non-Somalis, and the austere Salafist interpretation of Islam is far from universally accepted throughout the country. And even while al-Qaeda initially decided against seeking sanctuary in Somalia, it *has* proved to be a hotbed for terrorism and insurgency, largely as a result of its status as a collapsed state and near-constant anarchy, which has led to a power vacuum that violent non-state actors have filled.

Al-Shabaab has not demonstrated a proclivity to attack the West, but the group has conducted several high-profile attacks outside of Somalia, including the Kampala bombings in July 2010 in Uganda, the Westgate Mall Attack in Nairobi, Kenya, in September 2013, and an attack at a university in Garissa, Kenya, in April 2015. These attacks could foreshadow Shabaab's development into a force throughout the region and not one strictly resigned to Somalia.[123] Fighting against a range of adversaries, including the African Union Mission in Somalia (AMISOM), forces from the Transitional Federal Government (TFG), and the Kenyan military, the group's control of territory has ebbed and flowed since 2011, with the loss of territory (especially coastal territory) significantly impacting Shabaab's ability to raise money. Nevertheless, the group has consistently demonstrated resilience in the face of adversity, successfully transitioning "from an insurgent group that controlled territory to a terrorist group that commits indiscriminate attacks on civilians and combatants alike."[124] Attacks on civilians have been accompanied by criticism from core al-Qaeda leadership, which is perhaps one reason Shabaab did not claim the deadly car-bomb attack in Mogadishu in October 2017 that led to over 300 casualties.[125]

The evolution of the global jihadist movement transformed al-Qaeda, long the movement's primary bulwark, into a decentralized network of terrorist groups operating in Yemen, Iraq, Algeria, Somalia, and elsewhere. It is crucial to understand how this evolution – perhaps what some might consider a devolution – occurred, in order to judge whether or not IS could follow a similar path. As of late July 2018, the counter-IS fight was winding down in northeastern Syria as the Islamic State's territory was reduced to less than 1 percent of what is was at its peak, mostly centered around the Hajin pocket and other towns and villages in the Central Euphrates River valley. Nevertheless, the group was estimated to still have between 20,000 and 30,000 fighters just in Iraq and Syria. And the Islamic State's ideology is still viable as a means of conveying specific grievances to young Muslims while also offering an attractive worldview that frames things in terms of "us" versus "them."

2

The Inner Workings of the
Islamic State

Al-Qaeda may have birthed several highly capable offshoots, but the transition of one of those off shoots – al-Qaeda in Iraq (AQI) – into the Islamic State was not a linear one. It involved bloody confrontations between erstwhile allies within the jihadist movement, and a lasting cleavage that has led to continued fighting and division between IS and al-Qaeda to the current day. Understanding this split is key to understanding IS, its inner workings, and its motivations.

Following the tumult brought forth by the Arab Spring, Syria descended into civil war. To al-Qaeda leadership, Syria was the opportunity the group was looking for to reassert itself on the world stage and once again become a relevant player in the heart of the Middle East. Al-Qaeda expanded into Syria in January 2012 with the establishment of Jabhat al-Nusra (JN), led by a Syrian AQI (now Islamic State of Iraq (ISI)) fighter, Abu Muhammad al-Joulani. Core al-Qaeda sought to uphold the chimera of deniability in its relationship with its nascent Syrian branch. In April 2013, the ISI declared JN its subsidiary, although Joulani scoffed at this arrangement and instead declared his loyalty to Zawahiri and core al-Qaeda. Core al-Qaeda's inability to control its affiliates had not only damaged its brand, but had now led to the emergence of what would become its most significant rival.[1] The fall-out resulted in ISI's expansion into Syria and its subsequent rebranding as the Islamic State (IS). Moreover, when the fissure occurred, the majority of foreign fighters in Nusra's ranks left the group to join IS.[2] Zawahiri publicly denounced the split between the groups in February 2014. No matter, the stage was set for the rise of IS.

In order to properly understand the rise and fall of IS, it is crucial to have a firm grasp of the group's capabilities – both how it is able to plan and conduct attacks (operational capabilities) and also how the group maintains itself as a cohesive entity (organizational capabilities). IS is a pioneering terrorist group in several ways, from its ability to raise and spend money to its multi-tiered approach to conducting terrorist attacks. IS's use of social media and encrypted apps to direct terrorist attacks overseas sets it apart from any terrorist groups of the past. As evidenced by the Paris November 2015 attacks and the Brussels March 2016 attacks, at its peak IS sustained the ability to strike into the heart of Europe while simultaneously managing a proto-state spanning Iraq and Syria.

Operational Capabilities

The Islamic State's ability to plan and execute attacks, against both conventional and unconventional forces on the battlefield, as well as abroad in Western cities, makes it a relatively unique organization in terms of its operational capabilities. Its fighters have mastered a diverse array of tactics, from VBIEDs to ambushes and hit-and-run attacks. Moreover, the leadership's exhortation for its followers to conduct attacks abroad, including so-called vehicular terrorism or ramming attacks, is a tactic pioneered by IS that has emerged as a new trend in terrorist attacks directed at the West. To remain relevant, as IS loses its last remaining territory in Iraq and Syria, it may seek to rely on launching spectacular terrorist attacks in the West to maintain morale and burnish the group's brand. This section will discuss the group's operational capabilities, which include financing, weapons, intelligence, the ability to maintain a safe haven, and training.

Financing

At the height of its territorial control in 2015, the Islamic State generated more than $6 billion – the equivalent of the gross domestic product of Liechtenstein.[3] While IS's territorial control has declined, it still retains financial power; IS's surviving leadership is alleged to have smuggled as much as $400 million out of Iraq and Syria and used it to invest in legitimate businesses – hotels, hospitals, farms, and car dealerships – throughout the region, including in Turkey, where some militants have also reportedly made large purchases of gold.[4] IS's financial holdings and funding model have made it the wealthiest insurgent group in history, and its diversified funding portfolio and ability to raise money through criminal activities provide it with an opportunity to survive and even make a comeback in Iraq and Syria over the next several years.[5]

Following its obstreperous rise to global infamy in 2014, IS was enshrined in media-fueled hyperbole. While, much of the time, the superlatives were misplaced, one area in which they were unquestionably warranted was in regard to its finances. Indeed, the war chest it amassed in 2014 and 2015 easily made it the richest terrorist organization in the contemporary era.[6] IS is different from previous terrorist groups because the territory it controlled provided extremely lucrative resources, such as oil, and a renewable funding source in the form of a taxable population. As former Assistant Secretary for Terrorist

Financing at the Department of the Treasury Daniel Glaser has noted, IS generated its wealth from three primary sources: oil and gas, which generated about $500 million in 2015, primarily through internal sales; taxation and extortion, which garnered approximately $300 million in 2015; and the 2014 looting of Mosul, during which IS stole about $500 million from bank vaults.[7]

To put IS financing in perspective, it is useful to consider not only IS's similarities to other groups but its differences as well. Indeed, there are far more differences than similarities, as IS is unique in the scale and scope of its financing activities. Like many other terrorist groups in the contemporary era, IS relies on a range of criminal activities, including – but not limited to – extortion, kidnapping for ransom, robbery and theft, and antiquities smuggling. IS may also have been involved with narcotics trafficking.[8] There is little evidence to suggest that foreign donations from nation-states have also been a significant funding source for IS, although wealthy individuals from the Gulf have been accused of financing terrorists in Syria.[9]

In addition to funding its organization from the bottom up, through petty criminality, IS also relied on a top-down funding structure from a range of sources associated with its control of territory. As mentioned in the introduction, IS is unique in recent history as one of the few terrorist groups to generate most of its funding from the territory it held – revenue amassed from taxation and extortion, the sale of oil and various oil-related products, looting, confiscation of property and cash, and fines levied against the population by the religious police for a litany of offenses.[10] IS's reputation as incorruptible – a defining characteristic inherited from its predecessors AQI and ISI – helped boost popular support.[11]

Most concerning, however, is that IS continues to make money from oil to this day, despite the drastic reduction in its territorial holdings. In late June 2018, four members of IS's Oil and Gas Network were killed during Coalition operations in the central Euphrates River Valley in Syria.[12] According to a United Nations Security Council report from the summer of 2018, IS has regained control of oil fields in northeastern Syria and continues to extract oil, both for its own use, and also for sale to locals.[13] So while significant progress has been made in combating IS's ability to raise money through oil, this revenue source has yet to be completely eradicated and probably never will be. Even when IS's predecessors did not control large swaths of territory in Iraq from 2006 to 2009, they were similarly able to raise substantial sums of money from oil, including by extorting local and regional distribution networks.

One of the core difficulties in degrading IS's considerable material wealth was that much of what it amassed was collected in and through the territory over which it presided. Indeed, as much as 80 percent of its fortune was acquired by mimicking one of the central functions of modern nation-states – that is, collecting taxes and tariffs from the local population.[14] In this sense, IS was unique in the recent history of insurgency. It was entrepreneurial and, to a large extent, self-sufficient.[15] As an upshot of this (and notwithstanding much spurious media coverage), there is scant evidence to suggest that foreign donations were ever a significant source of funding for it.[16] As the organization evolves in years to come, these revenue streams will probably change; indeed, external funding from sympathetic state and non-state donors could one day comprise a much larger proportion of its coffers.[17]

The war against IS has vividly shown the intractability of counter-terrorism financing. Sanctions, one of the principal traditional tools for this area of policy, were demonstrably insufficient, and even the impact of the Counter-IS Coalition's targeted, intelligence-led strikes on oil operations and cash storage sites in Iraq and Syria in 2015 proved to be impermanent. To cripple its material wealth, a combination of civilian and military measures was required, with global backing. Every potential facet of IS revenue had to be considered for targeting or sanctioning, and the most difficult areas to obstruct – taxation and extortion – became long-term targets for post-conflict stabilization.

As the organization continues to be degraded, its primary sources of revenue will change and its leadership may seek to secure external funding from sympathetic donors throughout the Arab and Islamic world, or nation-states in the Middle East that view IS as a potentially useful proxy in the region's ongoing internecine conflict. Still, this remains a remote possibility for two reasons. First, IS has demonstrated such an extreme sectarian agenda that its egregious behavior is beyond the pale even for states that normally sponsor terrorist groups. Second, the counter-threat finance measures devised and implemented by the international community, in partnership with private-sector entities including major banks, has made it extremely difficult for terrorist groups to take advantage of the licit financial sector to store, transfer, or launder illicit revenues.

Weapons

During its peak, IS could be considered one of the most well-funded terrorist groups in history, and, also, one of the most well-equipped.[18] The Islamic State managed to acquire an impressive arsenal of weapons to equip the army of its proto-state. IS fighters trained with small arms, but also learned how to use heavy-caliber weapons that could be used in more conventional-style skirmishes. Its fighters proved innovative, demonstrating the skill and alacrity to modify a range of weapons systems. The group displayed a remarkable ingenuity in training new recruits, adept at onboarding both battle-hardened jihadists with experience in previous fronts, and newly arrived Europeans with little or no knowledge of military tactics. Its fighters' willingness to die in suicide attacks was unprecedented in terms of overall numbers, lending credence to the saying that quantity can have a quality all of its own. Some scholars have argued that IS's ability to wage conventional warfare was so advanced that the organization of its military capabilities bore resemblance to the warfighting functions of the United States military in terms of combined arms concepts and command and control.[19]

Unlike many terrorist and insurgent groups that operated during the Cold War, IS was not forced to rely upon external states to provide it with weaponry. Instead, its fighters forcibly looted hundreds of millions of dollars' worth of weapons and equipment from Iraqi and Syrian military installations.[20] IS maintained a diversified source of weapons, including those acquired from other insurgents in Syria who defected to the Islamic State; weapons purchased from other insurgents who received them from foreign donors; weapons captured from defeated adversaries; and weapons bought from or traded for with corrupt members of the security forces in Syria and Iraq.[21] The group even managed to wrangle sophisticated anti-aircraft weaponry such as the Chinese-made FN-6, which was provided to Syrian rebels who were ultimately overrun by IS fighters.[22] Nearly 90 percent of the weapons and ammunition acquired by IS originated in China, Russia, and Eastern Europe.[23] Unlike in some conflicts where much of the weaponry on the battlefield is old or antiquated, the lion's share of IS's weaponry, and especially the ammunition it was using, was predominantly found to have been delivered to the region since the Syrian conflict began in 2011.[24]

IS was not the prototypical insurgent group – it was equipped more like a conventional military. Armored vehicles were purchased on the black market or scavenged from the Iraqi security forces which had retreated from the battlefield.[25] The use of "technicals," which are pick-up trucks modified with machine guns or anti-aircraft weaponry, provides the militants freedom of movement and much-needed mobility. IS fighters have used artillery and RPGs in Syria while also making use of Humvees and T-55 tanks captured from the Iraqi security forces.[26] Other types of weapons include M79 anti-tank rockets made in the former Yugoslavia, American-made M16 and M14 rifles, as well as assorted small arms and ammunition.[27] Many of the weapons and equipment that IS militants fought with were initially distributed to the Iraqi Army to provide it with both a qualitative and quantitative edge over its adversaries.[28] In October 2014, US planes dropped weapons intended for Kurdish fighters in Kobani, but instead ended up in IS-controlled territory and were ultimately commandeered by the militants.[29]

In terms of tactics, IS demonstrated interest and skill in experimenting with new technologies and elevated the use of suicide attacks to a new level. Between December 2015 and November 2016, IS conducted an astounding 923 suicide operations in Iraq and Syria alone.[30] Many of these attacks involved the use of VBIEDs. IS was able to record its attacks and then distribute the footage as propaganda.[31] This also set IS apart from other groups, including al-Qaeda and Hezbollah, both of which engaged in similar kinds of propaganda distribution, but never achieved the same scope or scale as IS did with its battlefield footage. Throughout the conflict there were reports of IS fighters using drones in a number of different ways, from surveillance and reconnaissance to actual attacks involving grenades and explosives.[32] And in keeping with the findings of Truls Hallberg Tønnessen, the primary strength of IS is not necessarily the acquisition and use of advanced technology, but the improvised use of less advanced and easily accessible technology to great (and lethal) effect.[22]

Intelligence

For the Islamic State, its intelligence capabilities served a dual purpose, having both internal and external objectives. Internally, IS sought to purge all potential spies and suspected collaborators. Externally, its intelligence service was used to attack its opponents, both within the region and farther abroad. Ominously, the intelligence skills IS fighters learned in Iraq and Syria could serve them well if they seek to return to their countries of origin or third-party countries to mount attacks. If IS is able to reconstitute its organization in the future, even in a far more limited form, its residual intelligence capabilities will probably be a major reason why.

IS relies on subversion and clandestine operations to execute attacks in both Syria and Iraq, including suicide bombings, assassinations, and other guerilla-style tactics, extending to offensive raids on critical military targets, such as Syrian Army bases. During the earliest stages of the conflict, in response to US airstrikes, IS fighters worked to stress the importance of operational security to fellow fighters, imploring them to assume a "covert posture submerged within the population," don masks that covered their faces, and even eschew any identifying information while operating in public.[34] In many ways, IS's intelligence service was one of its fundamental drivers of battlefield success and organizational cohesion. Soon after assuming leadership of the group, Baghdadi relied on IS's internal security apparatus to purge the organization of suspected informants.[35] When new recruits arrived from abroad, especially from Western countries, they were screened and vetted by IS fighters through a series of interviews, during which personal information was obtained and cross checked, passports were examined and donations were accepted,[36] IS maintained impeccable records of who was joining the organization in an effort to weed out spies and exact revenge on those who defected.

For IS, counterintelligence was a top priority. A captured IS computer even revealed a downloaded copy of the US Army and Marine Corps Counterinsurgency Field Manual (FM) 3-24, which the group presumably studied to better understand US operating procedures.[37] Intelligence agencies and security services in Western countries, particularly in Europe, remain highly concerned that sleeper cells of fighters will arrive back in their home countries with newly acquired skills in how to conduct surveillance, how to avoid detection, and how to build a clandestine network.[38] Those returning in order to plan an attack will do so surreptitiously, and many could seek to return to the illicit networks they belonged to before departing for Syria.[39]

The IS intelligence apparatus, also sometimes referred to as "Emni" (Arabic for "trust," "security," and "safety"), fulfills a wide range of internal security and external intelligence services, to include everything from rooting out informers to planning external attacks across the globe, including the Paris November 2015 and Brussels March 2016 attacks.[40] Former Baathists from Saddam Hussein's secret police played an instrumental role in helping to organize the Emni.[41] Some have compared the Emni to East Germany's Stasi, a brutal domestic intelligence agency that spied on citizens and foreigners alike.[42] Emni members successfully penetrated government institutions in Iraq, as well as various agencies within adversary forces, such as Kurdish intelligence, and within the ranks of Al-Nusra.[43] The Emni holds a special place within IS and, according to Rukmini Callimachi, is afforded "carte blanche to recruit and reroute operatives from all parts of the organization – from new arrivals to seasoned battlefield fighters, and from the group's special forces and its elite commando units."[44]

Before IS sought to expand into new territory, its intelligence operatives were sent to collect information on the existing political and ideological make-up of the area. Once IS actually moved into the territory, those individuals already identified as potentially resistant to the group would be rounded up and executed.[45] Such a sophisticated strategy should give pause to anyone who believes IS would be unable to once again infiltrate areas that have recently been reclaimed by Iraqi or Syrian forces, respectively. IS has also allegedly sent militants abroad to Turkey, Europe, and elsewhere as forward deployed assets, to be used as sleeper cells at some undetermined point in the future. As Bruce Hoffman notes, the Islamic State's "investment of operational personnel ensures that IS will retain an effective international terrorist strike capability in Europe irrespective of its battlefield reverses in Syria and Iraq."[46]

Sanctuary, Safe Haven, and Operational Space

As the world learned on September 11, 2001, when violent terrorist groups are allowed to persist unfettered in safe havens and sanctuary, they can develop the capability to plot and execute spectacular attacks. Without Raqqa as a headquarters, it remains debatable whether or not IS would have been able to plan an attack as sophisticated and coordinated as that launched in Paris, France, in November 2015. Sanctuary and control of territory – operational space – enable financing, which in turn helps facilitate the process of state building. As IS built its state, this in turn increased its legitimacy as an entity able to provide law and order and other basic trappings of a state, further attracting foreign fighters and their families to travel to the territory. The caliphate was becoming a reality.

Since the late 1990s, Sunni violent extremism has become a major threat to global stability and it now has more groups, members, and safe havens than at any other point in history.[47] And more so than any other insurgent group in recent memory, the Islamic State was able to hold and actually control vast swaths of territory across two sovereign countries. At its peak, the Islamic State controlled more than 100,000 km^2 of territory containing more than 11 million people, mostly in Iraq and Syria.[48] It maintained its de-facto headquarters in Raqqa, Syria, and its primary base of operations in Iraq was in Mosul. Throughout the course of the conflict, IS occupied parts of Idlib and Aleppo provinces, where training camps were established. At various points, in Aleppo, the group controlled the Jarabulus crossing to the west and the Tal Abayd crossing to the east, critical chokepoints that regulated the flow of men, money, and *matériel* coming into Syria from Turkey.[49] Losing the physical caliphate may tarnish its brand in the eyes of some, but the fact that it was able to successfully establish a caliphate in the first place will remain a viable propaganda tool for the group in recruiting new members and lifting the morale of the global jihadist movement as a whole. As Aaron Zelin remarked:

The most important take away is that it happened. No longer do individuals or jihadis have to point to a historical idealized past of the original Rashidun Caliphate. Rather, they can point to two to five years ago and that it was here and it was doing well from their perspective. As a result, it is about a lived nostalgia rather than just a pure utopian fantasy whether you agree or disagree with how well things actually were under IS rule. It's all about

how jihadis, supporters, and fence-sitters think of the experience. Many believe that if their enemies didn't attack them it
would have been successful.[50]

IS enjoyed safe haven in Syria largely unmolested for long enough to
allow it to really hold territory that it could use to train, produce media,
and begin implementing the foundational elements of its caliphate.
There is a direct connection between controlling territory and earning
money. Consider that, for long stretches of time during this conflict,
IS was earning well over $1 million per day from the sale of oil and
oil-related products.[51] Furthermore, IS checkpoints throughout the
territory it controlled provided the militants with multiple opportunities to "tax" those attempting to pass through. IS was so brazen in some
parts of the territory it controlled that it allowed municipal workers
and civil servants to remain in their jobs, including some city mayors
and other top local officeholders who were allowed to keep their posts,
provided they acknowledged the legitimacy of IS's rule.[52] Accordingly,
the control of territory meant the control of resources, including oil,
wheat, water, and ancient artifacts, all of which were sold to further
expand IS's financial portfolio.

Sunni disenfranchisement in both Iraq and Syria contributed to
the Islamic State's ability to establish sanctuary in those countries.[53]
Even after IS has been largely vanquished in Iraq and remains severely
attenuated in Syria, poor or non-existent governance remains a major
concern in both of those countries. These areas remain a concern
because IS has been able to orchestrate attacks when under immense
siege from the Coalition, taking advantage of ever-smaller swaths of
territory that the group can still utilize as a safe haven to plan, plot,
and incite from.[54] The US intelligence community remains extremely
concerned about IS developing an "alternate safe haven," that is,

another area outside of Iraq and Syria where its remaining fighters are able to congregate en masse to establish a robust presence and begin reconstituting.[55] Safe havens are spaces that are not simply ungoverned, but alternatively governed – they are governed by insurgents or terrorist groups who may seek to ally with or tolerate an IS presence in places like Libya, Afghanistan, Egypt's Sinai Peninsula, or throughout isolated archipelagos in Southeast Asia. Herein lie some of the dangers inherent in splintering, especially when certain regions already possess the militant infrastructure to allow splinter movements to flourish by providing a ready-made environment for terrorism and insurgency.

Training

By the summer of 2014, IS had already established logistical hubs for resupply, a functioning operational headquarters, training camps, and other vital infrastructure throughout Syria. Training for IS recruits, especially foreign fighters, was multi-purpose, at once designed to build a militant's practical skills, but also to "imbue him with a sense of solidarity with a larger cause."[56] After being properly vetted, new recruits would spend several weeks undergoing both religious and military training, tailored to align with their assigned role within the organization. Highly skilled recruits were selected to receive further training on more sophisticated weapons.[57] IS selected certain operatives for its "special forces program," which involved ten levels of training.[58] IS is far from the Navy SEALs, but a dedicated special forces program is a lot more than most insurgent groups are capable of achieving, with the exception of groups like Hezbollah, which is in a class of its own in many ways (and benefits from the largesse of Iran).

From 2012 to 2015, well over 100 jihadist training camps were identified in Syria and Iraq, used not only by IS but also by Nusra and a range of other violent militant groups.[59] A major part of what happens in IS training camps is religious instruction and ideological indoctrination.[60] As Graeme Wood has noted, "the religion preached by its most ardent followers derives from coherent and even learned interpretations of Islam."[61] Perhaps interestingly, it seems that many IS recruits were in need of strict lessons in how to interpret the Islamic State's austere view of Salafism – after all, only a mere 5 percent of incoming recruits were judged to have an "advanced" knowledge of Islam, while 70 percent were described as having only a "basic" grasp of the religion.[62] Even with a simplistic interpretation of religion, it was clearly still a significant motivating factor for recruits to join IS.[63]

IS also trains young children in their "Cubs of the Caliphate" camps, where children as young as 5 years old are indoctrinated in the group's ideology and taught how to kill.[64] Horgan et al. have described the six stages of child socialization to IS, including seduction, selection, and subjugation, among other disturbing aspects of the process.[65] In Syria, this has included an aggressive campaign targeting "youth, especially boys, to override parents' authority, create new power structures in society, and propagate [IS's] ideology."[66] The head of Germany's domestic intelligence agency has warned that the return of children "brainwashed" by the Islamic State poses a "massive danger" to his country in the near term and well into the future.[67] A captured French jihadist claimed that IS "made concrete plans" to send children (mostly Syrians) to Europe to conduct attacks against Western targets, but would only do so once the kids reach adolescence so that facial recognition software would not be as effective.[68]

Organizational Capabilities

IS's organizational structure may help it transition smoothly from a territorially based insurgent organization to an underground, clandestine terrorist group. Its network-like qualities and affiliate franchise groups contribute to its protean structure and ability to survive. Another important element to analyze is how IS went about building its state and the manner in which it constructed a bureaucracy to help it operate more effectively.[69] It even required recruits to fill out highly detailed "onboarding" documents which asked for name, address, phone number, and detailed information about the network that recruited them, a measure ostensibly implemented to enhance operational security.

This section also examines the "virtual caliphate" – that is, IS's ability to survive online through its use of information operations and social-media savvy. Even before Raqqa fell, the IS media machine kicked into high gear, working assiduously to dispel any notion of defeat as merely temporary and crafting a narrative of redemption, vengeance, and a future return to the glory days of the caliphate. The truth is that the establishment of the caliphate is a once-in-a-lifetime event and a feat unlikely to be repeated anytime soon. But IS will still attempt to use it as "proof of concept" in the future, demonstrating that it could be accomplished as a way of attempting to unify jihadists around its brand and core ethos.

Recruitment

In addition to recruiting within the region, IS was able to successfully recruit thousands of European Muslims to join its ranks. There were a significant number of Westerners counted among IS's ranks, including fighters from the United States, the United Kingdom, Australia, Scandinavia, and many European countries. There was also an outsized contingent of jihadist fighters from Trinidad and Tobago.[70] Why were so many young men and women from the outskirts of London, Paris, and Brussels so enamored with an ultra-violent, atavistic terrorist organization that sought to take the world back to the seventh century? This is the subject of ongoing debate between two French scholars of Islam, Gilles Kepel and Olivier Roy, concerning the topic of radicalization. What can explain so many French citizens going on to join IS? Why has France been among the most targeted countries in the West by jihadists? Kepel lays the blame squarely with religious extremism, while Roy argues that European jihadists who traveled to the caliphate and participated in gruesome actions are merely nihilists using Islam as a pretext to carry out sociopathic fantasies.[71]

According to Rik Coolsaet, "joining IS is merely a shift to another form of deviant behavior, next to membership of street gangs, rioting, drug trafficking and juvenile delinquency."[72] A 2012 report by the European Parliament titled "Europe's Crime–Terror Nexus: Links Between Terrorist and Organised Crime Groups in the European Union" noted the prevalence with which jihadist attacks involved links to criminality, including drug trafficking.[73] In some sense, a background in the criminal underworld left behind for militant Islam can play into the appeal of what has been called "jihadi cool," which blends "traditional notions of honor and virility, but also a strong undercurrent of oppositional, postmodern cool."[74] Thomas Hegghammer has referred to elements of this trend as "the soft power of militant jihad," while observing that "In Europe, radicals sometimes wear a combination of sneakers, a Middle Eastern or Pakistani gown and a combat jacket on top. It's a style that perhaps reflects their urban roots, Muslim identity and militant sympathies."[75]

IS's predecessor, AQI, was led by a criminal-cum-jihadist named Abu Musab al-Zarqawi, whose background included street gangs and prison time for sexual assault.[76] Indeed, IS seems to attract many jihadists with a similar profile, including the main link between the Paris November 2015 attacks and the Brussels March 2016 bombings, Salah Abdeslam, known for his penchant for drinking, smoking, and gambling, rather than his piety. Abdeslam was a regular patron (and brother of the manager) of a Molenbeek bar named Café del Beguines, a place known for drug dealing and other illicit activity and closed down after "compromising public security and tranquility."[77] Abdeslam was the only surviving member of the group of terrorists that formed the core of the French–Belgian nexus.[78] He has been back and forth to court, and his refusal to cooperate with authorities has made him something of a cult hero to aspiring jihadists, even cited as the inspiration for a March 2018 attack at a French supermarket.[79]

Molenbeek came under intense scrutiny following the Paris and Brussels attacks. It is a gritty neighborhood of Brussels where a "hybrid subculture of crime, violence, and jihadi activism has taken root."[80] It symbolizes the epicenter of the crime–terror nexus. It has a history with Islamic radicals and their networks, and is plagued by high levels of unemployment, and when compared with the rest of Belgian society its residents suffer from severe educational disparities, a disproportionately high involvement in the prison system, and isolation from wider Belgian society. Matthew Levitt described Molenbeek as "like another world, another culture, festering in the heart of the West."[81] In fact, Molenbeek was so insular that it was not particularly strange that a charismatic imam named Khalid Zerkani (a.k.a. "Papa Noel") with deep hatred for the West encouraged young Belgian men with ancestral roots in Morocco and other majority-Muslim countries to commit acts of criminality in order to finance jihad.[82]

Besides Abdeslam, several other notorious IS terrorists had criminal backgrounds, including the leader of the Paris attacks, fellow Belgian Abdelhamid Abaaoud. Others include Ahmed Coulibaly, a key figure in the Charlie Hebdo attacks; Mohamed Lahouaiej Bouhlel, the terrorist who killed 84 people by driving a truck through a crowd on Bastille Day in Nice, France; and Anis Amri, the Tunisian jihadist responsible for ramming a truck into a Berlin Christmas market.

Leadership

As has been well documented by now, the leadership core of the Islamic State congealed in Camp Bucca. Many of its top leaders have been eliminated – although, at the time of this writing, the so-called Caliph is still alive, on the run, and in hiding. With most of the original leadership gone, the chances increase that remaining fighters will splinter off and be absorbed by new groups elsewhere, even as "core IS" inevitably attempts to reconstitute itself back in parts of Iraq and Syria. The splintering of the group will lead to further decentralization and a situation in which there is a decreased threat from any one major jihadist group, but an increased threat from dozens of smaller outfits, some of which may eventually grow to become more lethal than the group from which they were originally derived.

IS is led by Abu Bakr al-Baghdadi, an Iraqi also known as Ibrahim Awad Ibrahim al-Badry, born in Samarra in 1971.[83] Captured by US forces near Fallujah in 2004, al-Baghdadi spent years at Camp Bucca, a detention facility where he is thought to have grown even further radicalized and anti-American, while also broadening his network among aggrieved Iraqi Sunni Arabs, including many from Anbar and Nineveh provinces.[84] Along with other Islamic State leaders – including Abu Muslim al-Turkmani, Abu Louay, and Abu Kassem – Baghdadi used his time as a networking opportunity to meet and organize with jihadists, ex-Baathists, and violent criminals.[85] Upon their release, they formed the core of what evolved into the Islamic State, after Baghdadi helped engineer the defection of al-Qaeda in Iraq from the broader al-Qaeda orbit.[86] Baghdadi obtained a doctorate in Quranic studies, for which he studied the theology of Islam's central text, from Saddam University in Baghdad. This education allowed him to burnish religious credentials that other jihadist leaders have never been able to claim, including al-Qaeda leaders Osama bin Laden and Ayman al-Zawahiri. The legitimacy afforded by his religious education was one of several factors – along with familial lineage traced back to the Prophet – that cleared Baghdadi's way to declare himself Caliph, or ruler of all Muslims, in a historic speech at the Grand Mosque in Mosul in June 2014.[87]

While the group's leadership cadre did include some prominent foreign fighters, such as a Chechen named Omar al-Shishani,[88] there were also former Baath party military and intelligence officers that held high-ranking positions during Saddam Hussein's regime, including Abu Ali al-Anbari and Abu Muslim al-Turkmani.[89] Two other former regime-loyalists-turned-IS-members were Fadel al-Hayali and Adnan al-Sweidawi, both of whom served as military officers and Baath party insiders.[90] Indeed, IS maintained a leadership council, a cabinet, and had ties to local leaders. The leadership council helped deal with religious issues and doctrine, but also apparently made decisions about executions. The cabinet maintained oversight on finance, security, media, prisoners, and recruitment, while local leaders were comprised of roughly a dozen deputies spread between Iraq and Syria.[91] IS operates in a more decentralized fashion than al-Qaeda ever did, with operations carried out by a network of regional commanders who each maintained responsibility for subordinates, who had their own autonomy, but were also able to collaborate and coordinate with the regional commanders on a variety of tactical issues.[92]

Before being killed in a US airstrike in August 2016, Baghdadi's deputy was Abu Muhammad al-Adnani, a Syrian jihadist who fought against US forces in Iraq and was captured in 2005. Like Baghdadi, Adnani was detained in Camp Bucca for a period of time. He would go on to become the terrorist group's chief spokesman, tasked with directing its media campaign and information operations.[93] In June 2014, al-Adnani was the first member of IS to officially declare a caliphate in Iraq and Syria. He was designated as a terrorist by the US Department of State in August 2014, and a $5 million bounty was subsequently placed on his head. Al-Adnani's legacy continues to live on through audio recordings. In the most notorious of these, a nine-minute audio recording titled "Die in Your Rage" from September 2014, he implores Muslims in Western nations to carry out lone-wolf attacks. In addition to serving as spokesman, al-Adnani headed IS's previously aforementioned *Emni,* or external operations unit, which was responsible for planning attacks outside of IS territory. Al-Adnani is thought to have had a hand in planning some of the most spectacular attacks ever conducted by the group, including the Paris November 2015 and the Brussels March 2016 attacks.[94]

Ideology

Just as salient as the military skills taught in IS's training camps was the religious instruction and indoctrination of IS recruits and members, including young children. The next generation of youngsters has already been brainwashed, force-fed a highly sectarian and *takfirist* worldview. The Islamic State has proven to be the most austere of all Salafi-jihadist groups, even eclipsing al-Qaeda in its austere interpretation of *sharia* law. As IS seeks to expand abroad following the collapse of its caliphate, it will probably need to do what al-Qaeda has successfully done to co-exist in certain locales – that is, tailoring its ideology (and tempering it where necessary) to fall more closely in line with local attitudes, as AQAP has done in Yemen and as its various iterations have attempted to do in Syria.

The brand of Islam practiced by the Islamic State has been described, perhaps most accurately, as "untamed Wahhabism" that views the killing of those deemed unbelievers as a necessity to furthering its mission of purifying the community of the faithful.[95] The group's ideology, defined by an extremely narrow interpretation of *sharia* on social and criminal issues, explains its use of beheading as a way of murdering its victims, who have included several Westerners, Christian and Yazidi religious minorities, Shiite Muslims (considered apostates), Kurds, Alawites, and even other Sunni Muslims whom IS deems worthy of elimination. It has been labeled "the most elaborate and militant jihad polity in modern history."[96]

After it seized Mosul in June 2014, IS publicized a "city charter" that called for the amputation of thieves' hands, mandatory prayers, the banning of all drugs and alcohol, and the desecration of shrines and graves considered to be polytheistic.[97] The group's adherence to such an austere, unforgiving brand of Islam is reminiscent of AQI's split with core al-Qaeda, and once again al-Qaeda senior leadership, including Ayman al-Zawahiri, viewed the group's extreme violence as ultimately counterproductive.[98] The public split with al-Qaeda has seemingly forced jihadists to choose sides,[99] although, in an interesting twist, some IS fighters probably get some of their ideological guidance on building an Islamic State from "The Management of Savagery," a manifesto penned by one of core al-Qaeda's main ideologues, Abu Bakr Naji.[100] Its ideology has been described as "aggressive" and "expansionist" with no recognition of modern-day political borders.[101] To be sure, IS regards state boundaries as "artificial creations of colonial powers designed to divide the Muslim world."[102] The fact that IS has announced the establishment of an Islamic state is proof in the eyes of many Muslims worldwide that Baghdadi will be able to resurrect the caliphate.[103]

For IS, the future is one in which a caliphate stretches across the globe. Indeed, the state-building project undertaken by IS was one in which Baghdadi saw his organization "taking a first step toward erasing the artificial boundaries imposed by colonial powers to divide Muslims."[104] The Islamic State's ideology is "an extremist reading of Islamic scripture" and one which espouses "sharply anti-Shiite sectarian views and harsh application of Islamic law."[105] IS's ideology promotes a worldview that essentially "classifies and excommunicates fellow Muslims."[106] That most IS recruits have a poor understanding of Islam is a benefit to recruiters, who in some ways prefer recruits with an unsophisticated command of their religion, as it makes them more malleable and less likely to question those who seek to indoctrinate them.[107] Furthermore, IS and its ideology will persist for generations. While the physical caliphate has been destroyed, the fact that it was established will help fuel the duration of the ideology well into the future.[108]

Human Resources and Bureaucracy

In the post-9/11 era, it became fashionable to talk about how terrorist organizations like al-Qaeda were "networked," assuming a transnational posture that showed scant resemblance to the vertically structured, top-down ethno-nationalist terrorist groups of the 1980s. But in fact, al-Qaeda, and the Islamic State after it, were both highly bureaucratic in nature, even though both groups maintained a global presence. And even though IS was extremely brutal in doling out punishment to those who "broke the rules," its leadership was also aware of the importance of providing services to the constituency it claimed to represent. During the midst of civil war, internecine violence, and widespread sectarian strife, IS provided predictability, however draconian. Its vast governance network, spearheaded by the *hisbah,* or religious police, dispensed swift justice for a wide range of offenses, but Syrians, Iraqis, and those foreigners who emigrated to the caliphate understood what they needed to do and how they needed to live in order to stay alive. This imbued IS with a sense of political legitimacy that few terrorist groups ever manage to acquire.

All told, IS attracted approximately 43,000 fighters from more than 120 countries.[109] The conflict in Syria has attracted more Westerners than any other conflict in the modern era, including the 1979–89 anti-Soviet jihad.[110] The number of foreign fighters arriving to join the Islamic State finally tailed off in September 2016, dropping from approximately 2,000 recruits crossing the Turkish–Syrian border each month, to only 50.[111] A vast majority of those fighters hailed from the Middle East, North Africa, and other regions typically associated with global jihad, such as the Caucasus and Central Asia. Besides foreign fighters and militants from Saudi Arabia, Tunisia, Lebanon, and Jordan, IS was comprised of thousands of Iraqis and Syrians.[112] After the initial US invasion of Iraq in 2003, a radical Salafi cleric from Aleppo named Abu al-Qaqaa became the primary point of contact for Syrian recruits who were eager to join AQI under the leadership of Zarqawi.[113] The group has also won recruits following large-scale prison breaks throughout Iraq, replenishing its ranks with hardened jihadists, violent sociopaths, and career criminals.[114] Moreover, the group deliberately recruited extremely young fighters, including many teenagers, while others were even younger.[115]

Included in the panoply of individuals recruited by IS were children as young as 6 years old, some of whom were trained to become suicide bombers.[116]

In line with IS's declared goal of establishing an Islamic caliphate, the group has devoted a robust portion of its funding to the nascent stages of state building. In August 2014, IS began paying municipal salaries, provided public works, maintained electricity, trash, and sewage services, offered health care and education to its supporters, and even attempted to enforce parking laws and regulations in areas it controlled or claimed to control.[117] In these areas, it also ensured the availability of basic necessities such as gas and food.[118] In Mosul, IS held a "fun day" for kids, distributed gifts and food during Eid al-Fitr, held Quran recitation competitions, started bus services, and opened schools. More so in Iraq than in Syria, IS has been aware of dealing with the local population in Sunni-predominant towns, villages, and cities.[119] An analysis of al-Qaeda in Iraq reveals that that group, too, was a bureaucratic and hierarchical organization that tried to keep an ironclad grip on the money it earned from a series of rackets.[120] So, it should come as little surprise that its progeny is as well.

IS may be wealthy, especially when compared to other terrorist groups, but it also maintains a vast human resources-type network to deal with medical expenses for fighters (and their families), legal support, safe houses, and administrative expenses (e.g., utilities) in the areas under its control and other logistical requirements of clandestine organizations.[121] It has consistently compelled mid-level bureaucrats and technocrats to remain in their positions in order to ensure continuity.[122] IS's use of former Assad-regime loyalists displayed a pragmatism that was vital to the success it had in holding on to territory it captured.[123]

In areas it controlled, IS went to work building its state, which included all the facets of a normal local government, from police cars and ambulances to traffic cops at intersections; it even opened a complaints desk, for civilians to voice their concerns, and nursing homes, for elderly relatives of jihadists and their extended families.[124] The provision of public services became an important component of constructing the state. IS sent out its members to repair potholes, administer post offices, distribute food to those in need, and even began a campaign to vaccinate its subjects against polio.[125] IS also had a Consumer Protection Authority office.[126] As Graeme Wood notes, "The Islamic State, like any other government, had to administer its territory and population, and was busy building bureaucracies for taxation, health, education, and other official functions."[127] In the areas in Syria under its control, IS set up an electricity office that monitored electricity-use levels, installed new power lines, and instructed work-shops on how to repair damaged ones.[128] In Libya, the IS state-building apparatus established an "Office of General Services" to ensure that businesses were officially registered so taxes could be collected.[129]

A census was conducted in Mosul, where citizens were counted and catalogued according to occupation. Business owners' names were recorded in ledgers, along with their religion and sect.[130] Its administration, bureaucracy, and governance structures have been described as "very sophisticated" and "capable of enduring for years."[131] The Islamic State's bureaucratic apparatus required recruits to complete paperwork that listed their prior education, employment experience, interests, and skills. This information was used to scout talented members and identify jobs that would best suit the capabilities of these individuals.[132] IS members created rules and regulations that governed "everything from fishing and dress codes to the sale of coun-terfeit brands and university admission systems."[133]

Media, Public Relations, and Propaganda

IS has displayed an adroit understanding of its media, and used it in a way no other terrorist group had done in recent memory. IS has relied on a sophisticated approach to media, especially social media, in spreading its message, sowing terror and fear, recruiting new members, and countering Western efforts to shape the narrative.[134] Perhaps most impressive has been the speed with which IS is able to produce its media campaigns, responding in real-time (by "live tweeting") to events as they unfold on the ground. This mode of communication has been described as a "swarmcast" for its interconnected, dispersed, and resilient form.[135]

IS dedicated attention and resources to spreading its message and diffusing its propaganda, exemplified by its pervasive use of social media, including active Twitter campaigns in each of the provinces where it operates and promotes its activities and the battles it fights.[136] As one commentator noted, "Gulf state fundamentalists, battle-hardened Chechens, and middle-class Londoners were all drawn into IS by its powerful messaging and the promise to, in a twist on an old phrase, be the evil you want to see in the world."[137] IS propaganda was directed at terrorizing foreign populations while also admonishing the group's followers to act, as evidenced by the rash of attacks in the West over the past several years, to include increasingly low-cost, opportunistic attacks using vehicles to ram pedestrians. Through a deliberate process of recruiting members with a background in production, editing, and graphic design, IS constructed the most elaborate media apparatus of any terrorist organization to date – a legacy that will assuredly be carried forth by the global jihadi movement as it plans its next move.[138]

The group has been successful at conducting information warfare for several reasons. First, information power-related personnel are accorded high levels of prestige or are otherwise well rewarded. Second, the caliphate narrative is incredibly effective, both for unifying their operations and messages, and for providing a compelling frame for those operations for their supporters and potential supporters. Third, the group's major themes are cleanly grouped and tightly focused, which makes message discipline easy. The themes are also germane to several important and diversified sub-narratives that are specifically targeted to different audiences.

To date, IS has taken advantage of social media to disseminate its message and ideology far beyond what al-Qaeda was ever able to achieve.[139] Despite the attention afforded to the Islamic State's execution videos, the group actually produces much more material, and on a broader range of topics, than what gets reported in the mainstream media.[140] Of all the messages propagated by IS, the establishment and implementation of the "caliphate" is a unique selling point, as it retains historical and religious resonance for the broader Muslim *ummah* and harkens back to a point in history when Islam experienced its Golden Age.[141] IS attempts to communicate the core narrative that its caliphate is a triumphant, model society to all of its potential recruits.[142] IS is more capable than al-Qaeda ever was and continues to grow as an organization and an ideology.[143] Many fear that the legacy of IS will live on through its media/propaganda, calling for the nostalgia of the caliphate.[144]

IS did use social media to broadcast the beheading of several Westerners it had kidnapped, but it also used Twitter, Instagram, YouTube, and Facebook to show its humanitarian efforts, including fighters handing out ice-cream cones to children, in an attempt to appeal to its constituents. It has even developed its own video game modeled after *Grand Theft Auto*.[145] IS has produced several popular series such as *Knights of Martyrdom* and *Risen Alive*, which emphasize the camaraderie of jihad by showing militants fighting together on the battlefield.[146] *Dabiq* is IS's magazine, which is an English-language production used to help lure more recruits.[147] The magazine is multi-faceted, reporting battlefield statistics but also laying out a thoroughly detailed religious explanation for its actions, especially its attempt to establish an Islamic caliphate in Syria and Iraq.[148]

Just like other millennials, the concept of "oversharing" extends to terrorists as well. The use of multiple media platforms has served as a cache of open source intelligence (OSINT) for intelligence and law enforcement authorities attempting to track, monitor, and combat IS.[149] Simply from monitoring jihadists' use of social media, Western authorities have been able to gain insight into foreign fighters traveling to Syria and Iraq to fight with the group, as well as to map the rift that developed and eventually led to a split between IS and Jabhat al-Nusra.[150]

Even though IS militants communicate openly on some social media forums, its media wing remains incredibly agile. When its accounts on Twitter and other sites are shuttered, new accounts appear almost immediately. It relies on services like JustPaste.it to distribute battle summaries, SoundCloud for the release of audio reports, Instagram to share photos, and WhatsApp to swap graphics and videos.[151] Other commonly used apps include Ask.fm, PalTalk, kik, and Tumblr.[152] The Islamic State dedicates a significant portion of its resources to media and propaganda.[153] Fawaz Gerges estimates that IS allocated one-third of its annual budget to a combination of propaganda and governance.[154]

The Islamic State's slogan is "Baqiya wa Tatamaddad" – "Remaining and Expanding." Rather than living under apostate regimes in the Middle East or morally bankrupt societies in Western nations, Muslims who join IS can enjoy an ideal Islamic community, and those who resist this call will be vanquished. This vision is furthered by videos that focus on the caliphate as a benevolent state committed to public works and Islamic welfare.[155] IS propaganda is meticulously tailored to different target groups it seeks to recruit, from criminals and gangsters to technically minded professionals.[156] Its members understand their audience better than the West does and it has been able to position itself as a group with countercultural appeal – so-called "jihadi cool."[157]

IS has a legion of "fanboys" who disseminate the group's propaganda.[158] "IS's social media success can be attributed to a relatively small group of hyperactive users, numbering between 500 and 2,000 accounts, which tweet in concentrated bursts of high volume."[159] Between June and October 2015, Twitter suspended or removed the accounts of over 125,000 IS sympathizers or members.[160] A RAND Corporation report from August 2016 noted that, if Twitter continued its campaign of account suspensions, this harassment could force IS supporters to lose valuable time reacquiring followers and could ultimately push some to use social media channels that are far less public and accessible than Twitter.[161] Once technology companies like Twitter and Facebook began policing their sites more aggressively, jihadists migrated to other platforms to communicate, including Telegram, which IS fighters used both to recruit and to plan terrorist attacks.[162]

3

The Coming Terrorist Diaspora

For many of the Islamic State's surviving fighters, the loss of Iraq and Syria may merely signal a temporary pause in the fight.[1] A significant percentage of militants will almost certainly seek out new battlefields to continue waging jihad.[2] The caliphate has indeed collapsed and the organization has splintered. Accordingly, to speak of IS as a monolith going forward might not make much sense. While IS may be a singular brand, it encompasses a wide swath of jihadists with similar but not necessarily identical objectives. There will continue to be, well into the foreseeable future, a medium-intensity yet highly capable insurgency, based along the Euphrates River Valley with tentacles stretching throughout parts of eastern Syria and northern and western Iraq. There will also be IS's international footprint, its provinces abroad, which will ebb and flow in operational tempo while also maintaining varying degrees of linkages to areas of the former caliphate.

In early February 2018, the United States began downsizing its military footprint in Iraq, shifting personnel and resources to other hotspots around the globe, including Afghanistan. As of April 2018, President Trump publicly called for the withdrawal of US troops from Syria, with the White House Press Secretary Sarah Huckabee-Sanders announcing: "[T]he military mission to eradicate IS in Syria is coming to a rapid end, with IS almost being completely destroyed."[3] But, as recent history has proven time and again over the past decade and a half, a violent Sunni jihadist group, whether it calls itself IS or rebrands under another banner, will reconstitute in parts of Iraq and Syria to challenge existing governance structures while planning new attacks and organizing into a formidable fighting force.

IS Affiliates Abroad

Just as al-Qaeda did before it, the Islamic State has spun off a constellation of franchise groups and affiliates around the globe, each of which has the potential to grow into a formidable terrorist organization in its own right. As of late 2018, the United States Department of State had designated IS franchise groups in Indonesia, the North Caucasus, Afghanistan, Algeria, Libya, the Sinai (as well as mainland Egypt), Somalia, Tunisia, the Philippines, Bangladesh, the Greater Sahara, and West Africa. This section will focus on the three most pernicious IS satellites, located in the Sinai, Afghanistan, and Libya, respectively, while also analyzing some of the other areas where IS affiliates have demonstrated serious potential to evolve into more dangereuos long-term threats. But to understand the scale of this threat, it is essential to have a comprehensive understanding of the nature of these groups, which, while IS-affiliated, may differ significantly across several important measures.

Table 3.1 assesses these franchise groups in order to determine what type of group the IS affiliate should be characterized as. There is a growing body of scholarship that differentiates between terrorism, insurgency, and guerrilla warfare, and an in-depth analysis of these differences is beyond the scope of this book.[4] This table looks at the size of the group, its primary targets, organizational structure,

Table 3.1 Analysis of IS affiliates

Affiliate	Size	Primary Targets	Structure	Strategy	Territorial Control	Reach	Typology
Afghanistan	500–1,000	Civilians Insurgents	Decentralized	Punishment	Geographically divided	Regional	Insurgents
Libya	500–800	Security forces	Hybrid	Guerrilla	Small pockets Contested	Transnational	Terrorists
Philippines	750	Civilians Security forces	Hybrid	Guerrilla	Dispersed Localized	Regional	Guerrillas
Sinai	500–750	Civilians Security forces	Decentralized	Punishment Guerrilla	Shifting Ungoverned	Local	Guerillas
West Africa	3,500	Civilians	Hybrid	Punishment	Large swaths	Regional	Insurgents
Yemen	100–250	Security forces	Decentralized	Guerrilla	Small pockets	Local	Insurgents

strategy,[5] extent of territorial control, and reach (defined as area of operations). The final column of the table classifies each affiliate according to typology. In other words, whether the group most closely resembles a terrorist organization, insurgent group, or guerrilla army. Indeed, just as insurgency and terrorism are not the same, the objectives of counterinsurgency and counterterrorism are different, too. Nuanced approaches to fighting adaptive adversaries require a different mix of tools – military, police, diplomatic, economic – to effectively counter the protean campaign of violence waged by IS affiliate groups.

Sinai Peninsula

The vast, ungoverned territory of Egypt's Sinai Peninsula has long been home to smugglers, terrorists, and an array of other non-state actors and it has once again become attractive territory to radicals and extremists.[6] With its fluctuating number of fighters, decentralized structure, and hybrid strategy of attacking both security forces and Egyptian civilians, the IS branch in the Sinai could most aptly be described as a guerrilla movement that relies on terrorist tactics, including raids, ambushes, and bombings, to keep the government from extending reach into the Sinai in any meaningful way. The Sinai has long been considered one of the world's most lawless areas, due in part to geography and a Bedouin culture that is nomadic and fiercely anti-authoritarian.

Egypt experienced a spike in violence following the ouster of Mohammed Morsi, a Muslim Brotherhood leader voted into office following Arab Spring protests.[7] The Sinai already has a dedicated IS franchise group that continues to gather momentum, particularly in the face of the ineptitude of Egyptian security forces. Signs of a merger between Egyptian groups and IS became apparent as early as 2014, when elements of Ansar Bait al-Maqdis (ABM) pledged allegiance to IS and made efforts to establish connections with IS fighters in Libya.[8] This connection could very well grow in the future, with money and weapons being exchanged between IS militants in Libya and Egypt.[9] The Sinai was critical terrain for the militants and became, in effect, "both a haven and a crossing point for smuggling fighters, weapons and illicit goods" between Egypt and the Maghreb.[10]

Throughout the Sinai, IS-affiliated militants pursue a hybrid strategy of attacking both Egyptian security forces and civilian non-combatants, the latter part of the strategy introducing a highly sectarian dimension to the conflict. IS fighters in the Sinai regularly clash with Egyptian security forces and have launched attacks over the past several years in which hundreds of Egyptian troops have been killed.[11] IS's Sinai affiliate has also demonstrated its penchant for conducting spectacular attacks, evidenced by the downing of Metrojet Flight 9268, when an IS bomb killed all 224 people onboard an airliner destined for St Petersburg, Russia. The group is also responsible for attacking Coptic Christian churches and firing rockets into Israel.

Weak Security Forces

Despite having a formidable conventional military, at least by regional standards, Egypt has struggled mightily to contain the growing insurgency in the Sinai. There are serious concerns that the Egyptian military's failure to adequately combat IS's Sinai affiliate could lead the group to eventually develop into a highly capable franchise group, similar to the evolution of al-Qaeda in the Arabian Peninsula (AQAP), al-Qaeda's Yemeni affiliate. Many argue that the Sisi government's approach to counterinsurgency is myopic, leading the population of the Sinai to support the militants.[12] This provides an opening for jihadists, as the government has little-to-no presence, economic conditions are dire, and local Bedouins have long operated with autonomy. In response to the growing anarchy in the Sinai, Israel has waged a covert air campaign over the past two years, relying on a mix of unmarked drones, jets, and helicopters to target militants; in what clearly marks a new development in the relationship between Cairo and Tel Aviv, these operations have all been launched with the tacit approval of Egypt's top military leadership, signaling how desperate Sisi is for help in containing the threat.[13] IS's Sinai-based affiliate has demonstrated the capability to wage a prolonged insurgency replete with terrorist tactics and guerrilla-style attacks against the security forces, thus increasing the possibility of a lingering low-intensity conflict that could plague ineffectually governed parts of Egypt for years.

Ungoverned Territory

The operational tempo of terrorist attacks seems to have increased in intensity from 2015 to 2018, while the insurgency itself is morphing and spreading into different territories within Egypt. By the spring of 2016, IS in the Sinai had moved into parts of the Western Desert, Upper Egypt, and Greater Cairo.[14] Repeated offensives by the Egyptian military to dislodge IS militants in the northern part of the Sinai have so far been unsuccessful.[15] The jihadists' reach and influence remains localized to the Sinai and other areas within the country, but has the potential to spread beyond Egypt's borders and grow into a regional threat. As evidence, IS's Sinai affiliate has broadened its targets, recently declaring war on the Palestinian militant group Hamas, sparking fears that IS could attempt to move into Gaza, bringing its fighters even closer to the Israeli border.[16] Now that ties between IS in the Sinai Hamas have been severed, the threat to Israel has been reduced, although not totally eliminated.[17] Israel's concerns are warranted, as the Sinai has traditionally been an anarchic region and one which is geographically ideal for violent Salafists, given its proximity to Israel.[18]

Sectarianism

Well before the Arab Spring, Egypt suffered from periodic spasms of religious and political violence, and has long been fertile soil for religious extremism, evidenced by the domestic terrorist campaigns waged by groups like Egyptian Islamic Jihad and Gama'a al-Islamiyyah. But the recent wave of attacks has assumed an even more virulent sectarian character and the tactics used by jihadist groups in the Sinai include roadside IEDs, suicide bombings, and assassinations.[19] Put simply, because of its geography, history, and cultural significance, Egypt is too valuable for jihadists to ignore.[20]

Egypt's Coptic Christian population has borne the brunt of these attacks, essentially under assault by Salafi-jihadists for much of the past two years. In April 2017, terrorists waged a week-long campaign of attacks against Christians, including bombings on Palm Sunday in Alexandria and Tanta,[21] and another shooting at a monastery one week later.[22] Toward the end of December 2017, 11 were killed in an attack on a Coptic Church near Cairo.[23] And it is not just Christians who are under attack. In November 2017, in what has been recorded as Egypt's deadliest terror incident to date, over 300 Sufi Muslims were killed in an attack on their mosque in the Sinai.[24]

Afghanistan and Pakistan (AFPAK)

IS has been operating in Afghanistan since approximately 2014 under the auspices of the Islamic State in Khorasan Province (ISKP) Through a series of coordinated and highly lethal attacks targeting Afghanistan's minority Shiite community, IS has established itself as one of the most poignant drivers of instability in that country, further intensifying the sectarian element of the conflict in Afghanistan.[25] ISKP has also frequently battled with the Taliban, especially in Nangarhar and Zabul provinces between 2015 and 2017, and the organization split in the summer of 2017, with one faction declaring loyalty to a former Lashkar-e-Taiba commander and the other, comprised mostly of Central Asians, coalescing behind an ex-Islamic Movement of Uzbekistan (IMU) leader.[26] The Central Asian faction dominates territory in northern Afghanistan while the Pakistani-led faction is more active in southern and eastern Afghanistan, closer to the Pakistani border.[27]

Although ISKP has clashed with Taliban fighters and launched attacks against the Afghan government and military – in January 2018, the group killed 11 soldiers at the Kabul military academy – it is most widely known for its brutal and unrelenting attacks against Afghan civilians and non-combatants, including the non-governmental organization Save the Children.[28] Attacks against civilians form part of ISKP's approach to insurgency, which follows a strategy of punishment. The essence of this approach is deliberately targeting non-combatants, either to provoke a government overreaction or to demonstrate to the civilian population that the security forces are weak and the state illegitimate. A July 2016 attack on Hazaras organizing a protest march in Kabul killed over 80 civilians and wounded another 250 people. Then, in late October 2017, the group orchestrated a wave of suicide bombings directed at Shiite targets, including several mosques, which killed more than 100 and wounded another 200.[29]

IS has also attacked hospitals, hotels, and military installations, and has launched attacks in both Afghanistan and Pakistan and appears to be gaining ground in the latter, especially in Baluchistan.[30] An October 2016 attack on a police training college in Quetta resulted in more than 60 dead and another 120 wounded, most of them cadets. Although IS claimed this attack, there was some speculation that the attack was actually committed by another militant group, Lashkar-e-Jhangvi (LEJ), and that IS "outsourced" the attack to LEJ.[31]

Violent Competition

Although its presence in Afghanistan initially surfaced in 2014, ISKP became an official IS affiliate in January 2015, starting with a group of defectors from the Pakistani Taliban, or Tehrik-i-Taliban Pakistan (TTP). The Pakistani militants helped IS to establish a foothold across the border in Afghanistan, in the southeastern districts of Nangarhar province.[32] The organization was then reinforced by approximately 200 IS militants from the core group in Iraq and Syria, who traveled to Afghanistan to bolster the nascent affiliate.[33] Soon after it was established, it sought to actively recruit and absorb disaffected Taliban fighters into its ranks.[34] By 2018, ISKP had grown into a formidable threat, continuing to absorb new fighters, including further defections from the Afghan Taliban and returning foreign fighters fleeing Iraq and Syria.[35] The spike in violence, worrying even by Afghan standards, could signal violent competition between ISKP and the Afghan Taliban, evidence of a process of outbidding wherein terrorist organizations engage in escalating violent competition to prove which group is the most dedicated and likely to prevail.[36]

Infrastructure for Jihad

Afghanistan is a country wracked by violence dating back decades, and, accordingly, already has an established infrastructure for jihad, making it an attractive place for terrorists and terrorist groups to relocate. By late 2015, ISKP fighters had already taken over territory in Nangarhar, Farah, and Helmand provinces.[37] Moreover, ISKP is just 1 of over 20 militant groups operating in the region.[38] It is difficult to estimate how many fighters ISKP has under arms, although US military officials have claimed that over 1,600 IS-linked militants have already been killed, though nobody quite knows how many fighters remain.[39] At the end of December 2017, Russian officials pegged the number at about 10,000 and growing.[40] More conservative estimates place the number somewhere around 700 active fighters, while other experts assert that the number is unknowable, yet probably falls somewhere between 500 and 1,000.[41]

Precisely accounting for the number of fighters in specific groups is always fraught with risk, although what most analysts can agree upon is that new recruits are flocking to Afghanistan regularly. ISKP frequently receives an influx of new recruits from those who leave the IMU.[42] The British government has voiced concerns that citizens from the UK have made their way from Iraq and Syria to join up with IS in Afghanistan.[43] The Iranian government has made it known that they are preparing for ISKP to receive an influx of fighters now that the caliphate has crumbled in Iraq and Syria.[44]

Persistent American Presence

Because Afghanistan has had a persistent American military presence for the past 17 years, it stands to reason that jihadists will continue to be attracted to this theatre for the opportunity to engage in combat with US troops. The situation is mutually reinforcing. As ISKP continues to gain strength, the United States feels pressured to become more involved, so as not to repeat the mistakes of Iraq in 2011, when a precipitous withdrawal from that country helped fuel the rise of IS there.[45] Indeed, the presence of IS is one of the reasons President Trump, at the urging of Secretary of Defense James Mattis, ultimately decided to keep US troops in the country. In April 2017, in a display of brute force, the United States dropped the "Mother of All Bombs," killing scores of insurgent fighters, yet the threat remains constant from an array of Afghan and foreign jihadists.[46]

Libya

Of all the IS satellites, Libya just may have the potential to be *the* most dangerous safe haven for the group in the near future. The territory is awash in weapons, there is no recognized government to speak of, and it serves as a focal point and crossroads for jihadists of all stripes, located across the Mediterranean Sea from Europe. Two deadly terrorist attacks in Europe have been tied back to Libya already. The danger emanating from this country is more than about just IS; it's the combination of potential threats coalescing to make Libya into the kind of safe haven that Afghanistan was in the decade prior to September 11, 2001.

Failed State

The 2011 intervention left Libya with dueling governments - one recognized by the United States and the international community, the other aligned with General Haftar. In the chaos, Libya also became a safe haven for the Islamic State.[47] The situation in Libya has been described, quite accurately, as one "marred by a prolonged period of political fragmentation, violent conflict, and economic dislocation."[48] "Libya has the most potential to replicate the Islamic State's model in Mesopotamia if things go right for it," according to North Africa expert Aaron Zelin.[49] The anarchy in Libya is now the fourth-largest foreign fighter mobilization in recent history, behind the ongoing civil war in Syria, the Afghan jihad of the 1980s, and the 2003 Iraq war.[50]

One troubling scenario that could boost IS's Libyan branch is the absorption of former al-Qaeda in the Islamic Maghreb (AQIM) fighters as that group continues to decline.[51] Libyan jihadists are believed to be planning attacks on the country's "Oil Crescent" and there is evidence to suggest regional cooperation between IS-affiliated militants in Libya and networks of associates in Morocco, Algeria, and Tunisia.[52]

All In for IS?

IS was well positioned to take advantage of the chaos that engulfed Libya in the immediate aftermath of the post-Qaddafi era, capitalizing upon decades of hatred for the long-time Libyan dictator. Early on, some of its members formed the Islamic Youth Shura Council.[53] Soon thereafter, its Libyan affiliate began building its network by poaching jihadists from existing groups, including Ansar al-Sharia.[54] Around 2012, the Katibat al-Battar al-Libiyah brigade (KBL), a notorious group of Libyan foreign fighters, had been active in both Syria and Iraq and brought important capabilities and expertise to the fledgling IS presence in the country.[55] By November 2014, IS accepted the Libyan start-up as an official *wilayat,* or franchise, with Libyan jihadists returning home from fighting abroad.[56] Several hundred jihadists returned to Libya, declared allegiance to IS, and set up shop in Derna.[57]

The Libyan branch has ebbed and flowed over time, expanding its physical and media presence by early 2015.[58] By the end of 2015, its fighters had assumed control over large sections of Sirte and, by the following summer, IS militants were attempting to consolidate control of territory near Misrata.[59] By early 2016, there were around 1,500 IS fighters in Sirte, but, following a bloody seven-month battle, IS was cleared from its stronghold by the end of the year, forced to withdraw from territory it once completely dominated.[60] The group has managed to maintain an on-again, off-again presence in Bengazhi, which has been plagued by violence for years.[61] IS is now once again attempting to re-establish itself as a legitimate governing entity in pockets of Libya, and Salafists have slowly been assuming control of critical internal security functions. Over time, the goal of IS is to gradually marginalize opposition to its rule and impose a semblance of order that has been elusive since NATO forces deposed Qaddafi nearly a decade ago.[62]

Hub for External Operations

In Libya, where as recently as late 2017 IS boasted approximately 6,500 fighters, the group has carved out space roughly 100 miles southeast of its former base of operations in Sirte.[63] Its members have successfully connected with existing jihadist networks as they began building an infrastructure in Sirte.[64] In addition, IS maintains training and operational bases throughout the central and southern parts of the country.[65] In a sign of Libya's growing importance as a hub for external operations, US bombers conducted airstrikes against IS training camps in Libya in late September 2017, killing dozens of jihadists linked to the Islamic State.[66]

To date, IS's Libyan affiliate has been tied to two major external operations, successfully tallying attacks on European soil, including the deadly Manchester concert bombing in May 2017 and the Berlin Christmas market attack in December 2016. The group has also launched devastating regional attacks, in Bardo and Sousse, Tunisia, respectively, with links back to Libya.[67] The country remains in a state of constant conflict and anarchy, awash in weapons, with various jihadists fighting, switching sides, and occasionally cooperating. Most alarming, the Islamic State maintains specialized entities in Libya, including the "Desert Brigade" and the "Office of Borders and Immigration," which is responsible for external operations, logistics, and recruitment.[68]

Other Locations

The collapse of the caliphate has major significance for Iraq and Syria, the two states where IS once maintained its sanctuary, but also for countries where fleeing foreign fighters might go next. The preceding section discusses IS hubs in the Sinai, Afghanistan, and Libya, but there are other potential hotspots of interest throughout the globe, several of which will be detailed below.

Turkey

At the top of this list should be Turkey, a logical landing spot for many IS militants based purely on geography, located directly north of and contiguous to both Iraq and Syria. IS activity in Turkey is clustered around major cities along the border with Syria (probably due to proximity, travel routes, and population density) and the majority of IS-linked attacks have a connection back to the core group in Iraq and Syria.[69] In early February 2018, "thousands" of IS fighters apparently fled Iraq and Syria while a substantial number "have gone into hiding in countries like Turkey."[70] These revelations are nothing new. Journalist and renowned IS expert Rukmini Callimachi's interview with a former IS fighter from Germany revealed that IS deliberately dispatched hundreds of its fighters to Turkey.[71] In the aftermath of IS's deadly attack on Istanbul's Reina nightclub in the early hours of January 1, 2017 – an attack which killed 39 and wounded 71 – it was revealed that IS had established robust cells operating throughout the country.[72]

Turkey could serve as a logistics hub to plot future attacks and, unlike many other terrorist sanctuaries such as Afghanistan, Libya, or Somalia, Turkey is *not* a failed state. This is important because militants have easier and more reliable access to communications, transportation, and financial networks. There is also the possibility that a spectacular attack could be engineered from Turkish soil, as one nearly was with the improvised explosive device airmailed from Turkey to Australia in August 2017.[73] Over the past decade, Turkey has slowly developed into a country with dense pockets of support for Salafi-jihadist groups, including IS and al-Qaeda, which have used it as a base to mobilize support for their operations.[74] Still, the Turkish military and internal security forces are well trained and highly capable, making it less likely that IS will be able to escalate its campaign beyond the level of low-intensity conflict. In any case, Turkey is more attractive as a logistical hub for planning and acquiring the resources necessary to plot and conduct terrorist attacks in either Europe or the Middle East.

Yemen

The IS presence in Yemen has ebbed and flowed over the past several years, although AQAP remains the dominant militant group in the country, even as both entities come under intense assault by an array of counterterrorism forces. By late 2016, IS in Yemen was mainly confined to the Qayfa front in al-Buyda' and was estimated to have approximately 100 fighters, although the US Department of Defense acknowledged that IS increased its presence from 2017 to 2018, with militants taking advantage of a power vacuum due to that country's ongoing civil war.[75] American airstrikes targeted IS training camps in al-Bayda' in mid-October 2017, killing scores of fighters in this collapsed state flanking Saudi Arabia's southern border.[76] The Trump administration has moved Yemen higher on the United States' list of counterterrorism priorities, as American policymakers and military officials are increasingly concerned that IS fighters fleeing Iraq and Syria will head to the southern parts of the country. In fact, in May 2018, IS for the first time issued instructions for its fighters to travel to the group's stronghold in al-Bayda'.[77]

Still, it is no certainty that IS will find sanctuary in Yemen, a country dominated by al-Qaeda in the Arabian Peninsula in the Sunni heartland of its remote tribal areas.[78] Indeed, the growth of the Islamic State and its announcement of expansion into Yemen in November 2014 helped AQAP by allowing the latter to contrast its style to the comparatively excessive and brutal methods of IS. AQAP specifically announced that, unlike IS, its fighters would never target "mosques, markets and crowded places," ensuring it would earn some degree of legitimacy among Yemen's civilian population.[79] And, despite a relentless onslaught from US airpower and American-backed forces, AQAP remains a major threat in Yemen and, compared to IS, is the far more powerful of the two groups, especially in the hinterlands of Shabwa and Abyan provinces.[80]

Even as IS has successfully staged coordinated, guerilla-style attacks throughout Yemen, the main driver of instability continues to be the ongoing proxy war between Iran, supporting the Houthi rebels, and Saudi Arabia, which, along with the United Arab Emirates, has been waging an unrelenting air war in Yemen, leading to further instability and various humanitarian crises.[81] But if Yemen receives an influx of foreign fighters from Iraq and Syria, IS could certainly grow into a more odious threat. There is already a fairly robust network of militant Salafist groups active throughout the country.[82] Yemen could prove to be a country where al-Qaeda retains its position as the dominant jihadist group and successfully consolidates the disparate cells and small groups of militants under its aegis – or, at least, influence – and that, over time, the majority of IS fighters may eventually gravitate to AQAP both to seek its protection and also to join forces merely to survive.[83] As of mid-2018, IS was struggling to recruit locally among tribes where they are fighting, since the focus of locals is mainly on battling the Houthis and not necessarily declaring loyalty to the Islamic State. Nevertheless, the battle fronts are prime recruiting grounds, so it seems inevitable that IS will continue to maintain at least a steady, low-level presence in Yemen for the foreseeable future.[84]

South Asia

When attempting to answer the question of where the Islamic State might reconstitute next, part of the answer may lie in an area where IS's remaining leadership feels the group *must* expand to remain relevant. An analogous situation unfolded with al-Qaeda in 2003 following the US invasion of Iraq. Al-Qaeda strategists felt that the group would be marginalized within global jihadist circles if it failed to establish a franchise group in a Muslim country "under siege" from non-Muslims. In a similar way, the Rohingya crisis in Myanmar – where a Muslim minority is being oppressed by a Buddhist majority – could serve as a motivating factor for the Islamic State to expand throughout South and Southeast Asia.[85] In January 2018, Malaysian authorities arrested two IS-linked Indonesian citizens who were allegedly planning to kill Buddhist monks in retaliation for the treatment of Rohingya Muslims in Myanmar.[86] Similarly, Akayed Ullah, the Bangladeshi immigrant who detonated a pipe bomb in the New York City subway in December 2017, was said to have visited a Rohingya refugee camp just before returning to the United States and detonating his explosives.[87]

As the Islamic State and al-Qaeda continue to compete for new recruits and territory, the international community should be on high alert for a new IS franchise breaking ground in virgin territory.[88] Yet even if this occurs, it will probably do so not as a result of a centrally directed, command-and-control-driven approach to expanding, but rather from local conditions favorable to a revolutionary movement that offers the promise of upending the status quo in a province, country, or region experiencing high levels of political and/or religious strife and where it is the norm, not the exception, to solve problems through the use of political violence, rather than negotiation or power sharing. In other words, we should look at this global network not as the direct result of a corporate strategy, but rather as an opportunistic, even parasitic, entity. According to this theory, the ideal territory for expansion is a fragile state plagued by persistent civil conflict and sectarian tensions, and with a population considered fertile for and receptive to the Islamic State's propaganda.[89] Myanmar is one such country, even though there are already indications that al-Qaeda in the Indian subcontinent has begun working with local jihadist groups on the ground there.

A new franchise group in Myanmar would allow IS to gain many of the benefits of affiliation by furthering its strategic reach, leveraging local expertise, spreading innovation, and increasing the group's legitimacy in a part of the world where until now it has lacked a sig-nificant presence. There are currently several important impediments to Myanmar developing into the next jihadist hub, especially a lack of logistical infrastructure that includes weapons, safe houses, and a robust network of travel facilitators.[90] That dynamic could change over the next few years with a sustained effort and assistance from returning foreign fighters and existing IS operatives in the broader region, including Bangladesh – making the country a ripe target for IS expansion.[91]

Another South Asian hotspot with a growing IS presence is Bangladesh, a nation with a history of Islamic militancy but long overshadowed by Pakistan. The Islamic State has launched dozens of attacks in Bangladesh against an array of targets, from aid workers to Catholic priests. The most notorious attack came against the Holey Artisan Bakery in Bangladesh's diplomatic quarter in July 2016, when attackers pledging allegiance to IS killed 29 people using bombs, machetes, and small arms.[92] Bangladesh may ultimately prove to be a future battleground between IS and al-Qaeda, with the latter acting through its franchise group al-Qaeda in the Indian Subcontinent, or AQIS.[93] Since 2013, hundreds of Bangladeshis have perished in ter-rorist violence throughout the country, mostly at the hands of AQIS militants.[94]

Another potential post-caliphate growth area for the Islamic State is the disputed Kashmir territory fought over between India and Pakistan, which could prove to be fertile ground for an IS affiliate. Even though several prominent jihadist groups are already active in the region, including Hizb-ul-Mujahideen (HM), Lashkar-e-Taiba (LeT), and Jaish-e-Mohammed (JeM), IS could seek to entrench its operatives in a conflict with great symbolic and religious significance for Muslims worldwide.[95] Moreover, because Kashmir is considered such a sacred cause to Pakistan, a growing IS presence in any future conflict in this territory might also earn the group external support from Pakistan's Inter-Services Intelligence (ISI) agency, which has a long history of providing various forms of both active and passive support to a bevy of jihadist groups.[96]

Southeast Asia

Throughout Southeast Asia, entrenched rivalries, repeated splintering of terrorist organizations, and infighting between factions of jihadi groups have limited their reach in the recent past. But there is a rich history of Islamic militancy in Southeast Asia, from the al-Qaeda-linked Jemmah Islamiyah and Abu Sayyaf Group, to older groups like the Moro Islamic Liberation Front (MILF). Geography is also a critical factor. In some ways, it facilitates terrorism and insurgency, since the islands, peninsulas, and archipelagos that dot the region are particularly difficult to govern. But in other ways, geography is a blessing for authorities in the sense that the Philippines and Indonesia are difficult to reach from the battlefields in Syria and Iraq and are dispersed across a vast distance, making it challenging for jihadists to concentrate or mass forces in any one area.

This is an important variable to consider, especially because Indonesia is the world's most populous Muslim nation and one which has struggled to keep a lid on extremism and radicalization. Jihadist violence in Jakarta and other parts of Indonesia has ebbed and flowed over the past several years.[97] It has included suicide attacks against police and even a suicide attack conducted against churches by a family that had returned from Syria.[98] Indonesia's counterterrorism chief has warned of sleeper cells in every province of the country.[99] The main effect of the collapse of the caliphate in the Middle East has been to reenergize, "expand and transform local extremist movements" throughout the region.[100]

Yet, even despite the distance, fighters from Southeast Asia are making successful return trips to their countries of origin. As of December 2017, 30 fighters from the Philippines had returned there from Syria and Iraq.[101] In an attempt to expand in Indonesia, IS has pursued an aggressive campaign of recruitment and propaganda dissemination.[102] The lines of communications stretch across battlefields, with Southeast Asian fighters in Syria communicating with militants back home in Indonesia and the Philippines to help recruit fighters and coordinate movement into Marawi.[103] Katibah Nusantara, the Southeast Asian wing of IS, was formed by Malay and Indonesian-speaking fighters in Syria.[104] In Southeast Asia, the lure of establishing links with the Islamic State is driven by local dynamics, but has had a galvanizing "effect of a general revival of *jihadi* fervor," especially in Indonesia.[105] There have been numerous reported cases of radicalization amongst guest workers and so-called "migrant maids" from the region being radicalized by IS propaganda.[106]

In many ways, the Philippines could prove to be an appealing destination for IS fighters to relocate and establish a home base.[107] The geography of the country – the Philippines is an archipelago consisting of more than 7,600 islands – makes counterinsurgency and maritime security difficult for the Filipino government. Moreover, the presence of longstanding insurgent groups that already embrace a radical Islamist agenda could allow IS to gain a foothold as it works to champion local grievances. It helps that Muslim insurgents in the area often clash with Christian militias, providing IS the sectarian angle it has been able to successfully exploit elsewhere, including in Afghanistan, Egypt, and Yemen.[108]

It was recently discovered that core IS in Iraq and Syria sent nearly

$2 million to militants in the Philippines to help the group wage the battle for the city of Marawi.[109] Southeast Asia has long been a hotbed of Islamic extremism and violence. It is also worth noting that jihadist militants linked to Abu Sayyaf and other groups operating in the region have demonstrated a remarkable ability to self-fund their organizations without the need for donations from external sources, relying instead on various criminal activities, including robbery, illicit smuggling, and kidnapping for ransom.

Neighboring Indonesia, for example – home to the world's most populous Muslim country – was one of several bases of key al-Qaeda leaders before the 9/11 attacks, and more recently has seen an uptick of arrests related to terrorist plots by Islamic extremists.[110] Still, the nucleus of jihadists actively fighting in – and possibly returning to – the Philippines and other Southeast Asian countries is relatively small compared to other countries in other regions, such as North Africa, in both absolute and relative terms. Nonetheless, as core IS unravels, the region is likely to continue to become increasingly useful to the group as a safety valve outside of the Middle East.

The Combating Terrorism Center at West Point's report on Islamic State activity in Southeast Asia reached several interesting conclusions, noting that IS relies on local militant groups to adopt its brand; in the Philippines specifically, the most common target of terrorists was the military, and small arms were used in most attacks; and an estimated 45 percent of IS attacks and plots in the region had both "financial and communication ties to Southeast Asian Islamic State operatives in Syria where group members sought to enable and guide attacks remotely."[111] A lack of cooperation between intelligence and militaries, including maritime forces, further complicates the issue of counterterrorism.[112]

The situation in Southeast Asia exemplifies some of the challenges in defining what exactly constitutes an IS fighter, and thus an IS affiliate. Some militants have declared allegiance to IS and others have been semi-recognized by IS central, meaning that IS media will claim credit for their attacks. In other cases, IS fighters in the region receive some material support, but does that constitute an ongoing relationship, or are these isolated incidents of support? Core IS recognized Isnilon Hapilon as its chief representative in Southeast Asia, but most of the fighters he commanded seem to have been killed in Marawi, as were a significant portion of the Maute group, although these groups are slowly reforming. Lastly, what are we to make of the Abu Sayyaf Group fighters in Sulu and Jolo, who never declared their loyalty to IS and were outside of the command-and-control network of Hapilon? Many experts consider ASG more akin to a network of gangs rather than an actual organization with an identifiable chain of command. Fighters might fly the black flag of IS for intimidation purposes or invoke the IS name when seeking to negotiate higher ransom payments for kidnapping victims.[113]

Russia and Central Asia

Of all the potential future jihadist hotspots, Central Asia could be the most unassuming and least-hyped region as a future home of returning foreign fighters seeking to make another run at the caliphate. According to the Soufan Group, the former Soviet Republic is host to the highest overall number of foreign fighters. There is a long history of jihadist mobilization throughout Russia, and, throughout Central Asia more broadly. The latter has spawned groups like the Islamic Movement of Uzbekistan, initially formed in opposition to Uzbek strongman Islam Karimov in the 1990s, although its fighters would soon go on to forge strong links with al-Qaeda and other elements of the global jihadist movement. Militants from the Ferghana Valley fought together in Tajikistan's civil war from 1992 to 1997, gaining experience and growing their networks.[114]

Central Asia is a region where the rule of law is weak, levels of corruption are high, and poverty, extremism, and radicalization are endemic.[115] Indeed, a study by the Royal United Services Institute (RUSI) geared toward understanding the variables that contribute to radicalization among Central Asian labor migrants working in Russia found that there is some evidence of structural factors leading to marginalization, exclusion, and alienation of Kyrgyz, Tajik, and Uzbek laborers in Russia, although the authors of the report stopped short of establishing causal links leading to radicalization.[116] Even without a causal link, however, some scholars have concluded that the working and living conditions for Central Asian labor migrants working in Russia were so miserable that many who radicalized and traveled to Syria and the Levant "expect that they are on a 'one way journey,' some to martyrdom but most for a completely new life, and do not plan to return."[117]

There are direct connections between countries from the Former Soviet Union (FSU) and the Middle East. Turkey has been a popular destination for Muslims from Central Asia, but Ankara has grown wary after attacks by members of the Central Asian global diaspora, particularly ethnic Uzbeks, in Istanbul, St. Petersburg, Stockholm, and New York City.[118] The result could lead Turkey, or other countries in the region, to deport former foreign fighters to third-party countries, as Turkey did with 16 IS fighters it deported to Malaysia in August 2017, in what terrorism expert Kim Cragin has dubbed "foreign fighter 'hot potato.'"[119]

Even Kazakhstan, a country of approximately 18 million where 70 percent of the population identifies as Muslim, and one which has traditionally been immune from the type of jihadist violence experienced by its smaller, poorer neighbors, has suffered from several terrorist attacks over the past few years.[120] Authoritarian leaders across the region have used the threat of IS influenced terrorist attacks as a tool to crack down further on dissent, as leaders in Kyrgyzstan have done.[121] During the Soviet era, religion was suppressed, pushing radicals to the margins and forcing them to remain well organized in order to survive. In addition to the IMU, several other jihadist groups operate throughout Central Asia, including Hizb ut-Tahrir al-Islam (Party of Islamic Liberation, HuT), the Jamaat of Central Asian Mujahidin, and the Uyghur Islamic Party of Eastern Turkestan (now known as the Turkestan Islamic Party, or TIP) separatist group, which has been extremely active in the Syria jihad.[122]

Toward the end of 2017, Russia overtook Saudi Arabia and Tunisia for the dubious distinction of being the largest exporter of IS fighters.[123] One factor that could play a key role facing Russia in the future is the struggle for supremacy between jihadist groups in the Caucasus. A competition for recruits and resources is intensifying between the two dominant jihadist entities, fostering decentralization of the insurgency.[124] And, despite the falling-out and subsequent competition for recruits and resources between the al-Qaeda-linked Caucasus Emirate and the IS-linked Wilayat Qawqaz, one issue with the potential to unite these feuding Sunni factions is a shared antipathy for the Russian government, especially as Putin continues to support the Shiite axis of Iran, the Assad government, and Lebanese Hezbollah against Sunnis in the Syrian civil war.[125]

In recent years, many high-ranking jihadists have switched allegiance from the Caucasus Emirate to Wilayat Qawqaz. The Islamic State, in their eyes, is the most legitimate force espousing the austere brand of Salafism popular among jihadists, particularly the younger generation.[126] The split between the two groups centers around which faction can demonstrate a stronger resolve to fight the adversary – in this case, the Russian state and security services.

In the past, Islamic militants have launched many high-profile attacks on Russian soil, including ones specifically targeting transportation infrastructure – suicide bombings in the Moscow Metro in 2004 and 2010, an explosion that derailed the Moscow – St. Petersburg express railroad in 2007, and suicide attacks at the Domodedovo Airport in 2011, a bus in the city of Volgograd in 2013, and in the St. Petersburg metro in 2017. For the most part, Putin responded to these attacks by sending Russian security services into jihadist enclaves such as Dagestan and Chechnya. Rhetorically, Putin and the Russian propaganda machine capitalize upon these attacks by portraying all Kremlin enemies, both foreign and domestic, as part of a vast terrorist conspiracy.

If returnees were to go back to Russia in large numbers, they would face a draconian security force unconstrained by human rights or laws regulating the use of force. Nevertheless, these returnees would come back to territories like Chechnya, Dagestan, and Ingushetia – areas with an existing jihadist infrastructure and the ability to occasionally launch attacks into Moscow and other urban areas of the Russian homeland.

Sub-Saharan Africa

As evidenced by al-Qaeda's attacks on American embassies in Kenya and Tanzania in 1998, there have long been connections between Salafi-jihadists and certain parts of East Africa, but, in the main, Africa more broadly never registered especially high on the list of attractive destinations for radical jihadists. That is no longer the case. The growing threat of the global jihadist movement now extends deep into Africa, beyond North Africa and into vast pockets of territory pockmarking the Sahel, the Lake Chad Basin, the Greater Sahara, and throughout East Africa, stretching from the Horn of Africa south all the way to Tanzania and Mozambique.[127] And while al-Qaeda was once the premier jihadist group on the continent, myriad splits and fissures have led to a dizzying array and patchwork of militant groups with fluctuating alliances and loyalties.[128] With the establishment of the United States African Command, or AFRICOM, in 2007, the US military has significantly ramped up operations in Somalia, Kenya, Niger, and elsewhere.[129]

The two primary jihadist groups, al-Qaeda and IS, are locked in a battle for recruits, financing, and territory. As of late April 2018, the al-Qaeda affiliate al-Shabaab in Somalia claimed to command between 4,000 and 6,000 jihadists. Al-Qaeda's Mali affiliate, the Group for Support of Islam and Muslims (JNIM), boasts approximately 800 fighters, while Boko Haram, an AQIM affiliate,[130] fields an estimated 1,500 fighters. On the other side of the ledger, IS in West Africa (a splinter group of Boko Haram) numbers around 3,500, while IS in the Greater Sahara, operating between Mali and Niger, is one of the smallest offshoots, with 450 active fighters.[131] IS maintains a footprint in Somalia as well, although its capabilities pale in comparison to those of al-Shabaab.[132] IS in Somalia is a breakaway faction of al-Shabaab, as is a smaller splinter group, Islamic State in Somalia, Kenya, Tanzania, and Uganda.[133] A range of other jihadist groups are also active on the continent, including Ansar Dine, al-Mourabitoun, and Ansaru.[134]

Accompanying the proliferation in jihadist groups and splinters and offshoots has been a sharp spike in attacks.[135] AQIM remains a potent force in parts of North and West Africa, launching over 100 attacks in the region in 2016 alone, including several high-profile attacks in places like Ivory Coast and Burkina Faso, previously unscathed by the type of attacks that frequently inflicted other nations in West Africa, including Nigeria.[136] According to a report by the Foundation of Defense for Democracies, "Between January 2007 and December 2011, jihadists conducted 132 successful, thwarted, or failed attacks against Western interests in Africa. This figure nearly tripled to 358 attacks between January 2012 and October 2017."[137]

East Africa

The Horn of Africa has long served as a cradle for militant jihad. Since the early 1990s, there has been a reputed al-Qaeda presence throughout the region. The 1998 embassy attacks in Kenya and Tanzania proved how widespread and entrenched al-Qaeda's infrastructure throughout East Africa had grown. The current manifestation of the threat, al-Shabaab, has withstood an onslaught from the US-backed African Union Mission in Somalia (AMISOM) peacekeeping forces and an array of other external military forces, from Kenya to Ethiopia. Al-Shabaab has repeatedly suffered defections from its organization, although it hasn't appeared to slow the group down in the least.[138] The organization has repeatedly demonstrated a remarkable ability to regenerate itself.[139] More recently, in an attempt to present an enlightened image and demonstrate to the local civilian population that it has its best interests in mind, al-Shabaab banned the use of plastic bags, a coup for environmental advocates but not likely to curb the group's appetite for suicide bombings and assassinations.[140]

And although the Islamic State is desperately seeking to establish a foothold in Somalia, al-Shabaab has staved off the challenge due to its unmatched capacity for violence, its ability to govern, and its propaganda and media efforts.[141] The numbers of people killed in al-Shabaab attacks is astronomical. Between September 2006 and October 2017, al-Shabaab deployed at least 216 suicide attackers who carried out a total of 155 suicide bombing attacks, killing at least 595 and possibly as many as 2,218 people.[142] Despite the egregious violence, the group has managed to present itself as a viable governing alternative to the current Somali government, exploiting the grievances of the population and working to minimize corruption.[143] Finally, its cooperation with both transnational jihadist groups like AQAP and local expertise have fostered innovation and improvement in the capacity to construct highly lethal IEDs.[144]

Because of such a robust al-Qaeda presence in the Horn of Africa, IS is unlikely to rely on the region as a hub for its operations. Unlike Boko Haram, al-Shabaab has at present been relatively successful at denying IS space to operate and minimizing the number of recruits who have defected to the IS-affiliate. West Africa, on the other hand, has been far more inviting to the Islamic State, even as it continues to compete with other regional terrorist groups like al-Qaeda in the Islamic Maghreb.[145]

West Africa

On the other side of the continent from the Horn of Africa, West Africa has also traditionally been a bastion of al-Qaeda support, although IS has been gaining ground since the end of 2017. Since 2013, a spate of highly lethal attacks has targeted foreigners throughout the region, including in Algeria, Mali, Burkina Faso, and Ivory Coast.[146] The increase in the sophistication of attacks in West Africa appears to be the result of the transfer of tacit knowledge between skilled jihadists from IS and al-Qaeda and local African militants. Indeed, the explosives, types of mines, shells, and weapons being used all indicate an advanced level of expertise compared to previous years.[147]

Al-Qaeda has successfully tapped into new markets, breaking ground in parts of the region previously unaffected by terrorism, such as northern sections of Burkina Faso, where local militants mix with transnational jihadists.[148] Burkina Faso has been greatly impacted by spillover violence originating across the border in neighboring Mali, where JNIM has battled the French military in its quest to control territory and establish *sharia* governance.[149] Al-Qaeda has had a major impact on the deadliest terrorist organization in the region, Boko Haram, from the beginning, helping the group launch its terror campaign in 2009, while urging its leadership to adopt and introduce suicide bombing as a tactic in 2011.[150]

Still, even though al-Qaeda has a longer history of operating throughout West Africa, the Islamic State is mounting an aggressive campaign to supplant its rival and establish its own strategic reach. IS is indeed preparing for a long-term presence throughout West Africa, and the behavior of the Islamic State in West Africa (ISWA) in Nigeria and Niger looks eerily similar to how the Islamic State built its state in Iraq and Syria, providing governance for locals in exchange for the ability to levy taxes on the local economy.[151] According to AFRICOM officials, ISWA is considered to be a longer-term strategic threat compared to Boko Haram, which is viewed as more parochial and Nigeria-focused.[152]

Now that a fissure has cleaved Boko Haram in two, the future of militant jihad in West Africa may hinge on which group – IS or al-Qaeda – is able to network with groups already present on the continent, and which is able to provide a more attractive alternative to fighters returning home from the Middle East. Even before overt signs of a split, there were hints that IS and Boko Haram were cooperating. In April 2016, a convoy of Islamic State fighters in Libya delivered a shipment of weapons, mostly small arms, machine guns, and rifles, to Boko Haram militants near the Chadian border.[153] To date, there is evidence that jihadists fleeing the caliphate have sought out Africa specifically, traveling to northeast Nigeria and parts of Libya.[154]

Europe

There is no real concern that IS would ever attempt to establish a caliphate in Europe, but given that over 4,000 European citizens traveled abroad to join jihadist groups in Iraq and Syria, it is critical to examine both the impact upon the continent, and also the role that Europe will probably play in the immediate aftermath of the collapse of the caliphate. According to some estimates, approximately 30 percent of European foreign fighters have returned home to their respective countries, while another 14 percent have been confirmed dead.[155] This means that Europe faces overlapping challenges of dealing with those who have already returned, preparing for those who still might return, and figuring out how to prevent this entire phenomenon from repeating itself in a few years, if another caliphate is declared in Libya, Afghanistan, or elsewhere.

The foreign fighter phenomenon in Europe reinforces the global nature of conflict in 2019 – what happens in Mosul has consequences in Molenbeek. In the three-year period between June 2014 and June 2017, there were 32 jihadist attacks in Europe alone: 17 in France, 6 in Germany, 4 in the United Kingdom, 3 in Belgium, 1 in Denmark, and 1 in Sweden.[156] Between June 2017 and June 2018, there were another dozen attacks, including 6 more in France, 2 in the UK, and 1 each in Belgium, Germany, Finland, and Spain.

France

Without question, France has been disproportionately affected by the cascading consequences of the civil war in Syria and the rise and fall of the Islamic State. Nearly 900 French citizens relocated to Iraq and Syria, although close to 200 have died in combat.[157] France has suffered devastating terrorist attacks on its own soil, more than 20 in the past 4 years alone, including the November 2015 Paris attacks which resulted in the death of 130 civilians and the Nice truck attack that killed 86 more. Some scholars have traced France's problem with jihadism back to French political culture, noting the aggressively secular nature of Francophone countries. This militant secularism, when combined with high rates of unemployment and urbanization, could be a uniquely influential factor in why so many French citizens join the jihad.[158]

While Muslims make up 4.9 percent of the overall population in Europe, in France the percentage is 8.8 percent.[159] Its prisons have become veritable breeding grounds for Islamic radicalization, a troubling trend throughout the continent more broadly, but one particularly acute for a country where crime and terror frequently overlap, and one to which an untold number of foreign fighters (and their families) may continue to return home.[160] More than half of the 20,000 suspects on France's so-called "S-List" (S standing for "state security") are thought to have links to jihadist groups, a staggering figure.[161] Young children who were part of the caliphate and lost their parents in the fighting are now returning to France, including to their home neighborhoods like Saint-Denis, where they are being placed with foster families or community centers for orphans.[162] But these neighborhoods remain incubators of jihadism, with extremely high levels of crime and unemployment, presenting serious concerns that these children – some of whom witnessed horrific atrocities in the Middle

East – could be recruited by radical Islamists intent on conducting attacks within France in the name of the Islamic State.[163]

Germany

Germany has also been a major source of foreign fighters and has suffered several high-profile attacks on its soil, the most devastating of which was carried out by Anis Amri, a Tunisian jihadist with links to IS in Libya. In this attack, 11 people were killed and another 55 wounded, when Amri drove a truck through a crowded Christmas market in Berlin in December 2016.[164] Nearly half of the 900 Germans who traveled abroad to fight with jihadist groups in Iraq and Syria had contact with extremist mosques in the country.[165] In response, Germany has moved to ban Islamist groups believed to be responsible for radicalizing citizens and encouraging them to travel abroad to fight with IS and other militant groups.[166]

Germany has experienced a major surge in the overall number of terrorism-related prosecutions in recent years, with over 900 cases filed in 2017 alone.[167] In a media interview, the head of Germany's Office for the Protection of the Constitution, Hans-Georg Masasen, warned of the dangers posed by "kindergarten jihadists" and women and children who were "brainwashed" by IS and intent on returning home to Germany.[168] Without question, the arrival of over 1 million migrants in the past few years, many of them Muslims, has placed a strain on the German government to dial down tensions between ethnic Germans and newly arrived asylum seekers from the Middle East, Africa, and South Asia. There are legitimate concerns that an influx of Muslims will lead to a rise in right-wing groups throughout Germany, including groups like PEGIDA, or Patriotic Europeans Against the Islamization of the West.

United Kingdom

The United Kingdom has a lengthy history with terrorism, and more recently with Islamic terrorism, following the London bombings of July 7, 2005, when several militants linked to al-Qaeda conducted suicide attacks against tube trains and a bus, killing 52 and injuring another 784 people. And while the UK remained mostly immune from terrorism directed and inspired by IS initially, there were several deadly attacks conducted over the span of a few short months in 2017, including a combined knife and vehicle attack on Westminster Bridge and Parliament in March; a suicide bombing in Manchester that killed 22 people outside of a concert in May; and another combined knife and vehicle attack at London Bridge and Borough Market in June.[169] Three months later, in September, a terrorist bombing at the Parsons Green Underground station wounded 30 people, though none were killed.

Britons were among the most prominent members of the Islamic State, including Mohammed Emwazi (a.k.a. "Jihadi John"), an IS executioner, and Junaid Hussain, perhaps IS's most well-known "virtual entrepreneur."[170] Organizations like al-Muhajiroun, a banned Islamist network once led by convicted terrorist Anjem Choudry, also recruited and encouraged British Muslims to travel to and fight in Iraq and Syria.[171] Moreover, networks like al-Muhajiroun and Sharia4Belgium had spent years – or in the case of the former, decades – laying the groundwork for and building the infrastructure that was in place by the time of IS's caliphate declaration in 2014.[172] Speaking in late 2017, Gilles de Kerchove, the European Union's counterterrorism coordinator, commented that approximately 25,000 British citizens are possibly Islamic radicals, with around 3,000 considered to be "a direct threat" by British intelligence agencies.[173] In one particularly chilling case, a British IS supporter named Umar Haque attempted to recruit young

THE COMING TERRORIST DIASPORA

children at a private Islamic school in London, some as young as 11 years old, and to teach them to launch terrorist attacks across the capital.[174]

Belgium

For a small and somewhat ordinary European country, Belgium has figured prominently in jihadist terrorism, with the greatest number of foreign fighters per capita of any country in the West.[175] There have been several terrorist attacks in Belgium linked to IS, including the March 2016 attacks in Brussels at the airport and Maalbeek metro station, which killed 32 people.[176] Several high-profile IS fighters were Belgians, including the charismatic jihadist Abdelhamid Abaaoud, the ringleader of the Paris November 2015 attacks.[177] Belgium was also home to militants such as Fouad Belkacem, the one-time leader of Sharia4Belgium, and Khalid Zerkani, a veteran of al-Qaeda training camps who recruited young Belgians and sent them to fight in Iraq and Syria.[178] Of the nearly 70 Belgians identified as fighting in Syria, almost all were members of Sharia4Belgium, which was particularly active in Antwerp, but elsewhere as well.[179]

Immediately after the Paris and Brussels attacks, a section of Brussels named Molenbeek came under intense scrutiny as a locus of jihad inexorably linked to terrorism. This municipality, right in the heart of Belgium's capital, was a place where 80 percent of the population was of Moroccan origin.[180] Compared to the rest of Belgium, its residents were poor, young, and suffered from high unemployment and crime rates.[181] According to a story in *Politico*, of more than 1,600 organizations registered in Molenbeek, more than 100 had links with crime, and an additional 51 were linked to terrorism.[182] In many ways, however, the Brussels attacks marked a turning point for Belgium's long-criticized security services. Once considered inept and aloof, the Belgian security services have made significant progress improving their counterterrorism capabilities. As Renard and Coolsaet point out, the most important change has been a "broader policy shift from a narrow counterterrorism approach solely based on law enforcement and intelligence gathering towards a more comprehensive approach that combines repression and enhanced prevention."[183]

This chapter focuses on Europe not because it has the prospect of turning into the next IS state-building project, but rather because the continent's citizens helped build the caliphate. Talk of "no-go" zones has been overhyped, but there have been neighborhoods that became notorious as radicalization hubs, including parts of major European cities like Paris, Brussels, London, and Barcelona. So there is no chance that IS, or whatever terrorist entity follows it, will seriously attempt to make Europe into a jihadist sanctuary. However, the same countries discussed above that supplied recruits to IS could end up doing so again, this time with its younger generation, if the Islamic State is able to successfully regenerate itself. The most likely place for this to happen could be back where it all began, in Iraq and Syria.

4

From "Remain and Expand" to Survive and Persist

While it has become fashionable to defy conventional wisdom and to proffer the final demise of IS, few serious analysts argue that the Islamic State has been defeated once and for all. Many believe that the group will rise again, most probably right back in Iraq, or perhaps more likely Syria, where it is currently reverting to its previous form as a "mobile, brutal Sunni Arab insurgent organization."[1] The future of IS in the Middle East is of a group that will hunker down, husbanding its resources and going to ground, laying the foundation for a long-simmering insurgency while it bides time. IS and its followers view the establishment of the caliphate as a watershed moment in history – this is *the* defining moment for contemporary Islam, the Salafi-jihadists' "Khomeini moment," which indicates a historical achievement that will reverberate well beyond the present day. And, moving forward, the remaining sinew of the organization will stop at nothing to return to this glory.

The defining characteristics of IS in the future are those of an organization that is well prepared, able to adapt and evolve, and poised to take advantage of any missteps by the governments in Syria and Iraq, as well as continued ineptitude and weak capacity of the security forces operating throughout the region.[2]

Preparation

There is no doubt that IS has prepared for the long haul in the valleys and gullies along the Euphrates River. Its fighters have stockpiled arms, fuel, water, and food in trenches.[3] Because IS controlled such large swaths of territory across Iraq and Syria – at its peak, the group occupied an area the size of Britain with 12 million under its sway – it was able to enjoy unmolested freedom of movement to prepare for the next phase of the conflict.[4] Militants pre-positioned large quantities of cash, which they buried under sand berms and hoarded weapons, ammunition, and bomb-making materials in pre-fabricated tunnels throughout parts of northern Iraq.[5] After declaring the caliphate in 2014, IS leadership recognized that it would inevitably return to these areas to re-instigate guerilla warfare.[6] The Iraqi security forces have reclaimed Mosul and ejected IS from the majority of its Iraqi strong-holds, but they have done so with the backing of the US military and its Coalition allies. But for the Islamic State, this is a generational struggle, and its remaining leadership probably believes that the United States will ultimately withdraw, and the sectarian strife that has defined post-Saddam Iraq will return with a vengeance, pushing Sunni Arabs back into the Islamic State's embrace.

It comes as little surprise that IS would prepare for the next phase of its lifecycle, because it has been following a similar pattern of behavior since its inception, dating back to the mid-2000s when IS was known as al-Qaeda in Iraq, led by the Jordanian terror chieftain Abu Musab al-Zarqawi.[7] Many of the Islamic State's surviving fighters are thought to be holed up, hiding in isolated terrain, such as desert or mountainous regions, and among civilian populations in Iraq, Syria, and Turkey.[8] As Hassan Hassan has pointed out in his research, as part of a "calculated strategy," the Islamic State's remaining fighters deliberately "melted away" in the border region between Iraq and Syria divided by the Euphrates River.[9] They live to fight another day, while mimicking the strategies of subversion and sabotage perfected by other Maoist-style insurgencies throughout recent history.

Adaptation

Above all else, it is critical to understand that the Islamic State is a learning organization. This is one of the key precepts of its success. In preparation for previous times of uncertainty, it has been revealed that the group has widely read Abu Bakr Naji's *The Management of Savagery*, a jihadi gospel of sorts for waging an unrelenting campaign of insurgency and violence against the enemies of Islam.[10] It is thus important to note that, while IS has indeed lost most of its territory, it still boasts a committed cadre of operatives, including members of its elite intelligence unit, the Emni, and militants with administrative and bureaucratic experience – what IS experts Benjamin Bahney and Patrick Johnston have dubbed "the glue of the IS organization from top to bottom."[11] These organizational skills are indispensable to the group's ability to survive, serving as "muscle memory" for how to galvanize fighters and marshal the resources necessary if the caliphate is ever to be restored.

Even in early 2018, there were already clear signs that IS had regrouped. In the Hamreen Mountains, in northern Iraq, a group of between 500 and 1,100 IS fighters calling themselves "the White Flags" reconstituted, coordinating attacks on local security services.[12] Throughout Kirkuk, IS fighters constructed fake checkpoints to ambush Iraqi security forces operating in the area. They also set out to destroy oil tankers and target Shiite civilians making religious pilgrimages.[13] In

Kirkuk and elsewhere, including Diayala and Salahaddin, IS sleeper cells helped organize what Hassan Hassan has called "rasd," roughly equivalent to scoping, or reconnaissance, of these areas to determine how best to operate before reorganizing small formations of fighters.[14] And despite the onslaught of US bombing raids, pockets of militants remain holed up in Hajin, north of Abu Kamal, and Dashisha, on the outskirts of Deir ez-Zor.[15]

Besides recapturing physical territory in the areas where it formerly governed, the Islamic State will continue to perpetuate the "virtual caliphate," tailoring messages to Western audiences that elicit sympathy while urging revenge (this subject will be covered in depth in chapter 5).[16] By inciting Muslims to commit acts of terror in its name, IS remains relevant by keeping its brand in the news cycle, ensuring its ability to recruit new members, including younger generations of Muslims who may revere the generation that came before them and was able to successfully establish a true Islamic caliphate. Again, al -Suri's ideas, promulgated during the late 1990s, have proved to be much more salient for how things have evolved into the modern era of terrorist attacks by al-Qaeda and IS, as well as by their affiliates. The trend of "do it yourself" terrorism carried out by inspired jihadists with no direct links to any established group is a major concern for the future evolution of terrorism. Joining a group is now considered less important than committing an act in the name of bin Laden, or, more recently, Baghdadi. Zawahiri is far less charismatic than bin Laden was, which partly accounts for his limited ability to inspire the kind of widespread growth of the movement al-Suri had envisioned. Still, as evidenced by their releasing media within a week of each other in late August 2018, both Zawahiri and Baghdadi remain focused on exhorting their followers to launch attacks against the West, with the IS leader urging "the supporters of the Caliphate" to conduct attacks using guns, knives, or bombs in the West.[17] But the path forward is anything but linear. The current situation in Syria is one of a highly fractious and atomized jihadist landscape.[18] Now, perhaps more than at any other point in the conflict, IS is vulnerable to having its fighters absorbed by al-Qaeda, which is a reverse of the process that began in 2014, when IS was consistently convincing large segments of al-Qaeda-related groups to join the Islamic State.[19] Al-Qaeda has even begun using "re-radicalisation" programs, complete with courses based on a "sharia-bureau approved curriculum of jihad" to indoctrinate fighters joining its organization after having recently been IS members.[20]

Opportunism

Even though the Islamic State has changed, the structural factors throughout the Middle East which facilitated its rise have not. In some instances, they have worsened. Civil wars, jihadist ideology fueled by sectarianism, a dearth of regime legitimacy, economic weakness, and external intervention by states still largely define regional politics.[21] In his book *Waging Insurgent Warfare*, Seth Jones details the three most important factors in increasing the probability of an insurgency: local grievances, weak governance, and greed – all three of which are apparent in Iraq and Syria.[22] Not only are these factors important in *starting* an insurgency, but also they factor into the duration of an insurgency. IS has been particularly adroit at capitalizing upon the grievances – both real and perceived – of Sunni Arabs in Iraq and Syria, and will be actively looking for the next opportunity to further exacerbate latent and existing ethnic and religious strife in local communities. There is also the potential that IS could seek to co-opt Sunni tribes in the region, as it has done before, especially in 2014–15, through a combination of money and coercion.[23]

Throughout parts of Hawija district in Iraq, Islamic State fighters return to their former strongholds in the dark of night, sometimes to threaten villagers, other times to exact revenge by assassinating their enemies.[24] In Syria, IS fighters continue to inhabit ever smaller chunks of territory due west of the Syrian–Iraqi border, while also demonstrating the ability to launch sporadic attacks in some of the suburbs around Syria's capital, Damascus. IS is constantly searching for new pipelines of recruitment and its ideology remains popular among residents of Palestinian refugee camps, in concert with the Khalid bin al-Walid Army.[25] There is a real sense that if the Islamic State's former urban strongholds, including areas like Tal Afar and Qaim, are not quickly addressed with a robust and comprehensive stabilization and reconstruction plan, they will soon fall back under the sway of those advocating violent extremism.[26] In addition to these areas, others considered "high-risk" include western Mosul, Hawija and its surrounding environs, and a swath of territory along the Tigris River from Baiji to Sharga.[27] Given the Iraq government's poor track record of assuaging Sunni grievances, few are sanguine that Baghdad will muster the political will to pacify the populations of Ramadi, Tikrit, Samarra, and Fallujah, cities that comprised a considerable portion of violence in the so-called Sunni Triangle.

As other rivalries flare up in Syria, the fight against IS is taking a back seat. Indeed, the Syrian Democratic Forces, backed by the United States, are focused on fighting elements of the Assad regime, while Turkey is focused on countering the People's Protection Units (YPG) and SDF in northern Syria. This all takes away from the fight against the Islamic State, which has used the respite to begin connecting cells and supply lines across Syria.[28] The Assad regime has done remarkably little to combat IS, instead preferring to focus on other anti-regime elements around Homs, Hama, and Aleppo. Indeed, many fleeing IS fighters appeared to be able to move with impunity through territory nominally controlled by the Assad regime, which was either unwilling or unable to prevent their freedom of movement.[29]

The post-conflict reconstruction challenges in Iraq, particularly in places like Mosul, are immense. As RAND researchers Shelly Culbertson and Linda Robinson highlight in their work, another wave of violence could easily devastate Iraq "in a matter of months" if stabilization activities are insufficient and underfunded.[30] In neighboring Syria, although post-conflict reconstruction seems years away at this point, if and when eastern portions of the country begin to be rebuilt, IS will probably rely on its Syrian members to infiltrate security and governance structures.[31] IS knows these cities, towns, and villages and the local populations that still live there. Even though the territory it once controlled has now been largely usurped, when it was attempting to govern, IS did so quite effectively, providing its subjects with security, justice, and a clear, if draconian, set of rules by which to live.[32]

Strategy

At its apex, the Islamic State's strategy could perhaps best be summarized through its oft-repeated slogan, *"Baqiya wa Tatamaddad,"* or "Remaining and Expanding."[33] But with the loss of the caliphate, IS, and the global jihadist movement writ large, is in flux once again. And since the movement is far from a monolith, it is difficult to conceptualize an overarching strategy, per se, although it has become clear that both IS and al-Qaeda are actively seeking to remain in areas where they are currently strong, while also opportunistically dispersing fighters and resources to new areas where they can refortify, and expand once again, with the ultimate goal of controlling large swaths of territory and people. IS is known for many things – its penchant for violence, its ability to raise funds, and its sophisticated propaganda apparatus – but perhaps its greatest strength, and the one characteristic that will help it survive, is its oft-overlooked willingness to evolve and change in response to conditions on the ground. Its surviving leadership remains extremely aware of the need to balance strategic considerations and encourage strategic learning via doctrine.[34]

The global jihadist movement's most prolific strategists believe in the objective of establishing a caliphate, even while they disagree over the strategy to achieve this goal, as well as the timeline.[35] There is already compelling evidence that the movement is invoking the nostalgia of the caliphate to begin framing its future strategy.[36] Raqqa has been recaptured, but the Islamic State proved to its followers – and to the world – that, despite the enormous odds against such a proposition, it is possible to construct a jihadi proto-state capable of both governing and defending its borders. Granted, that state has now been conquered, but the fact that it could be established in the first place is the narrative that IS will cling to in its future propaganda. Moreover, it will highlight that this state could only be realized by the will of God, and that the reason it no longer exists is due to the actions of the infidels and Crusaders, evoking images of an eternal battle between good and evil, believers and non-believers, faithful Muslims and everyone else. As Craig Whiteside argues:

To fuel the information campaigns of the next three decades, much like yesterday's jihadists look back to Qutb and Azzam, IS and its rivals (including al-Qaeda) will use the caliphate idea and the understanding of the importance of local control and governance as proof positive of how to advance this political goal in the future. No one can ever tell them it is impossible anymore.[37]

The ongoing split between IS and al-Qaeda has not prevented the former from relying on the strategic guidance provided by notable figures from the latter, including jihadist strategists such as Abu Musab al-Suri, Abu Bakr Naji, and Anwar al-Awlaki.[38] Overall, despite current fissures in the movement, its leaders and followers have far more in common than they may recognize. As Daniel Byman has argued, "If jihadists disagree on fundamental outcomes, then any unity of purpose or organization will be much harder to achieve. If the question is simply one of priorities, then changes in circumstances can bring different factions together in the name of expediency."[39] In the past, opposition to apostate regimes and Western imperialists has proven to be an attractive elixir in this regard. By slightly reframing its narrative and modifying its tactics, the global jihadist movement could seek to unite its own warring factions.

Sardonically, it may be the Coalition's destruction of the caliphate that helps the movement refine its overall strategy. IS proved that building a state could be done successfully, albeit temporarily, while al-Qaeda would suggest that the caliphate collapsed because its declaration was premature, and the focus should instead be on gradualism and educating the global *ummah*.[40] In recent years, al-Qaeda's strategy has morphed from one focused obsessively on attacking the West to one defined by a desire to win the support of local populations in the areas it operates in.[41] A troubling scenario is one in which the erstwhile strategies of IS and al-Qaeda successfully merge into a singular, coherent approach for the global jihadist movement more broadly – one defined by cultivating local support on a truly global level, while aggressively attacking nation-states and groups it deems as enemies, infidels, and adversaries.

Tactics

At the heart of the movement's future strategic direction will be the tactics adopted to achieve its objectives along the way. Along the same lines as the jihadists' approach to strategy, both IS and al-Qaeda offer unique refinements and approaches to tactical innovation that, if combined and harnessed in concert, could prove to have a devastating and destabilizing effect in various theatres throughout the globe.[42] Moreover, as commercial off-the-shelf technologies become ubiquitous and easier to acquire, it would come as little surprise if jihadist groups were to exploit advances in unmanned aerial systems, artificial intelligence (AI), and 3-D printing to close the gap between their capabilities and those of advanced militaries. Indeed, as Daveed Gartenstein-Ross has noted, "for jihadist organizations, the ability to innovate is a necessity, not a luxury."[43]

The Islamic State's unique contribution to tactical evolution has been impressive. IS has pioneered the use of the virtual planner model for external operations.[44] This innovation allows terrorists in one location to direct attacks in another part of the world with only an Internet connection and reliable encryption.[45] In many cases, jihadists are able to leverage local criminal networks that act as facilitators to help acquire the logistics and resources necessary for an attack.[46] Even as Western nations have devoted substantial resources to countering this threat, savvy tacticians within the global jihadist movement will continue to rely on encrypted online messaging applications to identify local recruits and provide them with directions and technical expertise to attack targets, a development that poses a formidable threat to countries with less than adequate military, intelligence, and law enforcement capabilities.[47] The devastating Paris November 2015 attacks could serve as the model operation from the terrorists' point of view.[48]

The other more recent tactic to take note of is al-Qaeda's focus on "winning hearts and minds" as a method of securing and cementing its legitimacy among local constituencies.[49] Al-Qaeda has repeatedly demonstrated a pragmatic approach to operating in amidst civil wars, as evidenced by its actions in Syria, Yemen, and Mali.[50] If the global jihadist movement recognizes the importance of popular support and subsequently tones down its sectarian rhetoric, it remains entirely possible that Salafi groups could emerge as more preferable alterna tives than the weak and corrupt regimes holding office throughout large swaths of the Muslim world.

Ongoing Debates in Jihadi Ideology

Sunni jihadism is a "social movement family with its general foundation in Sunni theology, more specifically in the concept and practice of Jihad, and to some extent in the specific doctrine of Salafism."[51] As Cole Bunzel points out, while IS and al-Qaeda are the "principal organizational expressions" of the jihadi movement, jihadism is both an ideology and a "highly developed system of thought deeply-rooted in certain aspects of the Islamic tradition," and, as such, the sum of the movement itself is far greater than its individual parts.[52] The split between IS and al-Qaeda is occurring amidst a wider disagreement permeating the ranks of some of the leading jihadist ideologues. The infighting is nothing new. There have been many well-publicized spats in the past between jihadist leaders. What used to be hashed out through long and highly esoteric handwritten letters exchanged between ideologues has now devolved into social media feuds playing out in the public domain in chat rooms on the Internet. Rik Coolsaet commented on the continued rift between the two groups, noting that "a small but strident camp of hardliners consider Daesh's official ideology insufficiently radical and are pushing for an even more extremist stance that would exclude all possible cooperation with other jihadist groups, including al Qaeda."[53]

The debate centers on several themes in particular – takfirism, *tatarrus*, *sharia* law, and when to declare a caliphate – but is also reflected in both organizational and operational differences between the global jihadist movement's two heavyweights. The subject which has led to the most caustic debate has been over who can claim to be a proper, devout, and righteous Muslim. IS has taken takfirism, or the practice of declaring other Muslims to be non-believers due to their supposed apostasy or heresy, to new extremes.[54] Yet, ultimately, its leadership eventually recognized that this practice might be counterproductive, especially as the group is losing territory and needs to rejuvenate its ranks with an influx of new recruits. In September 2017, IS religious leadership appeared to soften its stance on this matter, issuing a revocation of an earlier religious edict that broadened the scope of takfirism.[55] Still, the debate continued to rage, with the ideological rift mostly centered on whether those who remain reticent to excommunicate apostates and unbelievers should themselves be excommunicated.[56] Some of the Islamic State's hard-core ideologues view the group's commitment to takfir as even more important than prayer and other fundamental components of Salafism.[57] Apparently, there is even a hardcore group of IS militants, which Tore Hamming refers to as "the extremist wing of the Islamic State," that sees Baghdadi as "soft," leading to further fragmentation of the group.[58]

Another thread within this debate is over the concept of *tatarrus*, or whom and what constitute legitimate targets for jihadists' violence. "Al Qaeda has tried to learn its lesson from this and compared to 15 years ago, the group is far more discerning in its targeting, while the same cannot be said about IS. The differing approaches have been described as 'winning hearts and minds' (al-Qaeda) versus 'crushing necks and spines' (IS)."[59] This shift is reflected in the styles and organizational structures of the two groups. To succeed, al-Qaeda believes that the support of the population is crucial, part of its Maoist-style insurgent approach, while IS's focoist-style approach views violence as instrumental and redeeming.[60]

Even before the Arab Spring, as early as 2010, Bin Laden was advocating for a change in al-Qaeda's approach, calling for "an advisory reading and development of our entire policy."[61] In September 2013 Zawahiri authored "General Guidelines for Jihad," which called for a more restrained approach, one consistent with a population-centric strategy.[62] This extends to how harshly to implement *sharia* law, especially taking into consideration local and tribal mores and customs. And for those jihadists arguing that al-Qaeda has lost its way, the move to be more accommodating toward civilian populations is perfectly in line, and in fact synchronized, with its strategy of garnering lasting and widespread popular support before it declares a caliphate of its own, which has always been part of al-Qaeda's long-term strategy.

The IS–Al-Qaeda Dispute

The fall-out from the split between IS and al-Qaeda has led to a competition viewed by both sides as zero sum in nature, where progress by one of these groups signaled a loss for the other. One of the primary drivers of such a heated competition is that, in many ways, the ideology and objectives of the group are so similar. The Islamic State reverted to extreme levels of violence as one method of differentiating itself from its rivals, including al-Qaeda. Both groups are attempting to recruit from the same milieus and influence similar constituencies. The main differences are that IS sought to create a caliphate on a timeline considered premature by al-Qaeda, and IS pursued a far more sectarian agenda in attempting to achieve this objective. Whether and how these differences are ever resolved will have a major impact on the future of the movement writ large.

The split itself occurred at the leadership levels of these groups, so one of the most interesting questions is: to what extent do foot soldiers and mid-level commanders really care, in actuality, about the previous infighting and strategic disputes? For some of the fighters at these levels, there is an obvious parallel to conflicts between street gangs, where members like the Bloods and Crips "fly their colors" – or represent their gangs by wearing their distinctive colors – and continuously disparage their adversaries by posting "dis videos" online, mocking and threatening rivals.[63] The bitterness and divisiveness of the feud has played out on social media, with leaders on each side hurling vituperation and casting opprobrium on the other as "bad Muslims." The initial castigation came from al-Qaeda's leader Zawahiri himself, who fulminated against IS for being deviant from the al-Qaeda methodology.

The truth is, as outlined in chapter 1's discussion of al-Qaeda in Iraq, that the relationship was doomed from the start. The group that would eventually become IS has always been something of a rogue element, formed and led by Zarqawi, who fought hard to preserve the independence of his affiliate. Even after pledging his loyalty to bin Laden and assuming the al-Qaeda moniker, Zarqawi still ignored directions from al-Qaeda's core leadership and narrowly pursued his own sectarian agenda in hopes of igniting a Sunni–Shia civil war, first within Iraq, and then throughout the wider Islamic world. One of al-Qaeda's first steps to present itself as more evenhanded was denouncing blatant sectarianism and working to convince AQI to jettison sectarianism as a guiding principle. When, in July 2005, Zawahiri penned a letter to the leader of AQI chastising him for his group's wanton slaughter of Shiites, the former stressed the overall negative impact these actions were having on the al-Qaeda brand and urged him to eschew targeting other Muslims. When Zarqawi disregarded Zawahiri's advice, he cemented AQI's reputation as a ruthless organization where violence was almost an end in and of itself.

So while the initial rift began deepening in Iraq in the mid-2000s, it developed into an internecine struggle during the early years of the Syrian civil war. Following the fall-out, al-Qaeda has worked assiduously to reestablish itself as a major factor in the Levant; to accomplish this, it has been forced to overcome several significant setbacks related to its organizational unity and coherence.[64] Al-Qaeda's initial presence in Syria was through an affiliation with Jabhat al-Nusra, the Islamic State in Iraq's erstwhile Syria branch. In mid-2016, Nusra rebranded itself as Jabhat Fateh al-Sham and later merged with other terrorist splinter groups to form Hay'at Tahrir al-Sham (HTS), a jihadist umbrella organization, which put even more distance between itself and al-Qaeda. As of mid-2018, al-Qaeda had no formal affiliate in Syria but still commanded the loyalty of several high-profile militants. Some al-Qaeda loyalists announced the formation of yet another new group, Tanzim Hurras al-Din, or the Religious Guardians' Organization, in 2018. While HTS remains focused on events in Syria, Tanzim Hurras al-Din is headed by al-Qaeda veterans who may seek to use Syria as a base to launch high-profile terrorist attacks against the West.[65] This posture is a departure from al-Qaeda's recent focus on grassroots appeal in Syria and, if it comes to fruition, it will probably have significant ramifications for the group's return to its former glory. Another important angle is that there are several Jordanian jihadi veterans among Tanzim Hurras al-Din's leadership cadre who were close to Zarqawi and, as such, there is both historical and ideological affinity with IS, which increases the probability that Hurras might successfully poach IS members and bring them into the al-Qaeda fold.[66]

The rebranding process for al-Qaeda in Syria was undertaken partly out of necessity, but it was also strategic in nature. From a pragmatic standpoint, the rebrandings have served to put some distance between al-Qaeda and a host of imitators and rivals. This could be an effort by the group to learn from past mistakes, when the leadership's reluctance to publicly disavow Zarqawi traded short-term gains for long-term losses and eventually contributed to the split, an event that seemed like an existential threat to al-Qaeda throughout 2014. The strategic part of the rebranding is no different from a company's use of public relations and marketing to refashion its image – al-Qaeda now seeks to present itself as the "moderate alternative" to the Islamic State.[67] The IS brand was represented by the caliphate and the group's reliance on anomic violence, while al-Qaeda sought to position itself as an organization more adept at strategic planning and with more attractive prospects for enduring success in the future.[68]

Although the rebranding is considered a feint by many counterterrorism scholars, it just might have worked to recast al-Qaeda's image within Syria.[69] And so, even while the emergence of IS at one point threatened the existence of al-Qaeda, it also presented the latter with an opportunity. Al-Qaeda's calculated decision to distance itself from its former satellite organization was an effort to portray itself as a legitimate, capable, and independent force in the ongoing Syrian civil war. Another objective was to prove that the militants were dedicated to helping Syrians prevail in their struggle.[70] Finally, it would give core al-Qaeda a modicum of plausible deniability as it paves the way for its erstwhile allies to gain eligibility for military aid from a collection of external nations.[71]

Now that the Islamic State has lost its caliphate, al-Qaeda may be the only group viewed as militarily capable of challenging the Assad regime's grip on power, although, as of early 2019, that seems like a long shot. Al-Qaeda could certainly prove to be the longer-term threat to stability in Syria, primarily due to its grassroots support and local appeal. Unlike the Islamic State, al-Qaeda is perceived as an entity willing to work with the population and possessing the resources necessary to provide at least some of the trappings of governance. In the long term, al-Qaeda could resemble Lebanese Hezbollah – a violent non-state actor that has solidified political legitimacy while still retaining its ability to wage large-scale acts of terrorism and political violence.[72]

Depending on where it operates, al-Qaeda has shifted between protector, predator, and parasite, labels which are not mutually exclusive. In both Yemen and Mali, its members demonstrate a remarkable knack for pragmatism when operating in the midst of brutal civil wars. After infiltrating local rebel groups, al-Qaeda fighters parrot their grievances and champion parochial objectives. After ingratiating its fighters, al-Qaeda then ramps up proselytization efforts and introduces a narrative defined by a mixture of local and global themes. Unlike the Islamic State, al-Qaeda is willing to work with other groups, as it has been doing in Syria, where it typically puts locals in charge of units, battalions, and other military formations, lending a sense of local legitimacy to its face in the country. Moreover, al-Qaeda has displayed a penchant for cooperation beyond immediate conflict zones, as evidenced by on-again, off-again tactical cooperation with Iran.

One of the most debated issues within the global jihadist movement is the so-called "near versus far debate" about which enemies the militants should concentrate the bulk of their efforts fighting – local apostate regimes or Western countries, especially the United States, but increasingly also the United Kingdom, France, and Australia. Al-Qaeda in Syria has managed to boost its brand through the provision of local services, including water and electricity, while also working to support local bakeries and control market prices of basic foodstuffs. Its leadership publicly announced that it will refrain from attacking the West, at least temporarily, in order to avoid Western counterterrorism reprisals, while simultaneously conserving its resources to concentrate on overthrowing the Assad regime, by far the top priority of Syrian Sunnis.

Al-Qaeda's Syrian leadership also recognizes that it is infinitely more successful when it focuses on local issues instead of a more amorphous and contested struggle with the West. These tensions seem to be at least partly to blame for the continued fracturing and splintering of al-Qaeda in Syria and its multiple iterations and offshoots. The debate over whether to focus locally or to revert back to a relentless quest to conduct spectacular attacks in the West could lead to a long-term and enduring fissure within the global jihadist movement. With the movement already divided by the al-Qaeda – IS split, this issue, similar to the decision on when to attempt to establish the caliphate, is a core ideological debate that is unlikely to be settled anytime soon.

For all of al-Qaeda's attempts at moderation, IS has behaved in an entirely opposite manner, as it pursued an uncompromising strategy of sectarianism, barbarity, and conquest. IS fully embraced sectarianism, seemingly making the killing of Shiites its *raison d'être*. And while al-Qaeda's propaganda might still be peppered with derogatory references to Shiites, in general it favors a much more measured approach than IS. The groups are different in many ways, some subtle and others not. For example, rather than working with local groups, IS consistently acted as a conquering army, routing local militant leaders rather than working alongside them. In addition, locals were taxed, extorted, and closely policed by IS religious patrols to ensure strict adherence to *sharia* law.

IS's approach to warfare was reflected in its fighting style, whereby the group relied on conventional means of warfare, including artillery and tanks, in combination with some asymmetric tactics. When IS assumed control of a certain swath of territory, it often installed foreigners (Chechens, Tunisians, and Uzbeks) in command of the area. But its success came with a price. The more territory IS took over and the more brazen its displays of military might, the more likely the Coalition could no longer ignore its actions. The result was that, compared to other Salafi-jihadist groups operating in Syria, IS bore the brunt of Western counterterrorism operations, a development that suited al-Qaeda just fine.[73] The relentless stream of IS propaganda directed at the West – particularly the gruesome videos of beheadings, burnings, and crucifixions – left the Coalition with little choice but to set its sights on the caliphate.[74] The success IS experienced in building its proto-state elevated it to the top priority for the Coalition. Accordingly, al-Qaeda in Syria was given breathing room to patiently rebuild its credibility and political legitimacy among locals.[75] Gartenstein-Ross has described this as a "strategy of deliberate yet low-key growth."[76]

The future of al-Qaeda and IS will be largely defined by the competition between the two. There is little debate that, beginning around 2014, IS could successfully lay claim to be the undisputed leader of the global jihadist movement. Once its caliphate collapsed, that began to change, and its current decline may be accompanied by al-Qaeda's rise back to preeminence. There are clear signs that al-Qaeda has modified its tactics to take advantage of what it sees as a unique opportunity. In Syria's Idlib province, al-Qaeda successfully cultivated grassroots support and by mid-2017 was beginning to accept former IS fighters into its ranks, a development most would have thought unthinkable just a year or two earlier. Al-Qaeda's leadership realizes that its response to the Arab Spring was sclerotic and is now making amends, focusing its resources and energy on the concerns most salient to Sunnis, a strategy that has helped the group spread its roots throughout northwestern Syria. It has also used this strategy successfully throughout parts of Yemen, where it operates under various front organizations, branches of Ansar Sharia, and other Salafi groups.[77]

Al-Qaeda's more balanced and predictable approach to governing is geared toward winning the popular support of civilian populations. Life under the Islamic State, even for its own loyal subjects, was enforced by draconian religious interpretations and subsequent enforcement of punishments for those who were not fastidious and completely obedient. Al-Qaeda was far less stringent and could be indifferent to perceived offenses that would draw harsh rebuke from the Islamic State. The year 2018 marked the 30-year anniversary of al-Qaeda's founding and it is clear that the group has evolved, adapted, and learned over time. Its ability to establish widespread political legitimacy through a refurbished image could propel the group through well into its fourth decade.

This shift over time by al-Qaeda to a more tolerant organization was in part a result of Zawahiri's leadership. For all of the criticism he endures for lacking charisma, a critique most jihadist scholars find unassailable, Zawahiri does give al-Qaeda the benefit of continuity and a historical appreciation for what has traditionally worked and what has failed in the jihadists' ongoing struggle against their adversaries. With his direction, the group has made course corrections based on trial and error and actively sought to amend previous errors in doctrine and strategy.

Al-Qaeda in Syria has gone to great lengths to protect its image by rebranding its affiliate several times already. Bilaad al-Shaam, or the Land of the Levantine People, is highly coveted by multiple groups within the global jihadist movement for religious and geographical reasons. Zawahiri sees Syria as an opportunity to demonstrate relevance, juxtapose al-Qaeda to the Islamic State, and position his group as the more capable and pragmatic entity and, thus, the group worth siding with as the competition continues.

Perhaps the most interesting change in al-Qaeda's behavior since the death of bin Laden is that the group no longer seems obsessed with striking the West and, indeed, according to Bruce Hoffman, in 2015 Zawahiri issued strict orders to Mohammed al-Jolani not to use Syria as a launching pad to attack the West.[78] There are several possible reasons for this decision, including that al-Qaeda's infrastructure in Europe was not nearly as robust as that of the Islamic State, and thus any attack was pobably going to pale in comparison to what IS had already achieved.

Another, more nefarious possibility is that Zawahiri is merely playing the "long game" while strategically concealing al-Qaeda's Khorasan Group assets as IS is further attenuated. Again, this might be changing with the continued splintering of groups in Syria and the emergence of Tanzim Hurras al-Din. At least in terms of capability, if not intent, discerning a group's organizational structure could provide clues to its reach and ability to conduct external attacks. Do groups adopt a more decentralized structure to conduct external attacks, or are attacks outside of the group's main territory a byproduct of a flatter structure? Relatedly, it is possible that too much structure is assigned to jihadist groups by those attempting to analyze them. Al-Qaeda and

IS, in addition to their respective affiliates, may in reality be far less monolithic than scholars and analysts believe.

The Future Is the Past

There are three distinct possibilities for the future of the al-Qaeda–IS relationship: status quo, outbidding, and rapprochement, each of which will be described in detail below. Suffice to say that whatever form this relationship assumes moving forward, it will be shaped just as much by decisions undertaken by the groups and their leadership cadre as it will by exogenous factors, which include actions pursued by nation-states, and probably by broader geopolitical phenomena, as evidenced by previous changes ushered in by events like the Arab Spring.

Status Quo

A continuation of the status quo would see the two groups remain at odds in something of an uneasy co-existence, operating in similar locales and attempting to recruit new members from the same pool of people, while also competing for access to weapons, financing, and territory. This scenario features continued clashes and frequent spats of violence where the dispute gets kinetic, but still remains confined to low-intensity conflict marked by assassinations, defections, and online verbal disputes and harassment. In the Middle East and other areas where the global jihadist movement predominates, one particular cliché still has currency – *the enemy of my enemy is my friend*. After all, as described in other parts of this analysis, these groups have more commonalities than they have differences.

Outbidding

Another possibility for al-Qaeda–IS relations in the future is the prospect that the two groups ramp up the competition by engaging in escalatory attacks against each other (as well as against security forces) in a process known as outbidding, wherein violent non-state groups rely on extreme violence to persuade potential acolytes that their terrorist or insurgent organization has a stronger resolve to fight the adversary.[79] This situation has played out historically before, in Sri Lanka, Northern Ireland, Lebanon, and the Palestinian territories. It could once again become a defining feature of the conflicts in Syria, Afghanistan, Libya, and West Africa, where the competition between al-Qaeda and IS leads to a spike in suicide bombings, IEDs, and armed attacks. As part of this scenario, in areas where both groups maintain a presence, the result is a violent struggle to exert dominance and command the loyalty of the population by demonstrating superior military prowess vis-à-vis their rivals.

Rapprochement

The possibility of rapprochement between al-Qaeda and IS seems unlikely given the current state of affairs between the groups, but it should not be wholly jettisoned as a possibility. It may take a few years, but a marriage of convenience in which tactical cooperation becomes a necessity is an entirely realistic scenario.[80] The result of enervated enmity would lead to decreased violence between the groups and act as a force multiplier for Salafi-jihadism, vastly increasing the threat of more spectacular-style attacks around the globe.[81] By working together and pooling the resources of the two groups, the newly formed (or reformed) organization would be enhanced by tacit knowledge transfer of sophisticated bomb-making methods, and shared tactics, techniques, and procedures for improved operations security.

For this to happen, there would probably need to be progress on mitigating some of the previously discussed disputes between the two groups and a recognition that ideological differences should not limit operational capabilities. Where this becomes most concerning is if the groups reunite and dedicate a significant portion of their efforts to attacking the West; it is not difficult to imagine a blitzkrieg-style propaganda offensive highlighting the merger while simultaneously imploring jihadists to launch attacks worldwide. To be sure, there are serious obstacles to these groups reuniting, but stranger things have happened. Al-Qaeda seemingly overcame the Sunni–Shia divide by cooperating with Iran, especially once the group's leadership realized it could benefit from tactical cooperation with the mullahs in Tehran.[82] So, in the end, if each group recognized the net benefits of a partnership, a working relationship in the future is not entirely out of the question.

Several top terrorism scholars have voiced skepticism regarding future rapprochement, especially since al-Qaeda and IS are engaged competitively on two different levels – ideologically and militarily. Hassan Hassan, IS expert and co-author of *ISIS: Inside the Army of Terror*, is a fervent believer that no long-term merger will be possible, remarking, "Even if the two organizations find it operationally expedient to work together, their overall strategies and visions cannot be bridged. Each views the other's strategy as ineffective."[83]

Nevertheless, a major event like the death of Baghdadi could prompt change and, relatedly, the split is most pronounced at the leadership level. Among the lower ranks, there is more fluidity between groups, so there could be room for future collaboration and cooperation between al-Qaeda and IS "pools."[84] Bruce Hoffman agrees that the death of Baghdadi could lead to a voluntary amalgamation of the remaining IS fighters with al-Qaeda, or a bid from al-Qaeda (or its acolytes) to undertake a hostile takeover of the surviving IS remnants. Further, since the leaders in charge of IS's external operations and intelligence operations are former Ba'athists – and both pragmatists and survivors – there is a chance that they might ally themselves to whomever and whichever group offered the best prospects for survival and continuing the fight.[85]

What Happens Next?

The three possible futures for al-Qaeda and IS laid out above could each contribute in a different way toward a broader overview of the groups' relative strengths and weaknesses. The section below outlines four distinct potential contexts, beyond whether or not the two groups ever overcome their differences. These contextual scenarios assess the

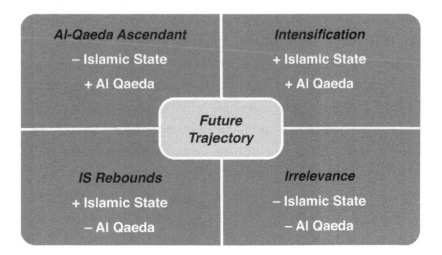

Al-Qaeda Ascendant	Intensification
– Islamic State	+ Islamic State
+ Al Qaeda	+ Al Qaeda

Future Trajectory

IS Rebounds	Irrelevance
+ Islamic State	– Islamic State
– Al Qaeda	– Al Qaeda

relative strength and weakness of each group and suggest a myriad of factors that might result from the outcome. It should be noted that in each of the scenarios described below, the groups remain as separate entities, but that does not entirely rule out on-again, off-again cooperation in specific regions at various times, although the cooperation does not signal anything close to reunification.

Intensification

In this scenario, both al-Qaeda and IS are at increased strength. This could result from any number of real-world developments, including a retrenched Western posture in the Middle East, North Africa, and South Asia. This scenario would see an expansion of the current wave of religious terrorism and could breathe new life into the global jihadist movement as a whole. Over the past two decades, there have been several times when analysts have predicted the demise of the movement – namely, almost immediately after the United States declared its Global War on Terror; once again following the death of Osama bin Laden; and more recently, following the recapture of the Islamic State's strongholds in Mosul and Raqqa and the destruction of its state-building project. But, rather than view the end of the caliphate as the beginning of the end of the movement, some see its establishment in the first place as proof of life, given the destructive energy it produced, luring legions of Muslims from around the world to make *hijrah* (emigration) to its state. Both al-Qaeda and IS could take advantage of exogenous shocks to the system, including another global financial crisis, which, in a world of finite resources, would directly impact nation-states' ability to counter these groups. Predatory insurgent organizations feast on the carcasses of states where civil wars have ravaged institutions and bureaucracies, the official organs of state power projection and legitimacy. Jihadist groups flourish in regions of the world characterized by state failure, lack of good governance, inability to establish widespread rule of law, weak security services, and high levels of corruption.

Irrelevance

Another possible future of the global jihadist movement is retrenchment, dissipation, and a move toward increasing irrelevance. In response to the establishment of the caliphate, there was a pendulum swing back in the other direction, as states moved to harden borders, information sharing and cooperation between intelligence services increased, and advances in technology favored counterterrorism forces. The use of biometrics and the integration of artificial intelligence into the targeting process could help Western militaries be both more effective and discerning in their hunt for terrorist leaders hiding in austere terrain. Another facet of this future potentiality is that the narrative crafted by the Islamic State and similar groups could fail to resonate with future generations and be exposed as bankrupt and contradictory. This scenario is embodied by a shift in the threat landscape where dangers posed by terrorist groups persist, but the gravest concerns to international security are manifested in nation-states and great power rivalries, not non-state actors. Furthermore, the threat of major combat between well-equipped nation-states could make proxy conflict less likely, as states seek to avoid escalatory actions that could lead to war.

Al-Qaeda Ascendant

A scenario in which al-Qaeda is ascendant and the Islamic State falters could result from an increase in external support to the former and increasing isolation of the latter. The percolating conflict between Sunni and Shia powers, represented by the bitter feud between Saudi Arabia and Iran, respectively, could lead some Sunni powers to become more tolerant of al-Qaeda and even sponsor it as a proxy force. Al-Qaeda would be well positioned to receive this type of support since it has worked diligently to refashion its image as a more moderate entity since the Arab Spring. IS is still considered too extreme and has never received external support, even from some of the more hardline boosters of Salafism throughout the Gulf. If al-Qaeda gets involved in certain conflicts that are both seminal and highly symbolic, such as Kashmir, it could further burnish its image as the real vanguard of Islamist rebels committed to defending Muslims. Further, if al-Qaeda focuses its resources on striking the West, and is able to do so success-fully, this may provide the momentum necessary to supplant IS as the leader of the global jihadist movement, and even poach IS fighters, as it has done already in parts of the Middle East and Africa.[86]

IS Rebounds

This scenario predicts the demise of al-Qaeda while the Islamic State rebounds and flourishes, in a replay of the situation during the period from 2014 to 2016. During this time, IS was ascendant and al-Qaeda was caught flat-footed, failing to anticipate the events surrounding the Arab Spring and then responding in a sclerotic manner, as other groups took advantage of the power vacuum to promote their own agendas and ideologies. Ultimately, al-Qaeda benefitted from the chaos that resulted from the Arab Spring, but continued success is far from a *fait accompli.*[87] There is no doubt that IS will indeed reconstitute itself and will almost certainly do so in Iraq and Syria, in addition to other potential locations. But the question is: to what extent does IS rebound and can it rise like a phoenix from the ashes to reclaim its past glory? It remains doubtful that the international community, having once been so negligent, could look away yet again as the group attempted to rebuild a state. The memories of past atrocities are still too fresh. But, most of all, for the countries most affected by the rise of IS – those in the region and others in the West where foreign terrorist fighters and their families are now attempting to return home – the terror and instability conjured by the Islamic State is still quite palpable. In fact, the pivotal time period that could engender this scenario was the 2017–18 timeframe, a time when the caliphate was decimated and al-Qaeda's strategy to quietly and patiently rebuild took shape. The result could be that al-Qaeda temporarily rises above IS as the target most concerning to Western counterterrorism forces, which once again attack al-Qaeda wherever it coalesces, elevating IS simply by default, as its fighters seek to "quietly and patiently rebuild" in their own right.

5

After the Caliphate: Preventing the Islamic State's Return

Whether it is al-Qaeda or IS, or a rejuvenated hybrid entity with off-shoots pockmarking the globe, how can the global jihadist movement be defeated once and for all? The track record for preventing another mass mobilization of jihadists in the future is not promising. Despite the fact that the West has been concerned with foreign fighters and their return for nearly three decades, there has been little tangible progress on crafting policy responses to dealing with the threat. Whether in the immediate aftermath of the end of the Soviet–Afghan war in the late 1980s, Bosnia and Chechnya in the 1990s, Iraq in the 2000s, or Syria in 2014, when it comes to preventing a worldwide flow of foreign fighters, the West always seems to be starting from scratch. As of 2018, there were an estimated 230,000 Salafi-jihadists worldwide, accounting for a 247 percent increase from 2001 to 2018. This means that the so-called Global War on Terror has failed to reduce the number of terrorists worldwide and, despite the massive resources dedicated by the West toward this mission, there are now more jihadist groups active than at any point since 1980.[1] A defining moment for this movement was the establishment of the caliphate.

But even as the jihadists' state-building project in Syria and Iraq begins to fade from recent memory, there is no time to lose in preparing to prevent the next attempt at building a caliphate, whether the destination is Sirte, Libya, or Nangarhar province in Afghanistan. Despite an intensified scrutiny on establishing robust counter-measures, there is still no unified policy in terms of preventing citizens from traveling abroad to join terrorist groups, or widescale agreement among states with respect to important issues such as citizenship deprivation, prosecution and length of sentences, punitive versus rehabilitative measures, or best practices and lessons learned regarding prison radicalization, recidivism, and deradicalization and disengagement initiatives. The patchwork of policies and widescale disparities in resources to enact these policies increase the likelihood of a future foreign terrorist fighter mobilization, even if it is not quite on the scale of IS's recent attempt to establish a caliphate.

The question now becomes, in the immediate aftermath of the caliphate's destruction: how will the international community ensure that it never returns? This will require a comprehensive response that is both carrot and stick. Returning foreign terrorist fighters, and in some cases their families, will need to be dealt with, while the campaign to counter IS on multiple levels – national, regional, and global – must simultaneously remain on the offensive to prevent splinter groups from reconstituting and to deny the group any opportunity to revive the *joie de vivre* it once inspired in tens of thousands of supporters, many of whom traveled to the Middle East to help build and defend the caliphate.

The physical manifestation of IS's state-building project has been crushed, but by no means has the ideology motivating tens of thousands of people to risk their lives defending the caliphate been weakened. If anything, the two-year period during which IS governed its own proto-state offered its followers proof of the concept that the establishment of a caliphate is more than just a jihadi talking point. Rather, it is an attainable goal worthy of dedicating one's life to. The sole reason for its destruction, the propaganda reminds IS adherents, is the Crusader-Zionist axis led by Western nations, especially the United States. Baghdadi proclaimed in an audiotape that was released in August 2018 that the United States "boasted of its so-called victory in expelling the state from cities and countryside in Iraq and Syria, but the land of Allah is wide and the tides of war change."[2] So, while the West breathes a collective sigh of relief that IS has been ousted from Raqqa and Mosul and nearly 70,000 IS fighters have been killed, the group's leader is confidently appealing to its supporters to remain loyal, patient, and steadfast until the moment is ripe for a revival.

Well before the collapse of the Islamic State's caliphate, countries around the world were concerned about a flood of returning foreign fighters. And while the numbers have been far lower than expected, for myriad reasons, the challenge of dealing with returnees is no less complex.[3] Preventing the return of the Islamic State is going to require a mixture of preventive and punitive measures, including discerning the proper way to deal with returnees, but also defending against future threats related to IS's core capabilities – social media and propaganda, financing, and the ability to harness new technologies to recruit and radicalize a fresh generation of followers.

There is little consensus in the West as to the best way to counter the threat. Moreover, with finite resources and a fleeting attention span, national governments must balance the threat posed by terrorism with a litany of other challenges, from climate change to energy insecurity. The global jihadist movement, while a major threat to international security, is merely one of many threats. Finally, some policymakers and military officials may conclude that the mission is complete. After all, the Islamic State's caliphate has been unquestionably destroyed. But in many ways, the challenges associated with the *aftermath* of the caliphate will be even more difficult to solve than the physical caliphate itself, which at least provided a clear target for the international community to focus on and work against. The exodus of fighters from Iraq and Syria seems poised to reset the cycle once more, the same cycle that has been repeating itself since the fatetul days of the Soviet–Afghan War, when Osama bin Laden and his group of "Afghan Arabs" spread throughout the globe and planted the seeds for what would grow into the global jihadist movement and all of its manifestations.

Dealing with Returnees

The prospect of returning foreign fighters and their families has understandably occupied much time and energy in policy and law-enforcement circles.[4] These fighters may attempt to return to their countries of origin, whether close to the battlefields of Syria and Iraq, or farther afield to Europe, Asia, and North America. Those states equipped with more robust national screening mechanisms, law enforcement, and intelligence structures stand a better chance of stopping the fighters at their border, blunting the impact of these returnees. But not all Western security services are created equal. Further complicating the issue is the inability to even agree on the definition of who constitutes a foreign fighter in the first place.[5] Moreover, the category of returnees is not nearly as homogeneous as it may seem. Just as foreign fighters who traveled to the Middle East left for different reasons and fought with different groups, those who return will do so for varying reasons as well.

The first subgroup of returnees might be labeled the "disillusioned." These individuals went to Syria looking for utopia, adventure, and a pure expression of religious identity, but instead found something much different.[6] Local Syrians did not respect them and, in many cases, viewed them as "adventure seekers," naïve about the harsh realities of what constituted on-the-ground truth in the ruins of Syria's civil war. Some foreign fighters were lured to the caliphate through guilt – IS propaganda targeted to Western Muslims repeatedly admonished them for remaining in their safe and comfortable environs in Europe, North America, and Australia, while their fellow Muslims were wantonly slaughtered by the Assad regime. After arriving in the caliphate, these individuals struggled with food, financing, and the tribulations of war. Upon returning to the West, they could mentor other radicalized youth. These fighters may require psychological treatment in addition to prison time.

The second subgroup could be labeled the "disengaged, but not disillusioned." Just as there are many reasons why militants go to fight, there are many reasons why they leave a conflict – marriage, battle fatigue, desire to be with family.[7] So they may have left, voluntarily, but remain committed to jihadism and the core tenets of Salafi-jihadism. Accordingly, individuals might grow disillusioned with IS as an organization, but not with jihad as a whole. These are among the most dangerous returnees who may be living back in their countries of origin. They might be on the authorities' watch-list, but as we have seen time and again, terrorist attacks are committed with regularity by so-called "known wolves," or individuals already on the radar of law enforcement and security services for their connections to extremist circles and ideology.

The third subgroup could be called the "operational" returnees. These are returning fighters who attempt to resuscitate dormant networks or create new ones, recruit members, or conduct homegrown-style attacks. They are likely to be pre-positioned and likely to attempt an attack under the command and control of IS remnants in the Middle East.[8] These individuals are the most dangerous and deadly.[9] The November 2015 Paris attacks are perhaps the clearest example; they were conducted by foreign fighters, who were trained in Syria and dispatched to France.[10] Operational returnees are of even more concern if one believes that hundreds of operatives have already been deployed to Europe, with hundreds more hiding out on Europe's doorstep in Turkey.[11] Turkey in particular remains an attractive staging ground for returning foreign fighters, given its proximity to the battlefield and the presence of pre-existing support networks.[12]

The fourth and final subgroup are those individuals captured on the battlefield and returned to their countries of origin against their will. This is a group that will require close assessment to determine which, if any, crimes have been committed, and whether or not there is ample evidence to move forward with a prosecution. Accordingly, many states have been unable to secure criminal convictions for returning foreign terrorist fighters, and even those who have been jailed ultimately received shorter prison sentences than many prosecutors would have hoped for.[13] As outlined in a report by the Radicalisation Awareness Network (RAN), there are three primary scenarios in these cases: prosecution; non-prosecution/resocialization (what I refer to as rehabilitation and reintegration); and dealing with children.[14] Each of these scenarios will be explored in more detail below.

Prosecution

Prosecuting foreign fighters who have returned is difficult on a number of levels. There are challenges regarding gathering admissible evidence that can be used in court, and even when prosecutions are secured, the length of prison sentences can be short. Further, there are warranted concerns about foreign fighters potentially radicalizing other prisoners, although special accommodations are now made to separate hardcore jihadists from the general inmate population in most prisons. But an unknowable question is: when these individuals serve their sentences and are released back into society, what kind of threat might they present?

In late May 2018, on the very same day he was released from jail, a Belgian jihadist went on a killing spree in the city of Liège.[15] It is almost certain that we are likely to see similar incidents playing out in the future. The resources required to track, monitor, and surveil individuals suspected of radicalization are immense and the mission itself seems somewhat unrealistic. European authorities lament that their already finite resources have been stretched thin by the sheer volume of potential suspects who need to be identified and tracked. The US-led coalition has scrutinized captured computers, documents, and cellphones to put together a global profile of IS members and sympathizers, a list with approximately 19,000 names on it that has been shared with Interpol.[16] The challenge is immense and the security forces will need more manpower simply to monitor and surveil these suspects, to say nothing of conducting investigations and pursuing prosecutions.

There are also widely different scenarios for a returning foreign fighter, their spouses or partners, and any children involved, some of whom may have no paperwork after being born in the caliphate. In turn, there are also myriad categories of prosecution, including prosecuting terrorist crimes within the territory of the so-called caliphate in Iraq and Syria, and raising the issue of how *foreign* national courts can prosecute terrorist crimes that have been committed in Syria and Iraq. There are also attempts to prosecute fighters taking place in Syria, through a combination of the Assad regime's judicial system and ad-hoc courts administered by non-state actors like the Kurds and other militia groups.

There are approximately 3,000 suspected members of IS awaiting trial in Iraq.[17] It is estimated that more than 100 of them are

Europeans.[18] Prosecuting terrorist crimes within the territory of the so-called caliphate in Syria and Iraq is a contentious issue. Under customary international law, Iraq has the legal obligation to prosecute war crimes that have been conducted on its territory, or to extradite those who have committed them. The situation in Syria is far more complex. As international law expert Tanya Mehra has described in detail, in Syria, "the judicial system has become a patchwork of 'ordinary' and 'special' courts that have jurisdiction."[19] Depending on their location within the territory of Syria, courts are run either by the Assad regime – which, after years of slaughtering its own people and using chemical weapons against civilians, lacks political legitimacy amongst most Syrians – or by armed groups scattered throughout the country, including the Syrian Democratic Forces, or SDF.[20] The SDF currently holds hundreds of IS prisoners. Moreover, as the SDF and other Kurdish groups are still actively engaged in fighting, including against Turkish forces on Syria's northern border, there are fears that the fighting will distract from their responsibility to guard IS fighters being held prisoner, increasing the chances for prisoner escapes.[21]

There is also the issue of how courts in states in the West can prosecute terrorist crimes that have been committed by its citizens while they were living under the caliphate. There have already been convictions of this kind in Canada, the United Kingdom, Belgium, Norway, and the Netherlands, with fighters prosecuted for crimes including attempted travel to Syria, recruitment, planning of an attack, and "terroristic murder."[22] Further, it is entirely conceivable that, in some instances, crimes committed in Syria and Iraq by European nationals could qualify as war crimes or crimes against humanity.

Dealing with the issue of prosecuting cases of terrorism is fraught with challenges. Many states lack well-developed jurisdictional infrastructures, and the capacity of their judiciaries, national courts, and other institutions could be severely under-resourced. These courts struggle to prosecute the cases they have and can be overwhelmed easily by having to handle just a small cluster of additional cases. Complex cases can be lengthy and time-consuming, while also depleting finite resources necessary for other criminal justice issues. There are also a number of unique circumstances facing courts in Western countries in prosecuting those citizens who have made it back home, as well as from the massive influx of Iraqi and Syrian migrants into Europe, some of whom might be victims, witnesses, or perpetrators of various crimes, to include terrorism.

So far, at least, it appears that many Western countries do not want to deal with their citizens who have been apprehended on the battlefield and are now being held in the Middle East.[23] But if these individuals are left to be prosecuted in Syria or Iraq, there are legitimate concerns that their prosecutions will certainly not meet fair-trial standards and could be politicized. A dearth of adequate funding for specialized war units or chambers needed to deal with these types of crimes means that these trials could be hasty, resulting in false convictions or what some perceive to be overly draconian sentences in proportion to the specific crime committed.[24]

The issue of whether or not to accept citizens who want to return home after leaving their countries of origin to help establish the caliphate crisscrosses legal, moral, and ethical seams. The governments of European countries are opposed to the death penalty, so leaving citizens of their country in Iraq and Syria is a dilemma, given concerns about the likelihood of receiving a fair trial. The case of a French woman named Emilie Konig is an archetypical example. After leaving France to live under the caliphate, Konig was captured during the war against IS and is now being held in the Kurdish region of Syria. The Kurds administer justice in this region, but, under international law, the territory is still part of Syria.[25] Understandably, many French citizens are wary of having individuals like Konig return to the country. The issue of how to deal with potential returnees has become a political lightning rod in many Western countries. In the meantime, many wives and children of IS fighters remain in limbo, as thousands languish in detainee camps throughout northern Syria while decisions on their fates are postponed.[26]

The United Kingdom is one of many European nations facing a tremendous strain on its resources, as more than 80 prisoners convicted of terror offenses between 2007 and 2016 were due to be released in 2018.[27] Its nationwide program to prevent radicalization and violent extremism, known as PREVENT, has been widely criticized for being ineffective and lacking a proper assessment and evaluation methodology. One case plaguing the UK is that of two members of the so-called "Beatles," British-born IS members known for their barbarism, which included the torture and murder of several Western captives.[28] There are serious jurisdictional issues in this case and much hand-wringing over who should prosecute these militants. The UK insists it does not want them back on British soil, while the United States is pressing London to bring the men to trial. If Britain doesn't prosecute them, they could ultimately end up at the notorious US prison at Guantánamo Bay, Cuba.[29] American policy is ambiguous, partly by design, but partly due to incoherence. The resulting inertia might afford policymakers and military officials with more time to figure out what to do with the captured terrorists.[30] Still, the dearth of strategy and seeming lack of urgency has attracted pointed criticism from a number of human rights groups.

Above all else, the most serious challenge to prosecuting foreign terrorist fighters remains the issue of evidence. To be useful, the evidence gathered to prosecute cases of terrorism must be able to pass muster in a legitimate court of law and it remains extremely dangerous to travel to a war-ravaged country to investigate and collect evidence. Some non-governmental organizations are on the ground in Iraq and Syria and have slightly changed the landscape by their presence alone.[31] Internet-based evidence is also a new element to consider, although with the phenomenon of spoofing, "deep fakes," and other forms of digital manipulation, many courts will understandably be wary of evidence generated via social or other online media.

Cross-border legal cooperation is a major hurdle as well, and not all courts are in agreement about the utility of, or ethical considerations surrounding, secret, restricted, or classified information and its use in court.[32] The other methods of documenting terrorism-related crimes are International Commissions of Inquiry and various resolutions passed by the United Nations Security Council (UNSC), including UNSCR 2379, which established an Investigative Team to support domestic efforts to collect, preserve, and store evidence, in Iraq, of acts committed by IS that may amount to war crimes, crimes against humanity, and genocide. There has also been a case in the United States – and there remains the possibility for similar cases in other Western countries – in which evidence taken from the battlefield was used successfully in court to prosecute individuals for crimes related to the support of terrorism.[33]

Rehabilitation/Reintegration

There are other options besides incarcerating returnees and, indeed, in many cases, this is the desirable approach, especially where the individual has not committed violent acts and demonstrates no propensity to do so in the future, although assessing this possibility is a precarious undertaking. Now that Western governments have made it clear that terrorism prevention, deradicalization, and countering violent extremism, especially among the youth, are among their top priorities, something of a cottage industry has emerged, with a long line of NGOs and other entities proclaiming to have the "silver bullet" to solve radicalization. The hard truth is that most programs do not work and even those that have shown promise often have difficulty demonstrating a correlation between the design of the program and its range of outcomes, to say nothing of establishing something like a causal link.

The United States Institute for Peace (USIP) has identified several promising themes across first-generation deradicalization programs implemented in the Middle East and South Asia. First, the intervention would address the affective – that is, a focus on social factors including emotional support, a sense of community, and social obligation. Second, it would target the pragmatic, or logistical factors, such as financial stability, education, vocational training, and other skill acquisition. And third, it would focus on the ideological bonds underpinning the thought processes and value system of the individual. [34]

There are widely different approaches both across and within regions. In Saudi Arabia, there has been an interesting evolution over time. At first, Saudi rehabilitation and reintegration programs focused almost exclusively on the ideological and psychological component, sending individuals to deradicalization sessions with imams and counselors, while also providing financial incentives to disengage from militancy. The recidivism rates from these programs were quite high and, to their credit, the Saudis shifted their approach. Reintegration programs now focus more on the returnees' families and do more to assist with rebuilding relationships between the individual and their family, society, and country.[35] By and large, however, one of the biggest differences between deradicalization programs in Europe and those in Muslim-majority countries is that the latter are almost always government-run and mandatory, which in turn calls into question their legitimacy and effectiveness, especially if the intent is to measure individuals' willingness to voluntarily turn away from jihad.[36]

France is a country with nearly 20,000 people considered to be at risk of radicalization by government authorities. In prison, the risk of radicalization is acute, because imprisoned jihadists may proselytize and recruit, an issue France has dedicated much time and attention to, but still struggles with. In prisons, case managers will meet with Islamists to discuss the contradictions in their ideologies, offering individual psychological treatment and meetings with case workers and chaplains.[37] But a parliamentary commission in France published a report noting that deradicalization programs in that country, especially those that existed outside of the penal system, "were hastily conceived and in some cases marred by severe deficiencies."[38] In Vilvoorde, Belgium, authorities responded to large numbers of youth leaving for Syria by implementing an intensive early-intervention program which built upon government engagement with communities and families to identify youth who may be at risk of radicalization.[39] The program in Denmark has come under fire for being too liberal and forgiving in its treatment of returnees. The program in Aarhaus is often lambasted by its critics as an example of appeasement and a fear of confronting the problem of militant Islam in a secular, European society. At the national level, Denmark seeks to arrest and prosecute returning foreign fighters with a proven involvement in terrorism, but others are assisted in gaining access to employment, housing, education, and psychological counseling.[40]

Programs designed to counter violent extremism and reintegrate "at-risk individuals" have been roundly lambasted as ineffective, and in some cases worse – counterproductive. There are numerous examples of failed programs, with shortcomings ranging from an inability to measure outcomes to actual spikes in violence following some interventions, as witnessed in Kandahar, Afghanistan, following a program featuring cash transfers as a development assistance tool.[41] Some practitioners lament that efforts to counter extremism should be organic and powered by grassroots initiatives.[42] Others insist that current efforts are futile because it will probably be years before we know which programs work best and why. Measurement, evaluation, and assessment in this area are notoriously difficult for social scientists, and the scores of self-proclaimed "deradicalization experts" who have cropped up with countering violent extremism (CVE) programs for sale amount to little more than modern-day snake-oil salesmen. This is not to dismiss some of the extremely important and necessary work being done, but rather to issue a rebuke to junk science and a suggestion to governments that progress in this area will be slow and probably characterized by setbacks and false positives.

Even after years of commissioned studies, carefully planned interventions, and generously sponsored government initiatives, there is still no "tried and true" method for deradicalization, reintegration, or countering violent extremism. It remains difficult to know what works and whether or not these programs are effective. There is a lack of reliable data on outcomes from rehabilitation programs and no uniform approach, which makes it impossible to conduct rigorous comparative analyses. Still, despite the problems plaguing these efforts, it is imperative that the international community keep trying to make progress. Moreover, there is a growing corpus of lessons learned that could inform the debate. One of the major findings from a global multi-year series of workshops on foreign terrorist fighters (FTFs) found that the international community would be well served by focusing on capacity-building efforts geared toward comprehensive community engagement and preventative measures.[43] This requires a whole-of-government approach and robust engagement with civil society, as well as public–private partnerships that might be focused on employment, education, or job training.

Generation Jihad: Born into the Caliphate

Among the many traumas of the Syrian civil war and spreading sectarian violence that characterizes large segments of the Middle East, the issue of children in the caliphate is perhaps the most egregious. What these children saw, and indeed what some of them were coerced to do, is impossible for most human beings to conceptualize. Some children witnessed killings, beheadings, and brutal atrocities, while others actually participated in these heinous acts. Many were brainwashed, indoctrinated with the virulent screed of sectarian hatred. As a result, most of these youngsters will never be the same – what will they grow up to be like as teenagers and adults? What impact could they have on neighbors and classmates at school? Court documents from proceedings in the UK have showed that children as young as 2 years old who have been exposed to IS indoctrination have demonstrated a fascination with guns and beheadings.[44]

IS pursued a deliberate and calculated strategy of targeting children and young teens, especially males, in order to "create new power structures in society," spread its ideology to young recruits, and sow the seeds for the next generation of future jihadists. The physical territory of the caliphate is gone, but its core messages, ideas, and narrative have already been implanted in countless numbers of young Muslims.[45] The Islamic State ran schools for children, where textbooks indoctrinated the pupils by focusing on a select few themes considered most important by IS leadership: encouraging violence, driving an apocalyptic narrative, establishing a purist "Islamic" state, and labeling it a caliphate.[46] The last part is especially crucial for the future of the Islamic State, as young children were brainwashed with the notion that what IS had achieved – and indeed what these children, their families, and neighbors helped to build and were an integral part of – was an achievement of historic proportions, a caliphate "based on prophetic methodology" that was the first and only *true* Salafi-jihadi state, an embodiment of political and religious authority for Muslims everywhere.

Future IS propaganda will seek to harness the legacy of its European fighters killed in battle, thus directly impacting the younger generation of children in marginalized neighborhoods, towns, and cities throughout Europe, from Malmo to Marseille. There are thousands of youngsters scattered across the continent who lost older siblings whom they probably looked up to. These deceased young men are now eligible to be lionized as IS martyrs in the heavily immigrant enclaves where they grew up, much in the same way that fallen Hamas militants are worshipped in Gaza, Tamil fighters were celebrated in Jaffna, or Irish Republican Army "volunteers" were revered in West Belfast. IS will deploy nostalgia in similar ways to how they have used it in the past and present – as a multidimensional propaganda tool. The "nostalgia narrative" will not only be deployed at a transnational level, through its central media units, and at the provincial level, through its provincial media units, but also at highly localized and even individual levels through on-the-ground networks.[47]

Yet the issue of dealing with the children of the caliphate is not as simple as some would like to pretend. These young people are *both* victims and perpetrators, a fact which cannot and should not be ignored. There is a growing body of evidence of atrocities committed by children associated with IS. In one instance, a 13-year-old British citizen executed a Kurdish prisoner. In another, a 7-year-old boy appears in a video holding a severed head. And the horrors are not merely relegated to the battlefield in Iraq and Syria. Europe has witnessed numerous cases where teens and pre-teens have been implicated in terrorist plots – a 13-year-old in the suburbs of Paris; a 12-year-old German Iraqi in Ludwigshafen, western Germany; and the United Kingdom has identified over 2,000 adolescents under 15 years old as "possible extremists."[48]

It is important not to look at the problem of "non-adults" as one singular cohort. Some children were more directly associated with violence than others, while certain groups of children were specifically groomed and recruited to form the future backbone of this group. A study by the International Centre for Counter-Terrorism – The Hague (ICCT) recommends dividing children into two distinct groups. Young children (aged 0 to 9) who were born in the caliphate or brought to IS-controlled territory at an extremely young age should be viewed and treated primarily as victims. All told, approximately 730 children were born in the caliphate to parents from elsewhere.[49] But older children should be scrutinized more closely. For the latter group, it will be critical to assess what level of indoctrination was involved, whether or not these children received training (and, if so, what kind and at what level), and, perhaps most importantly, their potential involvement in violent activities.[50]

Endgame for IS or New Beginnings?

Even though the main objective of the Coalition to Defeat IS was targeting and effectively defeating it, the degradation of a terrorist organization can lead to organizational fractures or splintering.[51] While causing IS to break apart might seem like a positive outcome, it is a double-edged sword in the truest sense, clichés aside. The fracturing of the Islamic State could lead to the emergence of new, and in some cases more violent and operationally capable, splinter organizations.[52] In Sub-Saharan Africa, Salafi-jihadism is spreading and countries with no prior experience of this threat have now been suffering from a spate of attacks. In the DRC and Mozambique, new groups have emerged, some using the Shabaab brand name even though there are no formal links with the Somali terrorist group.[53] So the threat is not just from off-shoots of the two primary Salafi-jihadist groups – IS and al-Qaeda – but also from *their* offshoots, compounding the challenge and presenting a nightmare scenario in which franchises eventually have enough clout to spawn derivative terrorist organizations in diverse locales, including in countries with little to no prior history of jihadism.

Dismantling IS is a necessary strategic objective, but policymakers, government officials, and military leaders must also be prepared to deal with splinter groups as they emerge in the aftermath of what seems to be a relatively successful campaign against the parent group. With IS, these splinters could form their own, new organization, or be absorbed into existing franchise groups or affiliates from North Africa to Southeast Asia.

As discussed earlier in this book, the Islamic State – a splinter of al-Qaeda in Iraq or AQI, which itself was previously a splinter of al-Qaeda – is one of many terrorist groups that resulted from the successful frac-turing of a pre-existing group.[54] It seems rather ominous that some of the most lethal and durable terrorist groups can trace their origins back to a splinter movement. The Liberation Tigers of Tamil Eelam (LTTE) coalesced between the late 1970s and early 1980s from a cacophony of Tamil rebel groups. Hezbollah, too, grew into the formidable politico-military force it remains today after its modest beginnings as a cast-off of the Afwaj al-Muqawama al-Lubnaniya (AMAL), formed in the early 1980s with help from Iran, supposedly in response to Israel's invasion of southern Lebanon. Other prominent splinter groups have flourished at various points in Algeria, Thailand, and Northern Ireland.

Splinter groups are often only slight variations of the original groups, with minor differences in ideology, but more significant discrepancies over strategy, tactics, and the utility of violence, some of the main points of contention discussed in the section on the IS–al-Qaeda dispute. That some of these groups were more savage than their predecessors is an unfortunate outcome of effective counterterrorism campaigns, which inevitably produce second- and third-order effects. Again, the Islamic State is instructive in this regard, as its emergence, consolidation of power, and declaration of a caliphate in the heart of the Middle East posed a far greater threat than al-Qaeda in Iraq ever did. IS generated significant income flows from a variety of sources, controlled swaths of territory on at least two continents, and could deploy operatives into Europe to conduct spectacular attacks in the West. It is certainly possible that if Islamic State is degraded to the point it is no longer such a threat, which is a process currently unfolding, whatever supplants IS could go through a similar transformation and ultimately metastasize into a more potent challenge than its predecessors.

The blueprint for start-up success as a terrorist organization – evidenced in Iraq and North Africa – is now widely known. After gaining a foothold in a failed state or ungoverned region, the group seeks to latch on to a marginalized ethnic or religious group, exploit local grievances, and lend guidance, resources, expertise, and manpower to the fight.[55] It is not difficult to imagine the Islamic State replicating this formula in any number of places, from Libya to Afghanistan and West Africa. These countries and regions are awash in weapons, and plagued by poor security forces and a weak rule of law, making them the ideal candidates for splinter groups seeking to regenerate and exploit new bases of operations, if they choose to relocate abroad.

The challenge for the international community will be preventing these regenerated slivers from emerging stronger than before. An apt analogy is that the remnants of a largely extinguished fire must be stamped out before the embers can accelerate into a massive conflagration that is difficult to contain. Destroying a terrorist organization – and potentially creating splinter groups in the process – is less important than denying the group the ability to control territory, raise money, and recruit legions of new followers. But this requires a sustained campaign, the consistent allocation of resources, and the political will to continue focusing on the issue long after it has dropped from the news cycle and daily media buzz, replaced by other pressing matters. It has been this last part that has proved capricious in the past. Moreover, despite a laudable effort by the international community to come together in the face of the unprecedented wave of foreign fighters who traveled to conflict zones over the past five years, there is still no universally accepted and agreed-upon strategy either for preventing a similar outflow of aspiring jihadists in the future or for how societies should handle the inevitable return of those who fight, survive, and then seek to come back to their countries of origin – some war-weary, disillusioned, and traumatized; others disengaged, but not deradicalized.

When considering the Islamic State, there are several potential outcomes if the ongoing Coalition counterterrorism campaign proves successful in smashing its core and causing it to splinter. One veritable certainty, however, is that the inclusion of the Islamic State into any future political framework in either Iraq or Syria is a non-sequitur.[56] The Islamic State has not shared any political platform anywhere close to being mildly acceptable to even the most dysfunctional or rogue nation-state. Were a political settlement in either Syria or Iraq to gain traction more broadly, it is possible that elements of the Islamic State could continue to prosper as a violent criminal organization, relying on extortion, smuggling, and robbery to survive. But a Hezbullah-like political entity is not even a remote possibility, nor does IS seem inclined to favor such a route.

As discussed in chapter 4, al-Qaeda in Syria could prove to be the final death knell of IS in that country, either by defeating its forces militarily or by absorbing the bulk of its remaining fighters into al-Qaeda's ranks. Between HTS and Tanzim Hurras al-Din, there is no shortage of militant Islamist groups which could be possible suitors for militants fleeing IS. Still, if the Islamic State feared it was facing extinction in Syria, its leadership might well decide to relocate the caliphate to Libya, or elsewhere where an existing offshoot might be bolstered.[57] It is possible that, following the atomization of the Islamic State, its remnants could be stamped out by security forces in areas where it currently operates. However, the two primary factors that led to the resuscitation of al-Qaeda in Iraq (AQI) into Islamic State – the Syrian civil war and Baghdad's marginalization of Iraqi Sunnis – show no signs of abating anytime soon, though prospects for the latter are more promising in the near term.

If none of the above futures play out, the United States will need to work with partner nations across the region to disrupt the blueprint that deftly enables splinter groups to reconstitute into more effective fighting forces. This can be accomplished in part by reducing the space for militants to operate and gain traction, including helping governments to address local grievances, promote good governance, and strengthen the rule of law. This will require a true "whole of government approach," including security cooperation in areas such as intelligence, surveillance and reconnaissance, and diplomacy; increased intelligence sharing; and continued punitive measures when necessary. The United States can help provide surveillance of poorly governed areas to help reduce threats within these territories, while also building the partner capacity of host-nation security forces to help stem migration (and other martial resource) flows to active areas of hostilities.

To the extent possible, the United States should continue working to mitigate the primary factors that led an al-Qaeda splinter to grow into the Islamic State in the first place – namely, pushing hard to end the Syrian civil war and exerting whatever leverage possible to cajole Baghdad into abandoning its overly sectarian stance against Iraqi Sunnis. To some degree, there has been progress on this front under the Abadi government. Without ameliorating what are essentially political issues, even successful counterterrorism tactics will allow room for splinter groups to emerge and grow stronger. There are several other important issues related to splinter groups that counterterrorism forces also need to take into account, including these groups' ability to finance their nascent organizations through a diverse range of activities, disseminate effective propaganda, and exploit new technologies.

Technology, especially technology that enables terrorist groups' ability to talk with one another and communicate their message to a broader audience, is a greater force multiplier in 2019 than it has been at any previous point in history. IS's leveraging of social media provided a tremendous boost to its ability to recruit and organize. It has also vastly improved terrorists' ability to plan and execute virtual plots. As Gartenstein-Ross observed, "Over the past few years, Syria-based IS operatives have found recruits online, spurred them to action, and played an intimate role in the conceptualization, target selection, timing, and execution of attacks. They have also used encrypted communication platforms to assist in bomb-making techniques and provide other forms of technical assistance."[58]

The West must develop a range of strategies to handle the threat posed by these different groups. The "hardcore fighters" who remain in Iraq and Syria will need to be killed or captured by Iraqi security forces and the anti-IS Coalition. The first priority should be detection, which goes hand in hand with increased information sharing and training partner nations to screen and investigate potential terrorists. This suggests an even greater role for multilateral cooperation. Another major hurdle will be marshaling the resources required to monitor, track, and surveil battle-hardened jihadists attempting to blend back into Western society. Efforts by the West to build the partner capacity of host-nation forces in weak and fragile states will not obviate the threat, but will be part of a more comprehensive solution geared toward combating the challenge posed by the "free agents," or roving bands of militants.

The trillion-dollar question is: how do you prevent a similar phenomenon of tens of thousands of people leaving their homes to travel to a war zone to support a violent, non-state armed group? Part of the answer is persuasion, and another part is prevention. Regarding the former, the challenge for Western countries is how to escape what Rik Coolsaet has called the "no-future subculture" that exists in many countries in Europe and elsewhere.[59] This viewpoint holds that French, Belgian, Dutch, and British citizens whose parents or grandparents emigrated from Algeria, Morocco, Somalia, or Pakistan feel no connection to the European societies in which they were raised, even while they have no clear links to their ancestral homelands. This creates an identity crisis which leaves them vulnerable to the allure of extremist interpretations of Islam, while others might see joining IS as a way to define their identities, seek adventure, or openly defy a society and culture they feel separated from to the point of actively wanting to oppose it.

To be fair, in many circles the conversation has grown to include not merely responses to terrorism, but efforts at prevention in the first place. One way states have approached this is to prevent individuals from traveling abroad to conflict zones in the first place through the use of administrative measures, including travel bans and control orders. These have proven to be quite effective in preventing the departure of individuals, although it is critical to establish safeguards and limits around their use.[60] This measure can also lead to unintended consequences, as witnessed with so-called "frustrated foreign fighters." After being denied the ability to travel abroad to wage jihad, they instead seek to conduct attacks in their countries of origin. There are numerous examples of attackers who fit into this category, with cases in the United States, Australia, Canada, Denmark, Spain, and France, to name a few.[61]

The physical entity that was the Islamic State's caliphate is over. Mosul and Raqqa have been retaken and, even though its leader Abu Bakr al-Baghdadi has not yet been killed or captured – at least, at the time of this writing in late 2018 – the core of the Islamic State is decimated. But its message still finds resonance among sub-populations of extremists throughout the world and will continue to do so well into the foreseeable future.

But to defeat IS in the long term, it will take more than measures in the physical world. To counter the threat IS will continue to pose in the future, it is crucial to understand what IS is and what IS is not, where it is truly dangerous and where its power and reach have limits. And, above all else, the Islamic State is an ideology. It represents the embodiment of Salafi-jihadism and all of its undercurrents – anti-American, anti-Jewish, and, of course, anti-Shia. This ideology motivates individuals and groups around the world to conduct attacks in its name, inspiring an amorphous and disconnected cadre of lone wolves and small groups of jihadists driven to act by its propaganda and overarching messages.

But for all of our acknowledgment of the threat posed by the Islamic State, there are many things it is not. For example, IS is not a monolithic actor, even though many in the West have lumped disparate and diverse threats under the Islamic State banner. This tendency is a legacy of the Cold War, when Washington became comfortable with defining grand strategy in terms of *us versus them*. "Them" now includes a range of state and non-state threats and not all terrorists are the same. Moreover, all Salafi-jihadi terrorist groups are not the same. Defining the Islamic State threat as unitary helps provide a much-needed structure and logic to Western counterterrorism strategy, but it also causes conceptual confusion. In some ways, attempting to make sense of IS is a fool's errand. This is not a centrally managed organization, but rather an opportunistic, disaggregated movement.

The Islamic State is also not an existential threat on the order of the challenge the United States faced throughout the course of the Cold War. IS is not a nuclear-armed nation-state, nor is it a near-peer adversary trained and equipped for conventional military operations. Countering IS demands a sober assessment of the group's organizational and operational capabilities, but, more poignantly, it requires an honest recognition of the international community's ability to affect the future trajectory of this movement. No counterterrorism strategy, no matter how comprehensive or robust, can address the grievances that led to the resuscitation of IS or pacify the virulent ideology that sustains the group.

Eliminating the physical embodiment of IS – the caliphate – is a necessary, but not sufficient, component of winning the long war against the group and in addressing the region's more fundamental challenges. And whatever iteration of violent extremism replaces IS, the West should be careful to realize that IS is more a symptom of the disease than the underlying cause. The most pragmatic approach to keeping this ideology confined to the margins is working to address the conditions that fueled IS's rise – sectarianism in Iraq and the Syrian civil war – while remaining honest about the threat posed by this ideology and the West's ability to counter this threat wherever it manifests itself over the course of the next generation.[62]

The establishment of the caliphate will be trumpeted by IS as an achievement of meteoric proportions. Indeed, even those opposed to the group and its ideology have to admit that for a violent non-state terrorist organization to establish a proto-state in this day and age is a rare event and a rather brazen, if not ambitious, feat. But it was also an aberration.

The fight against radicalization, extremism, and global jihad is not existential. Now that the caliphate has been crushed, the global jihadist movement will return to its peripatetic past, one characterized largely by infighting amongst militant groups and travel to new battlefields. The pendulum is now swinging away from a globally coordinated effort by centralized terrorist organizations and back to a focus on local and regional conflicts. But even in fragmented and atomized form, these groups present a threat, especially if the Islamic State's ideology persists and successfully convinces a new generation of Muslims that a caliphate is an attainable and desirable objective, and that the means to this end will include the relentless pursuit of never-ending global jihad.

Notes

Introduction

1 Rukmini Callimachi, "To Maintain Supply of Sex Slaves, ISIS Pushes Birth Control," *New York Times*, March 12, 2016.

2 Email exchange with Martha Crenshaw, June 2018.

3 Email exchange with journalist and author of *The Way of the Strangers: Encounters with The Islamic State*, Graeme Wood, June 2018.

4 Although most analysis focuses on the macro-, or group level, it is important not to discard the micro-level view of focusing on lone actors. For more, see Boaz Ganor, Bruce Hoffman, Marlene Mazel, and Matthew Levitt, "Lone Wolf: Passing Fad or Terror Threat of the Future?" in Matthew Levitt, ed., *Neither Remaining Nor Expanding: The Decline of the Islamic State*, Counterterrorism Lectures 2016–2017 (Washington Institute for Near East Policy, 2018), pp. 69–73.

5 https://www.newyorker.com/news/news-desk/isis-jihadis-have-returned-home-by-the-thousands.

6 https://www.usip.org/sites/default/files/The-Jihadi-Threat-ISIS-Al-Qaeda-and-Beyond.pdf, p. 7.

1 The Long Road to the Caliphate

1 See Mustaf Hamid and Leah Farrall, *The Arabs at War in Afghanistan*, London: Hurst & Company, 2015; see also Rodric Braithwaite, *Afgansty: The Russians in Afghanistan 1979–89*, New York: Oxford University Press, 2011.

2   Al Qaeda, Al-Qaeda, Al-Qa'ida, and several other variants are often used interchangeably in the literature. "Al-Qaeda" has been translated variously as the "base of operation," "foundation," "precept," or "method": Bruce Hoffman, "The Changing Face of Al Qaeda and the Global War on Terrorism," *Studies In Conflict & Terrorism*, 27:6, 2004, p. 551.

3   R. Kim Cragin, "Early History of Al-Qa'ida," *Historic Journal*, 51:4, December 2008, pp. 1051-2.

4   Ibid., p. 1056.

5   Brian Michael Jenkins, "Al Qaeda after Bin Laden: Implications for American Strategy," testimony before the Committee on Armed Services Subcommittee on Emerging Threats and Capabilities, United States House of Representatives, June 22, 2011.

6   Assaf Moghadam, "The Salafi-Jihad as Religious Ideology," *CTC Sentinel*, February 15, 2008.

7   Daniel Byman, "Explaining Al Qaeda's Decline," *Journal of Politics*, 79:3, 2017, p. 1107.

8   Brian A. Jackson, "Groups, Networks, or Movements: A Command-and-Control-Driven Approach to Classifying Terrorist Organizations and Its Application to Al Qaeda," *Studies in Conflict & Terrorism*, 29:3, 2006, p. 241.

9   Bruce Hoffman, *Inside Terrorism*, New York: Columbia University Press, 2006, pp. 285-8.

10 Byman, "Al Qaeda's Decline," p. 1107.

11 Seth G. Jones, *A Persistent Threat: The Evolution of al Qa'ida and Other Salafi Jihadists*, Santa Monica, CA: RAND Corp., 2014, p. 10.

12 Ibid., p. 11.

13 Daniel Byman, "Buddies of Burdens? Understanding the Al Qaeda Relationship with Its Affiliate Organizations," *Security Studies*, 23:3, 2014, p. 436.

14 Jones, *A Persistent Threat*, p. 2; see also Katherine Zimmerman, "America's Real Enemy: The Salafi-Jihadi Movement," American Enterprise Institute (AEI), July 2017, p. 4.

15 Douglas E. Streusand, "What Does Jihad Mean?" *Middle East Quarterly*, 4:3, June 1997.

16 Peter Bergen, *The Longest War: The Enduring Conflict Between America and Al Qaeda*, New York: Free Press, 2011, p. 23.

17 David Malet, "Why Foreign Fighters? Historical Perspectives and Solutions," *Orbis*, Winter 2010, p. 105.

18 Cragin, "Early History of Al Qa'ida," p. 1051.

19 Anonymous, *Imperial Hubris: Why the West is Losing the War on Terror*, Washington, DC: Brassey's, Inc., 2004, p. 129.

20 Bruce Hoffman, "Al Qaeda Trends in Terrorism and Future Potentialities: An Assessment," paper presented at a meeting of the Council on Foreign Relations, Washington, DC Office, May 8, 2003, p. 5.

21 David Aaron, *In Their Own Words: Voices of Jihad*, Santa Monica, CA: RAND Corp., 2008, p. 73.

22 Cragin, "Early History of Al-Qa'ida," p. 1066.

23 Anne Stenersen, *Al Qaeda in Afghanistan*, Cambridge University Press, 2017, pp. 165–75.

24 Jarret Brachman, "The Worst of the Worst," *Foreign Policy*, January 22, 2010.

25 Assaf Moghadam, "How Al Qaeda Innovates," *Security Studies*, 22:3, 2013, p. 477.

26 Bruce Hoffman, "Al Qaeda's Uncertain Future," *Studies in Conflict & Terrorism*, 36:8, 2013, pp. 640–1.

27 Nicholas J. Rasmussen, "Fifteen Years after 9/11: Threats to the Homeland," Statement for the Record: Hearing Before the Senate Homeland Security Governmental Affairs Committee, September 27, 2016.

28 Brian Michael Jenkins, *The Origins of America's Jihadists*, Santa Monica, CA: RAND Corp., 2017, p. 22. A complement to Jenkins's study is Alexander Meleagrou-Hitchens, Seamus Hughes, and Bennett Clifford, *The Travelers: American Jihadists in Syria and Iraq*, Program on Extremism, George Washington University, February 2018. This report focuses on American citizens who either traveled abroad or attempted to travel abroad to join jihadist groups in the Middle East. One of the primary findings is that travelers tend to be male, with an average age of 27, and

are "generally affiliated with IS upon arrival in Syria or Iraq." Minnesota, Virginia, and Ohio are the states with the highest proportional rates of recruitment.

29 Martin Rudner, "Al Qaeda's Twenty-Year Strategic Plan: The Current Phase of Global Terror," *Studies in Conflict & Terrorism*, 36:12, 2013, p. 959. See also Bruce Hoffman, "A First Draft of the History of America's Ongoing Wars on Terrorism," *Studies in Conflict & Terrorism*, 38:1, 2015, p. 81.

30 Daniel Byman, "War Drives Terrorism," *Washington Post*, June 21, 2016.

31 Byman, "Al Qaeda's Decline," pp. 1107, 1113.

32 Daniel Byman, "Judging Al Qaeda's Record, Part I: Is the Organization in Decline?" *Lawfare*, June 27, 2017.

33 Daniel Byman, *Al Qaeda, The Islamic State, and the Global Jihadist Movement: What Everyone Needs to Know*, New York: Oxford University Press, 2015, p. 13.

34 "Al Qaeda: Constitutional Charter, Rules and Regulations," Defense Intelligence Agency, AFGT-2002-600175.

35 Rajan Basra, Peter R. Neumann, and Claudia Brunner, "Criminal Pasts, Terrorist Futures: European Jihadists and the New Crime-Terror Nexus," International Centre for the Study of Radicalisation and Political Violence, November 10, 2016; see also Rajan Basra and Peter R. Neumann, "Crime as Jihad: Developments in the Crime–Terror Nexus in Europe," *CTC Sentinel*, 10:9, October 2017; and, Colin P. Clarke, "Crime and Terror in Europe: Where the Nexus is Alive and Well," International Centre for Counter-Terrorism (ICCT) – The Hague, December 13, 2016.

36 Brian Michael Jenkins, "The al Qaeda-Inspired Terrorist Threat: An Appreciation of the Current Situation," testimony before the Canadian Senate Special Committee on Anti-terrorism, December 6, 2010, p. 6.

37 Brian Michael Jenkins, "Stray Dogs and Virtual Armies: Radicalization and Recruitment to Jihadist Terrorism in the United States Since 9/11," Santa Monica, CA: Rand Corp., p. 14; see also Steven Simon and Jonathan Stevenson, "Al Qaeda's New

Strategy: Less Apocalypse, More Street Fighting," *Washington Post*, October 10, 2010.

38 Leah Farrall, "How Al Qaeda Works," *Foreign Affairs*, March/April 2011.

39 Byman, *Al Qaeda, The Islamic State, and the Global Jihadist Movement*, pp. 47–54.

40 Moghadam, "How Al Qaeda Innovates," p. 467.

41 Farrall, "How Al Qaeda Works."

42 Colin P. Clarke, "The Moderate Face of Al Qaeda," *Foreign Affairs*, October 24, 2017.

43 Martha Crenshaw, "Transnational Jihadism & Civil Wars," *Daedalus*, 146:4, Fall 2017, p. 68.

44 Tricia Bacon, "Hurdles to International Terrorist Alliances: Lessons from Al Qaeda's Experience," *Terrorism and Political Violence*, 29:1, 2017, pp. 79–101.

45 Barak Mendelsohn, *The Al Qaeda Franchise: The Expansion of al Qaeda and Its Consequences*, New York: Oxford University Press, 2016, p. 92.

46 Brian Michael Jenkins, "Al Qaeda in Its Third Decade: Irreversible Decline or Imminent Victory?" Santa Monica, CA: RAND Corp., 2012; see also Rick Nelson and Thomas M. Sanderson, "A Threat Transformed: Al Qaeda and Associated Movements in 2011," Center for Strategic and International Studies (CSIS), February 2011: https://csis-prod.s3.amazonaws.com/s3fs-public/legacy_files/files/publication/110203_Nelson_AThreatTransformed_web.pdf.

47 Bruce Riedel, *The Search for Al Qaeda*, Washington, DC: Brookings Institution Press, 2008, pp. 121–2.

48 Rohan Gunaratna and Aviv Oreg, "Al Qaeda's Organizational Structure and its Evolution," *Studies in Conflict & Terrorism*, 33:12, 2010, p. 1054.

49 Bruce Hoffman, "The Myth of Grass-Roots Terrorism: Why Osama bin Laden Still Matters," *Foreign Affairs*, 87:3, May–June 2008, pp. 133–8. See also Jenkins, "Al Qaeda after Bin Laden."

50 Steve Coll, *Ghost Wars: The Secret History of the CIA, Afghanistan,*

and Bin Laden from the Soviet Invasion to September 10, 2001, New York: Penguin, 2004, pp. 269, 380.

51 Lawrence Wright, *The Looming Tower: Al Qaeda and the Road to 9/11,* New York: Vintage, 2006, pp. 60, 264.

52 Hoffman, "The Changing Face," p. 551.

53 Coll, *Ghost Wars,* p. 474.

54 Rohan Gunaratna, *Inside Al Qaeda: Global Network of Terror,* New York: Berkley Books, 2002, p. 105.

55 Hoffman, "Al Qaeda's Uncertain Future," p. 636.

56 Moghadam, "How Al Qaeda Innovates," p. 469.

57 Gunaratna, *Inside Al Qaeda,* p. 73.

58 Coll, *Ghost Wars,* p. 474

59 Ali Soufan, *The Black Banners: The Inside Story of 9/11 and the War Against al-Qaeda,* New York: W. W. Norton, 2011, pp. 33–7.

60 Bacon, "Hurdles to Alliances," p. 86.

61 Juan Miguel del Cid Gomez, "A Financial Profile of Al Qaeda and Its Affiliates," *Perspectives on Terrorism,* 4:4, 2010, pp. 4–5.

62 Hoffman, "Changing Face," pp. 551–2.

63 Cragin, "Early History of Al-Qa'ida," pp. 1063–4.

64 Gunaratna and Oreg, "Al Qaeda's Organizational Structure," pp. 1054–64.

65 Fawaz Gerges, *ISIS: A History,* Princeton University Press, 2016, p. 71.

66 Chris Hedges, "Foreign Islamic Fighters in Bosnia Pose a Potential Threat for G.I.'s," *New York Times,* December 3, 1995.

67 David Malet, *Foreign Fighters: Transnational Identity in Civil Conflicts,* New York: Oxford University Press, 2013, pp. 185–6.

68 Evan F. Kohlmann, "The Afghan–Bosnian Mujahideen Network in Europe," Swedish National Defence College, November 28, 1995: www.aina.org/reports/tabmnie.pdf.

69 Mark Urban, "Bosnia: The Cradle of Modern Jihadism?" *BBC News,* July 2, 2015.

70 Cerwyn Moore and Paul Tumelty, "Foreign Fighters and the Case of Chechnya," *Studies in Conflict & Terrorism,* 31:5, 2008, pp. 412–33.

71 Murad Batal Al-Shishani, "The Rise and Fall of Arab Fighters in

Chechnya," *Jamestown Foundation*, January 31, 2006: https://jamestown.org/program/the-rise-and-fall-of-foreign fighters-in-chechnya.

72 Farrall, "How Al Qaeda Works"; see also Derek Henry Flood, "The Islamic State Raises its Black Flag over the Caucasus," *CTC Sentinel*, June 29, 2015.

73 Lorenzo Vidino, *Al Qaeda in Europe: The New Battleground of International Jihad*, Amherst: Prometheus Books, 2006, p. 203. See also Lorenzo Vidino, "The Arab Foreign Fighters and the Sacralization of the Chechen Conflict," *Al Naklah*, Spring 2006, pp. 1–11.

74 Carlotta Gall and Thomas de Waal, *Chechnya: Calamity in the Caucasus*, New York University Press, 1998, p. 208.

75 Ben Rich and Dara Conduit, "The Impact of Jihadist Foreign Fighters on Indigenous Secular-Nationalist Causes: Contrasting Chechnya and Syria," *Studies in Conflict & Terrorism*, 38:2, 2015, pp. 113–31.

76 Ali Soufan, *Anatomy of Terror*, New York: W. W. Norton, 2017, pp. 175–6.

77 Lorenzo Vidino, "How Chechnya Became a Breeding Ground for Terror," *Middle East Quarterly*, Summer 2005, pp. 1–10: http://foreignfighters.csis.org/history_foreign_fighter_project.pdf.

78 Maria Galperin Donnelly, Thomas M. Sanderson, and Zack Fellman, *Foreign Fighters in History*, Center for Strategic and International Studies (CSIS), April 1, 2017.

79 Mendelsohn, *The Al Qaeda Franchise*.

80 Byman, "Buddies of Burdens?" pp. 431–70.

81 Steven Brooke, "Strategic Fissures: The Near and Far Enemy Debate," in Assaf Moghadam and Brian Fishman, eds., *Self-Inflicted Wounds: Debates and Divisions within al-Qa'ida and its Periphery*, December 16, 2010, p. 45: https://ctc.usma.edu/self-inflicted-wounds.

82 Mendelsohn, *The Al Qaeda Franchise*, p. 110.

83 Bruce Riedel and Bilal Y. Saab, "Al Qaeda's Third Front: Saudi Arabia," *Washington Quarterly*, 31:2, Spring 2008, p. 37.

84 Thomas Hegghammer, "Islamist Violence and Regime Stability in Saudi Arabia," *International Affairs*, 84:4, 2008, p. 713.

85 Mendelsohn, *The Al Qaeda Franchise*, p. 115.

86 Brian Fishman, ed., *Bombers, Bank Accounts, & Bleedout: Al-Qai'da's Road In and Out of Iraq*, Combating Terrorism Center (CTC) at West Point, 2008: https://ctc.usma.edu/bombers-bank-accounts-and-bleedout-al-qaidas-road-in-and-out-of-iraq.

87 Brian Fishman and Joseph Felter, *Al-Qa'ida's Foreign Fighters in Iraq: A First Look at the Sinjar Records*, Combating Terrorism Center (CTC) at West Point, January 2, 2007: https://ctc.usma.edu/al-qaidas-foreign-fighters-in-iraq-a-first-look-at-the-sinjar-records.

88 Patrick B. Johnston, Jacob N. Shapiro, Howard J. Shatz, et al., *Foundations of the Islamic State: Management, Money, and Terror in Iraq, 2005–2010*, Santa Monica, CA: RAND Corp., 2016.

89 Brian Fishman, "Dysfunction and Decline: Lessons Learned from Inside Al-Qa'ida in Iraq," *Washington Quarterly*, March 2009. In 2006, AQI joined the Mujahedin Shura Council (MSC), which was a political–military front for several jihadist organizations, but, as Craig Whiteside notes, the council was "so dominated by AQI to the point that it is possible MSC was a sham organization used to convince Iraqis of its indigenous nature": Craig Whiteside, "The Islamic State and the Return of Revolutionary Warfare," *Small Wars & Insurgencies*, 27:5, 2016, pp. 768–9.

90 James J. F. Forest, Jarret Brachman, and Joseph Felter, *Harmony and Disharmony: Exploiting al-Qa'ida's Organizational Vulnerabilities*, Combating Terrorism Center (CTC) at West Point, February 14, 2006: https://ctc.usma.edu/harmony-and-disharmony-exploiting-al-qaidas-organizational-vulnerabilities; see also Byman, "Buddies of Burdens?" pp. 461–5.

91 Mendelsohn, *The Al Qaeda Franchise*, p. 123. After Zarqawi's death, AQI rebranded itself as the Islamic State of Iraq (ISI), without ever discussing the move with Al Qaeda core leadership.

92 Brian Fishman, "After Zarqawi: The Dilemmas and Future of Al Qaeda in Iraq," *Washington Quarterly*, 29:4, 2006, p. 21.

93 J. Peter Pham, "Foreign Influences and Shifting Horizons: The Ongoing Evolution of Al Qaeda in the Islamic Maghreb," *Orbis*, Spring 2011, pp. 240–54.

94 Geoff D. Porter, "Terrorist Outbidding: The In Amenas Attack," *CTC Sentinel*, 8:5, May 2015.

95 Christopher S. Chivvis and Andrew Liepman, *North Africa's Menace: AQIM's Evolution and the U.S. Policy Response*, Santa Monica, CA: RAND Corp., 2013.

96 Mendelsohn, *The Al Qaeda Franchise*, p. 133.

97 Jean-Luc Marret, "Al Qaeda in the Islamic Maghreb: A 'Glocal' Organization," *Studies in Conflict & Terrorism*, 31:6, 2008, p. 549.

98 Christopher S. Chivvis, *The French War on Al Qa'ida in Africa*, Cambridge University Press, 2015, p. 25.

99 Camille Tawil, *Brothers in Arms: The Story of Al-Qa'ida and the Arab Jihadists*, London: SAQI, p. 195.

100 Nicholas Schmidle, "The Saharan Conundrum," *New York Times Magazine*, February 13, 2009.

101 Chivvis and Liepman, *North Africa's Menace*, p. 4.

102 Manuel R. Torres Soriano, "The Road to Media Jihad: The Propaganda Actions of Al Qaeda in the Islamic Maghreb," *Terrorism and Political Violence*, 23:1, 2010, pp. 72–88.

103 Pham, "Foreign Influences," p. 245.

104 Rukmini Callimachi, "Paying Ransoms, Europe Bankrolls Qaeda Terror," *New York Times*, July 29, 2014.

105 Mendelsohn, *The Al Qaeda Franchise*, p. 134.

106 Eric Schmitt and Saeed al-Batati, "The U.S. Has Pummeled Al Qaeda in Yemen. But the Threat is Barely Dented," *New York Times*, December 30, 2017.

107 Michael Page, Lara Challita, and Alistair Harris, "Al Qaeda in the Arabian Peninsula: Framing Narratives and Prescriptions," *Terrorism and Political Violence*, 23:2, 2011, pp. 150–72.

108 Gregory D. Johnsen, *The Last Refuge: Yemen, Al-Qaeda, and America's War in Arabia*, New York: W. W. Norton, 2013, p. 261.

109 Alexander Meleagrou-Hitchens, "As American as Apple Pie: How Anwar al-Awlaki Became the Face of Western Jihad," The

International Centre for the Study of Radicalisation and Political Violence (ICSR), 2011; see also Scott Shane, "The Lessons of Anwar al-Awlaki," *New York Times Magazine*, August 27, 2015; and Haroro J. Ingram and Craig Whiteside, "The Yemen Raid and the Ghost of Anwar al-Awlaki," *The Atlantic*, February 9, 2017.

110 Bryce Loidolt, "Managing the Global and the Local: The Dual Agendas of Al Qaeda in the Arabian Peninsula," *Studies in Conflict & Terrorism*, 34:2, 2011, pp. 102–23.

111 Byman, "Buddies of Burdens?" p. 452.

112 "Al Qaeda is Losing Ground in Yemen. Yet It is Far from Defeated," *The Economist*, June 10, 2017.

113 Mendelsohn, *The Al Qaeda Franchise*, p. 140. See also Ty McCormick, "U.S. Attacks Reveal Al-Shabaab's Strength, Not Weakness," *Foreign Policy*, March 9, 2016.

114 Daveed Gartenstein-Ross, "The Strategic Challenge of Somalia's Al-Shabaab," *Middle East Quarterly*, 16:4, Fall 2009, pp. 25–36. For a more robust discussion of AIAI, see Kenneth J. Menkhaus, "Somalia and Somaliland: Terrorism, Political Islam, and State Collapse," in Robert I. Rotberg, ed., *Battling Terrorism in the Horn of Africa*, Cambridge, MA: World Peace Foundation, 2005, pp. 35–6.

115 Seth G. Jones, Andrew Liepman, and Nathan Chandler, *Counterterrorism and Counterinsurgency in Somalia*, Santa Monica, CA: RAND Corp., 2016, p. 9.

116 Daniel Benjamin and Steven Simon, *The Age of Sacred Terror: Radical Islam's War Against America*, New York: Random House, 2003, pp. 118–23.

117 Stig Jarle Hansen, *Al-Shabaab in Somalia: The History of a Militant Islamist Group, 2005–2012*, New York: Oxford University Press, 2013, pp. 28–32.

118 Ken Menkhaus and Christopher Boucek, "Terrorism Out of Somalia," Carnegie Endowment for International Peace, September 23, 2010: https://carnegieendowment.org/2010/09/23/terrorism-out-of-somalia-pub-41612.

119 Ken Menkhaus, "Non-State Actors and the Role of Violence in

Stateless Somalia," in Klejda Mulaj, ed., *Violent Non-State Actors in World Politics*, New York: Columbia University Press, 2010, p. 373.

120 David Shinn, "Al Shabaab's Foreign Threat to Somalia," *Orbis*, 55:2, 2011, pp. 203–15. See also Committee on Homeland Security, *Al Shabaab: Recruitment and Radicalization Within the Muslim American Community and the Threat to the Homeland*, Washington DC: Government Printing Office, July 27, 2011, p. 2.

121 Lorenzo Vidino, Raffaello Pantucci, and Evan Kohlmann, "Bringing Global Jihad to the Horn of Africa: al Shabaab, Western Fighters, the Sacralization of the Somali Conflict," *African Security*, 3:4, 2010, p. 224.

122 For more on this, see Richard Shultz and Andrea Dew, *Terrorists, Insurgents, and Militias: The Warriors of Contemporary Combat*, New York: Columbia University Press, 2007; and Clint Watts, Jacob Shapiro, and Vahid Brown, *Al-Qa'ida's (Mis)Adventures in the Horn of Africa*, Combating Terrorism Center, July 2, 2007.

123 Ken Menkhaus, "Al-Shabaab's Post-Westgate Capabilities," *CTC Sentinel*, 7:2, February 2014.

124 Christopher Anzalone, "The Resilience of al-Shabaab," *CTC Sentinel*, 9:4, April 2016.

125 Jason Burke, "Mogadishu Truck Bomb: 500 Casualties in Somalia's Worst Terrorist Attack," *Guardian*, October 16, 2017.

2 The Inner Workings of the Islamic State

1 Byman, "Al Qaeda's Decline," p. 1112.

2 Michael Weiss and Hassan Hassan, *ISIS: Inside the Army of Terror*, New York: Regan Arts, 2015, p. 186.

3 "Islamic State Has Been Stashing Millions of Dollars in Iraq and Abroad," *The Economist*, February 22, 2018.

4 Renad Mansour and Hisham al-Hashimi, "ISIS Inc.," *Foreign Policy*, January 16, 2018.

5 Phil Williams and Colin P. Clarke, "Iraqi and Syrian Networks," in

Kim Thachuk and Rollie Lal, eds., *Terrorist Criminal Enterprises*, Santa Barbara, CA: ABC-CLIO, 2018.

6 Ibid., pp. 27–46.

7 Daniel L. Glaser, "The Evolution of Terrorism Financing: Disrupting the Islamic State," in Levitt, ed., *Neither Remaining Nor Expanding*, pp. 43–7; Daniel L. Glaser, testimony before the House Committee on Foreign Affairs Subcommittee on Terrorism, Nonproliferation, and Trade, and House Committee on Armed Services Subcommittee on Emerging Threats and Capabilities, June 9, 2016; and Center for the Analysis of Terrorism, *ISIS Financing 2015*, Paris, May 2016.

8 Colin P. Clarke, "Drugs & Thugs: Funding Terrorism Through Narcotics Trafficking," *Journal of Strategic Security*, 9:3, Fall 2016; for more on how involvement in narcotics trafficking impacts terrorist groups, see Svante Cornell, "Narcotics and Armed Conflict: Interaction and Implications," *Studies in Conflict & Terrorism*, 30:3, 2007, pp. 207–27.

9 Scott Bronstein and Drew Griffin, "Self-Funded and Deep-Rooted: How ISIS Makes its Millions," *CNN*, October 7, 2014.

10 Stefan Heibner, Peter R. Neumann, John Holland-McCowan, and Rajan Basra, *Caliphate in Decline: An Estimate of Islamic State's Financial Fortunes*, London: The International Centre for the Study of Radicalisation and Political Violence, 2017. See also Rukmini Callimachi, "The Case of the Purloined Poultry: How ISIS Prosecuted Petty Crime," *New York Times*, July 1, 2018.

11 Johnston et al., *Foundations of the Islamic State*.

12 US Central Command, "Coalition Kills Daesh Criminal Leader, Followers," Combined Joint Task Force – Operation Inherent Resolve Public Affairs Office, June 19, 2018.

13 United Nations Security Council, "Twenty-Second Report of the Analytical Support and Sanctions Monitoring Team Submitted Pursuant to Resolution 2368 (2017) Concerning ISIL (Da'esh), Al-Qaida and Associated Individuals and Entities," New York, July 27, 2018, p. 8.

14 Mansour and al-Hashimi, "ISIS Inc."

15 Clarke, "Drugs & Thugs."

16 Heibner et al., "Caliphate in Decline."

17 Colin P. Clarke, Kimberly Jackson, Patrick B. Johnston, et al., *Financial Futures of the Islamic State of Iraq and the Levant*, Santa Monica, CA: RAND Corp., 2017.

18 "Islamic State Ammunition in Iraq and Syria: Analysis of Small-Calibre Ammunition Recovered from Islamic State Forces in Iraq and Syria," London: Conflict Armament Research, October 2014, p. 5.

19 Thomas Maurer, "ISIS's Warfare Functions: A Systemized Review of a Proto-State's Conventional Conduct of Operations," *Small Wars & Insurgencies*, 29:2, 2018, pp. 229–44.

20 "How ISIS Works," *New York Times*, September 16, 2014.

21 C. J. Chivers, "ISIS' Ammunition is Shown to Have Origins in U.S. and China," *New York Times*, October 5, 2014. See also Julia Harte and R. Jeffrey Smith, "Where Does the Islamic State Get Its Weapons?" *Foreign Policy*, October 6, 2014.

22 Kirk Semple and Eric Schmitt, "Missiles of ISIS May Pose Peril for Aircrews," *New York Times*, October 26, 2014.

23 Jamie Crawford, "Report Details Where ISIS Gets Its Weapons," CNN.com, December 14, 2017.

24 "Weapons of the Islamic State: A Three-Year Investigation into Iraq and Syria," *Conflict Armament Research*, December 2017, p. 146

25 Many of the Iraqi soldiers who refused to fight blamed their failure to stand their ground on officers, saying they were deliberately denied the resupply of basic necessities such as food and water: C. J. Chivers, "After Retreat, Iraqi Soldiers Fault Officers," *New York Times*, July 1, 2014.

26 Daniel Trombly and Yasir Abbas, "Who the U.S. Should Really Hit in ISIS," *Daily Beast*, September 23, 2014.

27 Gina Harkins, "5 Things to Know About Islamic State's Military Capabilities," *Army Times*, September 16, 2014.

28 "Arms Windfall for Insurgents as Iraq City Falls," *New York Times*, June 10, 2014.

29 Josh Rogin, "ISIS Video: America's Air Dropped Weapons Now in Our Hands," *Daily Beast*, October 21, 2014.

30 Charlie Winter, "War by Suicide: A Statistical Analysis of the Islamic State's Martyrdom Industry," International Centre for Counter-Terrorism (ICCT) – The Hague, ICCT Research Paper, February 2017.

31 Peter Bergen and Emily Schneider, "Now ISIS Has Drones?" CNN. com, August 25, 2014.

32 Michael S. Schmidt and Eric Schmitt, "Pentagon Confronts a New Threat from ISIS: Exploding Drones," *New York Times*, October 11, 2016.

33 Truls Hallberg Tønnessen, "Islamic State and Technology – A Literature Review," *Perspectives on Terrorism*, 11:6, 2017.

34 Trombly and Abbas, "Who the U.S. Should Really Hit in ISIS."

35 Nigel Inkster, "The Resurgence of ISIS," International Institute for Strategic Studies (IISS), June 13, 2014.

36 Charles Lister, "Profiling the Islamic State," Brookings Institution Doha Center Analysis Paper, No. 13, November 2014, p. 17: www. brookings.edu/research/profiling-the-islamic-state.

37 Carter Malkasian, "If ISIS Has a 3-24 (II): Trying to Write the Field Manual of the Islamic State," *Foreign Policy*, October 7, 2014.

38 Daniel Byman and Jeremy Shapiro, "Homeward Bound? Don't Hype the Threat of Returning Jihadists," *Foreign Affairs*, September 30, 2014.

39 Colin P. Clarke, "Round-Trip Tickets: How Will Authorities Know When Foreign Fighters Have Returned?" *Lawfare*, September 24, 2017, https://www.lawfareblog.com/round-trip-tickets-how-will-authorities-know-when-foreign-fighters-have-returned.

40 Anne Speckhard and Ahmet S. Yayla, "The ISIS Emni: The Origins and Inner Workings of IS's Intelligence Apparatus," *Perspectives on Terrorism*, 11:1, 2017.

41 Lorenzo Vidino, Francesco Marone, and Eva Entenmann, *Fear Thy Neighbor: Radicalization and Jihadist Attacks in the West*, Ledizioni: Italian Institute for International Political Studies (ISPI), 2017, p. 66.

42 Christoph Reuter, "Secret Files Reveal the Structure of the Islamic State," *Der Spiegel*, April 18, 2015.

43 Vera Mironova, Ekaterina Sergatskova, and Karam Alhamad, "ISIS Intelligence Service Refuses to Die," *Foreign Affairs*, November 22, 2017.

44 Rukmini Callimachi, "How a Secretive Branch of ISIS Built a Global Network of Killers," *New York Times*, August 3, 2016.

45 Michael Rubin, "How Does ISIS Do Intelligence?" American Enterprise Institute, AEIdeas, December 5, 2016.

46 Bruce Hoffman, "The Evolving Terrorist Threat and CT Options for the Trump Administration," in Aaron Zelin, ed., *How Al Qaeda Survived the Islamic State*, Washington Institute for Near East Policy, 2017, p. 11.

47 James R. Clapper, "Worldwide Threat Assessment of the US Intelligence Community," Senate Armed Services Committee, Statement for the Record, February 9, 2016, p. 4.

48 Seth G. Jones, James Dobbins, Daniel Byman, et al., *Rolling Back the Islamic State*, Santa Monica, CA: RAND Corp., 2017.

49 Caleb Weiss and Bill Roggio, "Islamic State Assaults City in Syrian Kurdistan," *FDS's Long War Journal*, September 18, 2014.

50 Email exchange with Aaron Zelin, June 2018.

51 Clarke et al., *Financial Futures*.

52 Yochi Dreazen, "From Electricity to Sewage, U.S. Intelligence Says the Islamic State is Fast Learning How to Run a Country," *Foreign Policy*, August 18, 2014.

53 Jones et al., *Rolling Back the Islamic State*, p. 50.

54 Nicholas J. Rasmussen, "World Wide Threats: Keeping America Secure in the New Age of Terror," Hearing Before the House Committee on Homeland Security, November 30, 2017.

55 Paul Cruickshank, "A View from the CT Foxhole: Nicholas Rasmussen, Former Director, National Counterterrorism Center," *CTC Sentinel*, 11:1, January 2018.

56 Byman and Shapiro, "Homeward Bound?"

57 Lister, "Profiling the Islamic State," p. 17.

58 Callimachi, "How a Secretive Branch of ISIS Built a Global Network of Killers."

59 Bill Roggio and Caleb Weiss, "Over 100 Jihadist Training Camps Identified in Iraq and Syria," *FDD's Long War Journal*, June 21, 2015.

60 Hassan Hassan, "The Secret World of ISIS Training Camps – Ruled by Sacred Texts and the Sword," *Guardian*, January 24, 2015.

61 Graeme Wood, "What ISIS Really Wants," *The Atlantic*, March 2015.

62 Ishaan Tharoor, "It Turns Out Many ISIS Recruits Don't Know Much About Islam," *Washington Post*, August 17, 2016; see also Simon Cottee, "'What ISIS Really Wants' Revisited: Religion Matters in *Jihadist* Violence, but How?" *Studies in Terrorism & Conflict*, 40:6, 2017, pp. 439–54; and Aya Batrawy, Paisley Dodds, and Lori Hinnant, "Leaked ISIS Documents Reveal Recruits Have Poor Grasp of Islamic Faith," *The Independent*, August 16, 2016.

63 Lorne L. Dawson and Amarnath Amarasingam, "Talking to Foreign Fighters: Insights into the Motivations for *Hijrah* to Syria and Iraq," *Studies in Conflict & Terrorism*, 40:3, 2017, pp. 190–210.

64 Lizzie Dearden, "ISIS Releases Video of Child Soldiers Training for Jihad in Syria Camp for 'Cubs of the Caliphate,'" *Independent*, February 23, 2015.

65 John G. Horgan, Max Taylor, Mia Bloom, and Charlie Winter, "From Cubs to Lions: A Six Stage Model of Child Socialization into the Islamic State," *Studies in Conflict & Terrorism*, 40:7, 2017, pp. 645–64.

66 Kinana Qaddour, "ISIS's War on Families Never Ended," *Foreign Policy*, February 1, 2018.

67 Jamie Dettmer, "Germany Alarmed by 'Kindergarten Jihadists,'" *Voice of America*, February 2, 2018.

68 Romina McGuinness, "ISIS Trained Child Soldiers to Launch Attacks on EU, Claims French Jihadist," *Express*, June 29, 2018.

69 Callimachi, "The Case of the Purloined Poultry."

70 Simon Cottee, "ISIS in the Caribbean," *The Atlantic*, December 8, 2016.

71 Robert F. Worth, "The Professor and the Jihadi," *New York Times Magazine*, April 5, 2017.

72 Joby Warrick and Greg Miller, "New ISIS Recruits Have Deep Criminal Roots," *Washington Post*, March 23, 2016.

73 Tamara Makarenko, "Increasingly Vulnerable," *The Cipher Brief*, April 27, 2016.

74 Simon Cottee, "The Challenge of Jihadi Cool," *The Atlantic*, December 24, 2015. See also Thomas Hegghammer, "The Soft Power of Militant Jihad," *New York Times*, December 18, 2015.

75 Hegghammer, "The Soft Power of Militant Jihad."

76 Mary Anne Weaver, "The Short, Violent Life of Abu Musab al-Zarqawi," *The Atlantic Monthly*, July/August 2006.

77 Andrew Higgins, Kimiko de Freytas-Tamura, and Katrin Bennhold, "In Suspects' Brussels Neighborhood, a History of Petty Crimes and Missed Chances," *New York Times*, November 16, 2015.

78 Jean-Charles Brisard and Kevin Jackson, "The Islamic State's External Operations and the French–Belgian Nexus," *CTC Sentinel*, 9:11, 2016.

79 Alissa J. Rubin and Milan Schreuer, "Sole Surviving Suspect in Paris Attacks Stands Trial in Belgium," *New York Times*, February 5, 2018. See also Rory Mulholland and Danny Boyle, "Heroic French Officer Arnaud Beltrame Dies after Switching Himself for Hostage in France Supermarket," *Telegraph*, March 24, 2018.

80 Simon Cottee, "Europe's Joint Smoking, Gay-Club Hopping Terrorists," *Foreign Policy*, April 13, 2016.

81 Matthew Levitt, "My Journey to Brussels' Terrorist Safe Haven," *Politico*, March 27, 2016.

82 Anthony Faiola and Souad Mekhennet, "The Islamic State Creates a New Type of Jihadists: Part Terrorist, Part Gangster," *Washington Post*, December 20, 2015.

83 Terence McCoy, "How ISIS Leader Abu Bakr al-Baghdadi Became the World's Most Powerful Jihadist Leader," *Washington Post*, June 11, 2014.

84 Tim Arango and Eric Schmitt, "U.S. Actions in Iraq Fueled the Rise of a Rebel," *New York Times*, August 10, 2014.

85 Andrew Thompson and Jeremy Suri, "How America Helped ISIS," *New York Times*, October 1, 2014. See also Terrence McCoy, "How the Islamic State Evolved in an American Prison," *Washington Post*, November 4, 2014.

86 William McCants, "The Believer," Brookings Institution, September 1, 2015: http://csweb.brookings.edu/content/resear ch/essays/2015/thebeliever.html.

87 Hannah Strange, "Islamic State Leader Abu Bakr al-Baghdadi Addresses Muslims in Mosul," *Telegraph*, July 5, 2014.

00 Will Cathcart, "The Secret Life of an ISIS Warlord," *Daily Beast*, October 27, 2014.

89 "The Anatomy of ISIS: How the 'Islamic State' is Run, from Oil to Beheadings," *CNN*, September 18, 2014.

90 Ben Hubbard and Eric Schmitt, "Military Skill and Terrorist Technique Fuel Success of ISIS," *New York Times*, August 27, 2014.

91 "How ISIS Works," *New York Times*.

92 Hubbard and Schmitt, "Military Skill and Terrorist Technique Fuel Success of ISIS." See also Ruth Sherlock, "Inside the Leadership of Islamic State: How the New 'Caliphate' is Run," *Daily Telegraph*, July 9, 2014.

93 Eric Schmitt, Rukmini Callimachi, and Anne Barnard, "Spokesman's Death Will Have Islamic State Turning to Its 'Deep Bench,'" *New York Times*, August 31, 2016.

94 Joby Warrick, "ISIS's Second-in-Command Hid in Syria for Months. The Day He Stepped Out, the U.S. Was Waiting," *Washington Post*, November 28, 2016.

95 David D. Kirkpatrick, "ISIS' Harsh Brand of Islam is Rooted in Austere Saudi Creed," *New York Times*, September 24, 2014.

96 David Motadel, "The Ancestors of ISIS," *New York Times*, September 23, 2014.

97 Daveed Gartenstein-Ross and Amichal Magen, "The Jihadist Governance Dilemma," *Washington Post* Monkey Cage Blog, July 18, 2014: https://www.washingtonpost.com/news/monkey-cage/ wp/2014/07/18/the-jihadist-governance-dilemma/?utm_term=. 8a6eb2d717ee.

98 For more on the falling-out between IS and al-Qaeda, see J. M. Berger, "The Islamic State vs al Qaeda," *Foreign Policy*, September 2, 2011.

99 William McCants, "State of Confusion," *Foreign Affairs*, September 10, 2014.

100 David Ignatius, "The Manual that Chillingly Foreshadows the Islamic State," *Washington Post*, September 25, 2014.

101 Robin Simcox, "ISIS' Western Ambitions," *Foreign Affairs*, June 30, 2014.

102 Daniel Byman, "The State of Terror," *Slate*, June 13, 2014.

103 Aaron Y. Zelin, "ISIS is Dead, Long Live the Islamic State," *Foreign Policy*, June 30, 2014.

104 Joby Warrick, *Black Flags: The Rise of ISIS*, New York: Anchor, 2016, p. 260.

105 Cole Bunzel, "From Paper State to Caliphate: The Ideology of the Islamic State," Brookings Institution, March 9, 2015: https://www.brookings.edu/research/from-paper-state-to-caliphate-the-ideology-of-the-islamic-state.

106 Hassan Hassan, "The Sectarianism of the Islamic State: Ideological Roots and Political Context," Carnegie Endowment for International Peace, June 13, 2016: http://carnegieendowment.org/2016/06/13/sectarianism-of-islamic-state-ideological-roots-and-political-context-pub-63746.

107 Lizzie Dearden, "ISIS: Islam is 'Not Strongest Factor' Behind Foreign Fighters Joining Extremist Groups in Syria and Iraq – Report," *Independent*, November 16, 2016.

108 Email exchange with J. M. Berger, June 2018.

109 Eric Schmitt, "U.S. Secures Vast New Trove of Intelligence on ISIS," *New York Times*, July 27, 2016.

110 Seth G. Jones, "Jihadist Sanctuaries in Syria and Iraq: Implications for the United States," testimony before the Committee on Homeland Security Subcommittee on Counterterrorism and Intelligence, US House of Representatives, July 24, 2014, p. 1.

111 Griff Witte, Sudarsan Raghavan, and James McAuley, "Flow

of Foreign Fighters Plummets as Islamic State Loses Its Edge," *Washington Post*, September 9, 2016.

112 "Foreign Fighters Flow into Syria," *Washington Post*, October 11, 201. See also David D. Kirkpatrick, "New Freedoms in Tunisia Drive Support for ISIS," *New York Times*, October 21, 2014.

113 Peter Neumann, "Suspects into Collaborators," *London Review of Books*, 36:7, April 3, 2014.

114 Tim Arango and Eric Schmitt, "Escaped Inmates from Iraq Fuel Syrian Insurgency," *New York Times*, February 12, 2014.

115 Jytte Klausen, "They're Coming: Measuring the Threat from Returning Jihadists," *Foreign Affairs*, October 1, 2014.

116 Kate Brannen, "Children of the Caliphate," *Foreign Policy*, October 27, 2014.

117 Megan A. Stewart, "What's So New About the Islamic State's Governance?" *Washington Post* Monkey Cage Blog, October 7, 2014.

118 "The Anatomy of ISIS," *CNN*.

119 Aaron Y. Zelin, "When Jihadists Learn How to Help," *Washington Post* Monkey Cage Blog, May 7, 2014.

120 Benjamin Bahney, Howard J. Shatz, Carroll Ganier, et al., *An Economic Analysis of the Financial Records of al-Qa'ida in Iraq*, Santa Monica, CA: RAND Corp., 2010; for more micro-level data on the group's financial bureaucracy, see Benjamin W. Bahney, Radha K. Iyengar, Patrick B. Johnston, Danielle F. Jung, Jacob N. Shapiro, and Howard J. Shatz, "Insurgent Compensation: Evidence from Iraq," *American Economic Review*, 103:3, 2013, pp. 518–22.

121 Howard J. Shatz, "To Defeat the Islamic State, Follow the Money," *Politico*, September 10, 2014.

122 Janine Davidson and Emerson Brooking, "ISIS Hasn't Gone Anywhere – And It's Getting Stronger," Council on Foreign Relations, Defense in Depth, July 24, 2014.

123 Mariam Karouny, "In Northeast Syria, Islamic State Builds a Government," Reuters, September 4, 2014.

124 Jessica Stern and J. M Berger, *ISIS: The State of Terror*, New York: HarperCollins, 2016, p. 114.

125 William McCants, *The ISIS Apocalypse*, New York: St. Martin's Press, 2015, p. 152.

126 Aaron Zelin, "The Islamic State of Iraq and Syria Has a Consumer Protection Office," *The Atlantic*, June 13, 2014.

127 Graeme Wood, *The Way of the Strangers*, New York: Random House, 2017, p. xxii.

128 Andrew Shaver, "Turning the Lights Off on the Islamic State," *Washington Post* Monkey Cage Blog, October 16, 2014.

129 Sudarsan Raghavan, "Inside the Brutal but Bizarrely Bureaucratic World of the Islamic State in Libya," *Washington Post*, August 23, 2016.

130 Ghaith Abdul-Ahad, "The Bureaucracy of Evil: How Islamic State Ran a City," *Guardian*, January 29, 2018.

131 Aymenn al-Tamimi, "The Evolution in Islamic State Administration: The Documentary Evidence," *Perspectives on Terrorism*, 9:4, 2015; see also Rukmini Callimachi, "The ISIS Files," *New York Times*, April 4, 2018.

132 Brian Dodwell, Daniel Milton, and Don Rassler, *The Caliphate's Global Workforce: An Inside Look at the Islamic State's Foreign Fighter Paper Trail*, Combating Terrorism Center at West Point, April 2016, p. 18: https://ctc.usma.edu/the-caliphates-global-work force-an-inside-look-at-the-islamic-states-foreign-fighter-paper-trail.

133 Shiv Malik, "The ISIS Papers: Behind 'Death Cult' Image Lies a Methodical Bureaucracy," *Guardian*, December 7, 2015.

134 Laura Ryan, "IS is Better Than Al Qaeda at Using the Internet," *Defense One*, October 10, 2014.

135 Ali Fisher and Nico Prucha, "ISIS is Winning the Online Jihad Against the West," *Daily Beast*, October 1, 2014.

136 Rod Nordland, "Iraq's Sunni Militants Take to Social Media to Advance Their Cause and Intimidate," *New York Times*, June 28, 2014. For more on the group's use of social media, see Rita Katz, "Follow ISIS on Twitter: A Special Report on the Use of Social

Media by Jihadists," Insite Blog on Terrorism & Extremism, June 26, 2014.

137 Jacob Siegel, "Has ISIS Peaked as a Military Power?" *Daily Beast*, October 22, 2014.

138 Colin Clarke and Charlie Winter, "The Islamic State May Be Failing, But Its Strategic Communications Legacy is Here to Stay," *War on the Rocks*, August 17, 2017. See also Nafees Hamid, "The British Hacker Who Became the Islamic State's Chief Terror Cybercoach: A Profile of Junaid Hussain," *CTC Sentinel*, 11:4, April 2018.

139 Bennett Seftel, "What Drives ISIS," *The Cipher Brief*, May 5, 2016.

140 Aaron Y. Zelin, "Picture or It Didn't Happen: A Snapshot of the Islamic State's Official Media Output," *Perspectives on Terrorism*, 9:4, 2015.

141 Charlie Winter, "The Virtual 'Caliphate': Understanding Islamic State's Propaganda Strategy," *Quilliam Foundation*, July 2015, p. 28.

142 Charlie Winter and Jordan Bach-Lombardo, "Why ISIS Propaganda Works," *The Atlantic*, February 13, 2016.

143 Daveed Gartenstein-Ross, Nathaniel Barr, and Bridget Moreng, "How the Islamic State's Propaganda Feeds into Its Global Expansion Efforts," *War on the Rocks*, April 28, 2016.

144 Colin P. Clarke and Haroro J. Ingram, "Defeating the ISIS Nostalgia Narrative," Foreign Policy Research Institute (FPRI), After the Caliphate Project, E-Notes, April 18, 2018.

145 Lorraine Ali, "Islamic State's Soft Weapon of Choice: Social Media," *Los Angeles Times*, September 22, 2014.

146 Ezzeldeen Khalil, "Gone Viral: Islamic State's Evolving Media Strategy," *Jane's Intelligence Review*, October 2014, p. 15.

147 Josh Kovensky, "IS's New Mag Looks Like a New York Glossy – With Pictures of Mutilated Bodies," *New Republic*, August 25, 2014. The name "Dabiq" was chosen for the magazine because Dabiq is a small village in Syria that is believed by some IS fighters to be the place where one of the final battles of the Islamic apocalypse will take place. See William McCants, "ISIS Fantasies of an Apocalyptic

Showdown in Northern Syria," Brookings Institution, October 3, 2014: https://www.brookings.edu/blog/markaz/2014/10/03/isis-fantasies-of-an-apocalyptic-showdown-in-northern-syria.

148 Harleen K. Gambhir, "Dabiq: The Strategic Messaging of the Islamic State," *Institute for the Study of War*, August 15, 2014, p. 2.
149 James P. Farwell, "The Media Strategy of IS," *Survival*, 56:6, December 2014 / January 2015, pp. 49–55.
150 Marc Lynch, Deen Freelon, and Sean Aday, "Syria's Socially Mediated Civil War," United States Institute of Peace (USIP), Peaceworks No. 91, 2014, p. 15.
151 Scott Shane and Ben Hubbard, "ISIS Displaying a Deft Command of Varied Media," *New York Times*, August 30, 2014.
152 Jytte Klausen, "Tweeting the *Jihad*: Social Media Networks of Western Foreign Fighters in Syria and Iraq," *Studies in Conflict & Terrorism*, 38:1, 2015, pp. 1–22.
153 Clarke and Winter, "The Islamic State May Be Failing, But Its Strategic Communications Legacy is Here to Stay."
154 Gerges, *ISIS: A History*, p. 270.
155 Greg Miller and Souad Mekhennet, "Inside the Surreal World of the Islamic State's Propaganda Machine," *Washington Post*, November 20, 2015.
156 Mia Bloom, "Constructing Expertise: Terrorist Recruitment and 'Talent Spotting' in the PIRA, Al Qaeda, and ISIS," *Studies in Conflict & Terrorism*, 40:7, 2017, pp. 603–23.
157 Cottee, "The Challenge of Jihadi Cool."
158 J. M. Berger, "How IS Games Twitter," *The Atlantic*, June 16, 2014; see also Simon Cottee, "Why It's So Hard to Stop IS Propaganda," *The Atlantic*, March 2, 2015.
159 Jonathon Morgan and J. M. Berger, "The IS Twitter Census: Defining and Describing the Population of IS Supporters on Twitter," Brookings Institution, March 5, 2015.
160 Jack Moore, "ISIS's Twitter Campaign Faltering Amid Crackdown," *Newsweek*, February 18, 2016. See also Dustin Volz, "Islamic State Finds Diminishing Returns on Twitter: Report," Reuters, February 18, 2016.

161 Elizabeth Bodine-Baron, Todd C. Helmus, Madeline Magnuson, and Zev Winkelman, *Examining ISIS Support and Opposition Networks on Twitter*, Santa Monica, CA· RAND Corp., 2016. Still, others are skeptical at how effective this tactic is over the long term. For a more pessimistic view on the effectiveness of shutting down IS Twitter accounts, see Amarnath Amarasingam, "What Twitter Really Means for Islamic State Supporters," *War on the Rocks*, December 30, 2015.

162 Mia Bloom, Hicham Tiflati, and John Horgan, "Navigating ISIS's Preferred Platform: Telegram," *Terrorism and Political Violence*, 2017, pp. 1–13.

3 The Coming Terrorist Diaspora

1 Margaret Coker, Eric Schmitt, and Rukmini Callimachi, "With Loss of Its Caliphate, ISIS May Return to Guerilla Roots," *New York Times*, October 18, 2017. See also Yaroslav Trofimov, "Faraway ISIS Branches Grow as Group Fades in Syria, Iraq," *Wall Street Journal*, May 18, 2018.

2 Julian E. Barnes, Valentina Pop, and Jenny Gross, "Europe Doesn't Expect Fresh Influx of Returning ISIS Fighters," *Wall Street Journal*, October 17, 2017.

3 Julie Hirschfeld Davis, "Trump Drops Push for Immediate Withdrawal of Troops from Syria," *New York Times*, April 4, 2018.

4 For some of the best works to discuss these differences, see Assaf Moghadam, Ronit Berger, and Polina Beliakova, "Say Terrorist, Think Insurgent: Labeling and Analyzing Contemporary Terrorist Actors," *Perspectives on Terrorism*, 8:5, October 2014; Seth G. Jones, *Waging Insurgent Warfare: Lessons from the Vietcong to the Islamic State*, New York: Oxford University Press, 2017, pp. 8–9; David Kilcullen, "Countering Global Insurgency," *Journal of Strategic Studies*, 28:4, 2005, pp. 597–617; and Hoffman, *Inside Terrorism*, p. 35.

5 The category strategy is consonant with that presented by Jones in *Waging Insurgent Warfare*, ch. 3.

6 Mohamed Fadel Fahmy, "Egypt's Wild West," *Foreign Policy*, August 24, 2011: https://foreignpolicy.com/2011/08/24/egy pts wild west-2.

7 Sahar F. Aziz, "Rethinking Counterterrorism in the Age of IS: Lessons from Sinai," *Nebraska Law Review*, 95:2, pp. 307–65.

8 For more on ABM, see Mokhtar Awad and Samuel Tadros, "Bay'a Remorse? Wilayat Sinai and the Nile Valley," *CTC Sentinel*, 8:8, August 2015.

9 Mokhtar Awad, "IS in the Sinai," in Katherine Bauer, ed., *Beyond Syria and Iraq: Examining Islamic State Provinces*, Washington Institute for Near East Policy, 2016, p. 21.

10 Sudarsan Raghavan, "Militant Threat Emerges in Egyptian Desert, Opening New Front in Terrorism Fight," *Washington Post*, March 14, 2018.

11 Erin Cunningham, "Bomb Blast in Egypt's Sinai Peninsula is Deadliest Attack on Army in Decades," *Washington Post*, October 24, 2014; Kareem Fahim and David D. Kirkpatrick, "Jihadist Attacks on Egypt Grow Even Fiercer," *New York Times*, July 1, 2015.

12 Zack Gold, "Sisi Doesn't Know How to Beat ISIS," *Foreign Policy*, November 30, 2017: https://foreignpolicy.com/2017/11/30/ sisi-doesnt-know-how-to-beat-isis.

13 David D. Kirkpatrick, "Secret Alliance: Israel Carries Out Airstrikes in Egypt, With Cairo's O.K.," *New York Times*, February 3, 2018.

14 Mokhtar Awad, "The Islamic State's Pyramid Scheme: Egyptian Expansion and the Giza Governorate Cell," *CTC Sentinel*, 9:4, April 2016.

15 Sudarsan Raghavan and Heba Farouk Mahfouz, "Egypt Launches Major Offensive Against Islamic State Militants," *Washington Post*, February 9, 2018.

16 Loveday Morris, "Islamic State Declares War on Rival Hamas With Video Execution," *Washington Post*, January 4, 2018.

17 Phone interview with Zack Gold, July 2017.

18 Colin P. Clarke, "How Salafism's Rise Threatens Gaza," *Foreign*

Affairs, October 11, 2017: https://www.foreignaffairs.com/articles/israel/2017-10-11/how-salafisms-rise-threatens-gaza.

19 Zack Gold, "Security in the Sinai: Present and Future," ICCT Research Paper, March 2014: https://www.icct.nl/download/file/ICCT-Gold-Security-In-The-Sinai-March-2014.pdf.

20 Mokhtar Awad, "Why ISIS Declared War on Egypt's Christians," *The Atlantic*, April 9, 2017.

21 Declan Walsh, "Attacks Show ISIS' New Plan: Divide Egypt By Killing Christians," *New York Times*, April 10, 2017.

22 Declan Walsh, "Gunmen Kill Police Officer Near St. Catherine's Monastery in Egypt," *New York Times*, April 18, 2017.

23 "Gunman Kills 11 in Attacks on Coptic Church, Christian-Owned Shop in Egypt," Reuters, December 29, 2017.

24 Declan Walsh and Nour Youssef, "Militants Kill 305 at Sufi Mosque in Egypt's Deadliest Terror Attack," *New York Times*, November 24, 2017.

25 Hassan Hassan, "Its Dreams of a Caliphate Are Gone. Now ISIS Has a Deadly New Strategy," *Guardian*, December 30, 2017.

26 Sudha Ratan, "The Trump Administration's New Afghan Problem: The Islamic State," *The Diplomat*, April 3, 2018.

27 Antonio Giustozzi, "Taliban and Islamic State: Enemies or Brothers in Jihad?" Center for Research & Policy Analysis, December 14, 2017: https://www.crpaweb.org/single-post/2017/12/15/Enemies-or-Jihad-Brothers-Relations-Between-Taliban-and-Islamic-State.

28 Zabihullah Ghazi and Mujib Mashal, "Deadly ISIS Attack Hits an Aid Group, Save the Children, in Afghanistan," *New York Times*, January 24, 2018. See also Bart Jansen, "11 Afghan Troops Die in Islamic State Attack on Kabul Military Academy, Latest in Violent Surge," *USA Today*, January 29, 2018.

29 Jawad Sukhanyar and Mujib Mashal, "Twin Mosque Attacks Kill Scores in One of Afghanistan's Deadliest Weeks," *New York Times*, October 20, 2017.

30 "ISIS On Rise in Pakistan," *The Hindu*, January 8, 2018: https://

www.thehindu.com/news/international/isis-on-rise-in-pakistan
-report/article22397277.ece.

31 Salman Masood, "Pakistan Reels After Attack on Police
Training College Leaves 61 Dead," *New York Times*, October
25, 2016.

32 Borhan Osman, "The Islamic State in 'Khorasan': How it Began
and Where it Stands Now in Nangarhar," Afghanistan Analysts'
Network, July 27, 2016: https://www.afghanistan-analysts.org/
the-islamic-state-in-khorasan-how-it-began-and-where-it-stand
s-now-in-nangarhar.

33 United Nations Security Council, "Twenty-First Report of the
Analytical Support and Sanctions Monitoring Team Submitted
Pursuant to Resolution 2368 (2017) Concerning ISIL (Da'esh), Al
Qaeda and Associated Individuals and Entities," January 26, 2018.

34 Mirwais Harooni and Kay Johnson "Taliban Urge Islamic State to
Stop 'Interference' in Afghanistan," Reuters, June 16, 2015.

35 Animesh Roul, "Islamic State Gains Ground in Afghanistan as Its
Caliphate Crumbles Elsewhere," *Jamestown Terrorism Monitor*,
16:2, January 26, 2018: https://jamestown.org/program/islamic-
state-gains-ground-afghanistan-caliphate-crumbles-elsewhere.

36 Matthew Dupee, "Red on Red: Analyzing Afghanistan's Intra-
Insurgency Violence," *CTC Sentinel*, 11:1, January 2018. See also
Najim Rahim and Rod Nordland, "Are ISIS Fighters Prisoners or
Honored Guests of the Afghan Government?" *New York Times*,
August 4, 2018.

37 "Afghan Official: Islamic State Present in at Least 3 Provinces,"
Associated Press, June 29, 2015.

38 Bennett Seftel, "'Persistent, Expanding and Worrisome': ISIS
Rebounds in Afghanistan," *The Cipher Brief*, January 5, 2018.

39 Mujib Mashal, "In Tangled Afghan War, a Thin Line of Defense
Against ISIS," *New York Times*, December 25, 2017.

40 Ayaz Gul, "Russia Says About 10,000 IS Militants Now in
Afghanistan," *VOA News*, December 23, 2017.

41 Amanda Erickson, "How the Islamic State Got a Foothold in
Afghanistan," *Washington Post*, March 21, 2018.

42 Merhat Sharipzhan, "IMU Declares it is Now Part of the Islamic State," *RFERL*, August 6, 2015.

43 Larisa Brown, "UK Jihadis 'Have Joined Slaughter in Afghanistan': Minister Fears 'Porous Borders' Have Allowed Extremists to Leave Syria for the Country," *Daily Mail*, January 29, 2018.

44 Tom O'Connor, "Where Will IS Be in 2018? Iran Says Afghanistan and Pakistan Are Next as Islamic State Loses Iraq and Syria," *Newsweek*, December 12, 2017.

45 Idrees Ali, "Air Strikes Hit Islamic State in Afghanistan Under New Rules: U.S.," Reuters, April 14, 2016.

46 W. J. Hennigan, "Air Force Drops Non-Nuclear 'Mother of All Bombs' in Afghanistan," *Los Angeles Times*, April 13, 2017.

47 Jo Becker and Eric Schmitt, "As Trump Wavers on Libya, an ISIS Haven, Russia Presses On," *New York Times*, February 7, 2017

48 Noha Aboueldahab, Tarek M. Yousef, Luiz Pinto, et al., "The Middle East and North Africa in 2018: Challenges, Threats, and Opportunities," Brookings Institution, December 21, 2017.

49 Aaron Y. Zelin, "The Islamic State's Model," *Washington Post* Monkey Cage Blog, January 28, 2015.

50 Aaron Y. Zelin, "The Others: Foreign Fighters in Libya," Washington Institute for Near East Policy, Policy Note No.45, 2018.

51 Malek Bachir and Akram Kharief, "The Slow Death of al Qaeda in Algeria," *Middle East Eye*, February 1, 2018.

52 Khalid Mahmoud, "AFRICOM Expects ISIS Attack on Libya's Oil Crescent," *Asharq Al-Aswat*, January 3, 2018; see also Jeff Seldin, "Defense, Intelligence Officials Warn Against Underestimating Islamic State," *VOA News*, December 31, 2017.

53 Aaron Y. Zelin, "The Islamic State's First Colony in Libya," Washington Institute for Near East Policy, PolicyWatch 2325, October 10, 2014.

54 Benoit Faucon and Matt Bradley, "Islamic State Gained Strength in Libya by Co-Opting Local Jihadists," *Wall Street Journal*, February 17, 2015.

55 Johannes Saal, "The Islamic State's Libyan External Operations Hub: The Picture So Far," *CTC Sentinel*, 10:11, December 2017.

56 Frederic Wehrey and Ala' Alrababa'h, "Rising Out of Chaos: The Islamic State in Libya," *Diwan*, March 5, 2015.

57 Paul Cruickshank, Nic Robertson, Tim Lister, and Jomana Karadsheh, "ISIS Comes to Libya," *CNN*, November 18, 2014.

58 Andrew Engel, "The Islamic State's Expansion in Libya," PolicyWatch 2371, February 11, 2015.

59 David D. Kirkpatrick, Ben Hubbard, and Eric Schmitt, "ISIS's Grip on Libyan City Gives It a Fallback Option," *New York Times*, November 28, 2015. See also Jon Lee Anderson, "ISIS Rises in Libya," *New Yorker*, August 4, 2015.

60 Sudarsan Raghavan, "A Year After ISIS Left, A Battered Libyan City Struggles to Resurrect Itself," *Washington Post*, January 8, 2018.

61 Issandr El Amrani, "How Much of Libya Does the Islamic State Control?" *Foreign Policy*, February 18, 2016.

62 For more, see Christopher S. Chivvis, *Toppling Qaddafi: Libya and the Limits of Liberal Intervention*, Cambridge University Press, 2013.

63 "How Real is the Threat of Returning IS Fighters?" *BBC News*, October 23, 2017.

64 Aaron Y. Zelin, "The Islamic State's Burgeoning Capital in Sirte, Libya," Washington Institute for Near East Policy, Policywatch 2462, August 6, 2015. See also Aaron Y. Zelin, "The Islamic State's Territorial Methodology," Washington Institute for Near East Policy, Research Note No. 29, January 2016.

65 Bennett Seftel, "ISIS Grows and Festers in Lawless Libya," *The Cipher Brief*, January 26, 2018.

66 Ryan Browne, "US Strikes ISIS Targets in Libya for a Second Time in Less Than a Week," CNN.com, September 28, 2017.

67 Johannes Saal, "The Islamic State's Libyan External Operations Hub: The Picture So Far," *CTC Sentinel*, 10:11, December 2017.

68 Frederic Wehrey, "When the Islamic State Came to Libya," *The Atlantic*, February 10, 2018.

69 Marielle Ness, "The Islamic State's Two-Pronged Assault on Turkey," CTC Beyond the Caliphate: Islamic State Activity Outside the Group's Defined Wilayat, January 2018.

70 Eric Schmitt, "Thousands of ISIS Fighters Flee in Syria, Many to Fight Another Day," *New York Times*, February 4, 2018. See also Mike Giglio and Munzer Awad, "The Escape: How ISIS Members Fled the Caliphate, Perhaps to Fight Another Day," Buzzfeed, December 19, 2017.

71 Callimachi, "How a Secretive Branch of ISIS Built a Global Network of Killers"; Jack Moore, "Hundreds of ISIS Fighters are Hiding in Turkey, Increasing Fears of Europe Attacks," *Newsweek*, December 27, 2017.

72 Erin Cunningham and Karim Fahim, "Islamic State Claims Responsibility for Istanbul Nightclub Attack," *Washington Post*, January 2, 2017. See also Ahmet S. Yayla, "The Reina Nightclub Attack and the Threat to Turkey," *CTC Sentinel*, 10:3, March 2017.

73 Ahmet S. Yayla, "ISIS Airmail: The Bomb Shipped from Turkey to Australia," *Wall Street Journal*, August 9, 2017.

74 Colin P. Clarke and Ahmet S. Yayla, "Erdogan's Fatal Blind Spot," *Foreign Policy*, February 15, 2018.

75 Hans Nicholas and Mosheh Gains, "Pentagon Confirms U.S. Ground Operations in Yemen," NBCnews.com, December 20, 2017.

76 Alex Horton, "In a First, U.S. Launches Deadly Strikes on ISIS Training Camps in Yemen," *Washington Post*, October 17, 2017.

77 Hassan Hassan, "ISIS Has Stepped Up Campaigns in Yemen, Egypt, and Afghanistan. The Coalition Fighting It Should Be Worried," *The National*, May 23, 2018.

78 Nadwa al-Dawsari, "Foe Not Friend: Yemeni Tribes and Al Qaeda in the Arabian Peninsula," Project on Middle East Democracy (POMED), February 2018.

79 Elisabeth Kendall, "Impact of the Yemen War on Militant Jihad," POMEPS Studies 29: Politics, Governance, and Reconstruction in Yemen, January 12, 2018: https://pomeps.org/2018/01/12/impact-of-the-yemen-war-on-militant-jihad.

80 Sudarsan Raghavan, "Still Fighting Al Qaeda," *Washington Post*, July 6, 2018.

81 Ben Watson, "The War in Yemen and the Making of a Chaos State," *Defense One*, January 28, 2018.

82 Peter Salisbury, "Yemen: National Chaos, Local Order," Chatham House Research Paper, Middle East and North Africa Programme, December 2017, p. 23.

83 Email exchange with Bruce Hoffman, July 2018.

84 Email exchange with Elisabeth Kendall, July 2018.

85 Colin P. Clarke, "Expanding the ISIS Brand," *National Interest*, February 17, 2018.

86 "Malaysia Arrests Two ISIS Militants Over Planned Attacks on Police Stations and Buddhist Monks," *The Straits Times*, January 22, 2018.

87 Jeffrey Gettleman, "A Mysterious Act of Mercy by the Subway Bombing Suspect," *New York Times*, December 18, 2017. See also Sadanand Dhume, "Bangladesh Exports a New Generation of Terrorists," *Wall Street Journal*, December 28, 2017.

88 Jason Burke, "Al Qaeda Moves In to Recruit from Islamic State and Its Affiliates," *Guardian*, January 19, 2018.

89 Daniel L. Byman, "What Happens When ISIS Goes Underground?" Brookings Institution, January 18, 2018: https://www.brookings.edu/blog/markaz/2018/01/18/what-happens-when-isis-goes-un derground.

90 Vera Mironova and Ekaterina Sergatskova, "Will Former ISIS Fighters Help the Rohingya?" *Foreign Affairs*, September 22, 2017.

91 C. Christine Fair, "Political Islam and Islamist Terrorism in Bangladesh: What You Need to Know," *Lawfare*, January 28, 2018.

92 Rukmini Callimachi, "ISIS Seems to Tailor Attacks for Different Audiences," *New York Times*, July 2, 2016.

93 For more on AQIS, see Alastair Reed, "Al Qaeda in the Indian Subcontinent: A New Frontline in the Global Jihadist Movement?" International Centre for Counter-Terrorism (ICCT) – The Hague, ICCT Policy Brief, May 2015: https://icct.nl/publication/al-qaeda-in-the-indian-subcontintent-a-new-frontline-in-the-glob al-jihadist-movement.

94 Fair, "Political Islam and Islamist Terrorism in Bangladesh."

95 Amira Jadoon, "An Idea or a Threat? Islamic State Jammu & Kashmir," Combating Terrorism Center, February 9, 2018: https://ctc.usma.edu/idea-threat-islamic-state-jammu-kashmir.

96 For more on this subject, see Steve Coll, *Directorate S: The C.I.A. and America's Secret Wars in Afghanistan and Pakistan*, New York: Penguin Press, 2018.

97 Richard C. Paddock, "In Indonesia and Philippines, Militants Find a Common Bond: ISIS," *New York Times*, May 26, 2017.

98 Jeffrey Hutton, "Suicide Bombers Strike Jakarta, Killing 3 Police Officers," *New York Times*, May 25, 2017; Alex Horton, "Family of Suicide Bombers Kills At Least 7 in Indonesia Church Attacks," *New York Times*, May 13, 2017.

99 Michael Peel, "Militant Islamists Shift Focus to Southeast Asia," *Financial Times*, June 18, 2017.

100 Sidney Jones, "How ISIS Transformed Terrorism in Indonesia," *New York Times*, May 22, 2018.

101 Ryan Browne and Barbara Starr, "U.S. Military Official: 50 ISIS Foreign Fighters Captured Since November," CNN.com, December 12, 2017.

102 Edward Delman, "ISIS in the World's Largest Muslim Country," *The Atlantic*, January 3, 2016.

103 Richard C. Paddock, "He Aimed to Fight in Syria. ISIS Had a Broader Plan: Southeast Asia," *New York Times*, September 3, 2017.

104 Joseph Chinyong Liow, "IS in the Pacific: Assessing Terrorism in Southeast Asia and the Threat to the Homeland," testimony before the Subcommittee on Counterterrorism and Intelligence Committee on Homeland Security, House of Representatives, April 27, 2016.

105 Kirsten E. Schultze and Joseph Chinyong Liow, "Making Jihadis, Waging Jihad: Transnational and Local Dimensions of the ISIS Phenomenon in Indonesia and Malaysia," *Asian Security*, 2018: https://www.tandfonline.com/doi/abs/10.1080/14799855.2018.1424710?journalCode=fasi20.

106 Nava Nuraniyah, "Migrant Maids and Nannies for Jihad," *New York Times*, July 18, 2017.

107 Patrick B. Johnston and Colin P. Clarke, "Is the Philippines the Next Caliphate?" *Foreign Policy*, November 28, 2017.

108 Felipe Villamor, "ISIS Threat in Philippines Spreads in Remote Battles," *New York Times*, October 23, 2017. See also James Griffiths, "ISIS in Southeast Asia: Philippines Battles Growing Threat," CNN.com, May 29, 2017.

109 Lindsay Murdoch, "Marawi Uprising Funded by $1.9 Million from Islamic State," *Sydney Morning Herald*, October 25, 2017.

110 Chandni Vatvani, "9 Suspected Terrorists Arrested in Indonesia," *Channel News Asia*, October 24, 2017.

111 Marielle Ness, "Beyond the Caliphate: Islamic State Activity Outside the Group's Defined Caliphate: Southeast Asia," *CTC Sentinel*, January 2018.

112 Will Edwards, "ISIS' Reach Extends to Southeast Asia," *The Cipher Brief*, August 20, 2017.

113 Email exchange with Zachary Abuza, July 2017.

114 Thomas M. Sanderson, "From the Ferghana Valley to Syria and Beyond: A Brief History of Central Asia Foreign Fighters," Center for Strategic and International Studies, January 5, 2018: https://www.csis.org/analysis/ferghana-valley-syria-and-beyond-brief-history-central-asian-foreign-fighters.

115 Svante Cornell, "Central Asia: Where Did Islamic Radicalization Go?" in Katya Migacheva and Bryan Frederick, eds., *Religion, Conflict, and Stability in the Former Soviet Union*, Santa Monica, CA: RAND Corp., 2018.

116 Mohammed S. Elshimi, "Understanding the Factors Contributing to Radicalisation among Central Asian Labour Migrants in Russia," RUSI Occasional Paper, April 2018: https://www.sfcg.org/wp-content/uploads/2018/04/RUSI-report_Central-Asia-Radicalisation_ENG_24042018.pdf.

117 Thomas F. Lynch III, Michael Bouffard, Kelsey King, and Graham Vickowski, "The Return of Foreign Fighters to Central Asia: Implications for U.S. Counterterrorism Policy," Center

for Strategic Research, Institute for National Strategic Studies, National Defense University, Strategic Perspectives No. 21, October 2016: http://inss.ndu.edu/Portals/68/Documents/strat perspective/inss/Strategic-Perspectives-21.pdf. See also Anna Dyner, Arkadiusz Legiec, and Kacper Rekawak, "Ready to Go? ISIS and Its Presumed Expansion into Central Asia," Polish Institute of International Affairs (PISM), Policy Paper No.19 (121), June 2015.

118 Goktung Sonmez, "Violent Extremism among Central Asians: The Istanbul, St. Petersburg, Stockholm, and New York City Attacks," *CTC Sentinel*, 10:11, December 2017. See also Andrew E. Kramer, "New York Turns Focus to Central Asian Militancy," *New York Times*, November 1, 2017; Sajjan Gohel, "How Uzbekistan Became Ripe Recruiting Territory for ISIS," CNN.com, November 1, 2017.

119 Kim Cragin, "Foreign Fighter 'Hot Potato,'" *Lawfare*, November 26, 2017.

120 Reid Standish, "'Our Future Will Be Violent Extremism,'" *Foreign Policy*, August 1, 2017.

121 Reid Standish, "Scenes from Central Asia's Forever War," *Foreign Policy*, August 7, 2017. See also "Kyrgyzstan: State Fragility and Radicalisation," International Crisis Group, October 3, 2016; and Bruce Pannier, "Are Central Asia's Militants Already Coming Home from the Middle East?" Radio Free Europe / Radio Liberty, May 25, 2018.

122 Eleanor Ross, "Why Extremist Groups are Gaining Strength in Central Asia," *Newsweek*, April 12, 2017. See also Thomas Joscelyn, "The Turkistan Islamic Party's Jihad in Syria," *FDD's Long War Journal*, July 10, 2018; and also Colin P. Clarke and Paul R. Kan, "Uighur Foreign Fighters: An Underexamined Jihadist Challenge," International Centre for Counter-Terrorism – The Hague (ICCT), Policy Brief 8, no. 5, 2017.

123 Jack Moore, "Russia Overtakes Saudi Arabia and Tunisia as Largest Exporter of ISIS Fighters," *Newsweek*, October 24, 2017.

124 Andrew S. Bowen, "ISIS Comes to Russia," *Daily Beast*, July 10, 2015.

125 Ekaterina Sokirianskaia, "Russia's North Caucasus Insurgency

Widens as ISIS' Foothold Grows," *World Politics Review*, April 12, 2016.

126 Colin P. Clarke, "How Russia Became the Jihadists' No. 1 Target," *Politico Magazine*, April 3, 2017.

127 John Campbell, "The Islamic State 'Presence' in the Sahel is More Complicated Than Affiliates Suggest," Council on Foreign Relations (CFR), June 1, 2018.

128 Jacob Wirtschafter and Karim John Gadiaga, "Africa Becomes the New Battleground for ISIS and al Qaeda as They Lose Ground in the Mideast," *USA Today*, October 25, 2017.

129 Wesley Morgan, "Behind the Secret U.S. War in Africa," *Politico*, July 2, 2018.

130 Jacob Zenn, "Boko Haram's Al Qaeda Affiliation: A Response to Five Myths about Boko Haram," *Lawfare*, February 1, 2018.

131 Ryan Browne, "US Wars of Growing African Terror Threat," CNN. com, April 19, 2018. The author is also thankful to Jason Warner for help with estimates of IS fighters in various African affiliates. Email exchanges with Jason Warner, July 2018.

132 Jason Warner and Caleb Weiss, "A Legitimate Challenger? Assessing the Rivalry between al-Shabaab and the Islamic State in Somalia," *CTC Sentinel*, 10:10, November 2017.

133 Jason Warner, "Sub-Saharan Africa's Three 'New' Islamic State Affiliates," *CTC Sentinel*, 10:1, January 2017.

134 Bennett Seftel, "Al Qaeda Thrives Across Weak West African States," *Cipher Brief*, September 14, 2017.

135 Cristina Maza, "ISIS and Al Qaeda Terrorists Increase Attacks on Western Targets in Africa, Report Reveals," *Newsweek*, February 26, 2018.

136 Caleb Weiss, "Al Qaeda Has Launched More Than 100 Attacks in West Africa in 2016," *FDD's Long War Journal*, June 8, 2016. See also Drew Hinshaw and Zoumana Wonogo, "Al Qaeda Attacks in Burkina Faso Kill At Least 30," *Wall Street Journal*, January 17, 2016.

137 Daveed Gartenstein-Ross, Jacob Zenn, Sarah Sheafer, and Sandro Bejdic, "Evolving Terror: The Development of Jihadist Operations

Targeting Western Interests in Africa," Foundation of Defense for Democracies, February 2018: https://www.thefdd.org/analysis/2018/02/25/evolving-terror-the-development-of-jihadist-operations-targeting-western-interests-in-africa.

138 Yaroslav Trofimov, "In Somalia – or Afghanistan – Can Insurgent Defections Change a War's Course?" *Wall Street Journal*, February 8, 2018.

139 Sunguta West, "The Resurgence of al-Shabaab," Jamestown Foundation, Terrorism Monitor, February 8, 2018: https://jamestown.org/program/resurgence-al-shabaab.

140 Rukmini Callimachi, "Al-Qaeda Backed Group Has a New Target: Plastic Bags," *New York Times*, July 4, 2018

141 Warner and Weiss, "A Legitimate Challenger?"

142 Jason Warner and Ellen Chapin, "Targeted Terror: The Suicide Bombers of al-Shabaab," Combating Terrorism Center, February 13, 2018: https://ctc.usma.edu/targeted-terror-suicide-bombers-al-shabaab. Despite this massive death toll, Warner and Chapin's detailed analysis concluded that the attacks actually attempt to avoid targeting non-combatant civilians.

143 Tricia Bacon, "This is Why al-Shabaab Won't Be Going Away Any Time Soon," *Washington Post* Monkey Cage Blog, July 6, 2017.

144 Daisy Muibu and Benjamin P. Nickels, "Foreign Technology or Local Expertise? Al-Shabaab's IED Capability," *CTC Sentinel*, 10:10, November 2017.

145 "The Fight Against the Islamic State is Moving to Africa," *The Economist*, July 14, 2018.

146 Clayton Thomas, "Al Qaeda and U.S. Policy: Middle East and Africa," Congressional Research Service (CRS) Report R43756, February 5, 2018.

147 Olivier Monnier, "Islamic State, al Qaeda Support Fuels Attacks in West Africa," *Bloomberg*, February 5, 2018.

148 "The Social Roots of Jihadist Violence in Burkina Faso's North," International Crisis Group, Report No. 254, October 12, 2017: https://www.crisisgroup.org/africa/west-africa/burkina-faso/254-social-roots-jihadist-violence-burkina-fasos-north.

149 Caleb Weiss, "Al Qaeda Branch in Mali Claims Burkina Faso Attacks," *FDD's Long War Journal*, March 5, 2018.

150 Jacob Zenn, "Demystifying al Qaeda in Nigeria: Cases from Boko Haram's Founding, Launch of Jihad and Suicide Bombings," *Perspectives on Terrorism*, 11:6, 2017.

151 "IS Affiliate Establishes Stronghold in West Africa," Reuters, April 29, 2018.

152 John Vandiver, "ISIS, Routed in Iraq and Syria, is Quietly Gaining Strength in Africa," *Stars and Stripes*, February 17, 2018.

153 Helene Cooper, "Boko Haram and ISIS Are Collaborating More, U.S. Military Says," *New York Times*, April 20, 2016.

154 Carla Babb, "Congressman Says Africa Next 'Hot Spot' for Islamic State," *VOA News*, December 7, 2017.

155 International Centre for Counter-Terrorism (ICCT) – The Hague, "Foreign Fighters Phenomenon in the EU: Profiles, Threats and Policies," 2016: https://icct.nl/publication/report-the-foreign-fighters-phenomenon-in-the-eu-profiles-threats-policies.

156 Vidino et al., *Fear Thy Neighbor*, pp. 15–16.

157 Marc Hecker and Elie Tenenbaum, "France vs. Jihadism: The Republic in a New Age of Terror," IFRI, January 2017: https://www.ifri.org/en/publications/notes-de-lifri/notes-de-lifri/france-vs-jihadism-republic-new-age-terror.

158 William McCants and Christopher Meserole, "The French Connection," *Foreign Affairs*, March 24, 2016: https://www.foreignaffairs.com/articles/2016-03-24/french-connection.

159 Conrad Hackett, "5 Facts About the Muslim Population in Europe," Pew Research Center, November 29, 2017.

160 Gilles Kepel, Tamara Cofman Wittes, and Matthew Levitt, "The Rise of Jihad in Europe: Views from France," Washington Institute for Near East Policy, PolicyWatch 2806, May 19, 2017: https://www.washingtoninstitute.org/policy-analysis/view/the-rise-of-jihad-in-europe-views-from-france.

161 Laurence Peter, "How France is Wrestling with Jihadist Terror," *BBC News*, July 28, 2016.

162 Mitch Prothero, "Their Parents Fought with ISIS. Now France is

Trying to Figure Out What to Do with Them," Buzzfeed, February 19, 2018.

163 Fidelma Cook and Jake Wallis Simons, "Jihadi Capital of France," *Daily Mail*, November 18, 2015.

164 George Heil, "The Berlin Attack and the 'Abu Walaa' Islamic State Recruitment Network," *CTC Sentinel*, 10:2, February 2017.

165 Daniel H. Heinke, "German Foreign Fighters in Syria and Iraq: The Updated Data and Its Implications," *CTC Sentinel*, 10:3, March 2017.

166 Caroline Copley and Madeline Chambers, "Germany Bans Islamist 'True Religion' Group, Raiding Mosques and Flats," Reuters, November 15, 2016.

167 "Germany Terrorism Prosecution Cases Soar," *Deutsche Welle*, October 22, 2017.

168 Jamie Dettmer, "Germany Alarmed by 'Kindergarten Jihadists,'" *VOA News*, February 2, 2018.

169 Liam Stack, "Terrorist Attacks in Britain: A Short History," *New York Times*, June 4, 2017.

170 Alexander Meleagrou-Hitchens and Seamus Hughes, "The Threat to the United States from the Islamic State's Virtual Entrepreneurs," *CTC Sentinel*, 10:3, March 2017; see also "Who Are Britain's Jihadists?" *BBC News*, October 12, 2017.

171 Michael Kenney, Stephen Coulthart, and Dominick Wright, "Structure and Performance in a Violent Extremist Network," *Journal of Conflict Resolution*, 61:10, 2017, pp. 2208–34.

172 Email exchange with Michael Kenney, June 2018.

173 Lizzie Dearden, "UK Home to Up to 25,000 Islamist Extremists Who Could Pose a Threat, EU Official Warns," *Independent*, September 1, 2017.

174 Michael Holden, "Teacher Tried to Create 'Army of Children' to Launch Terror Attacks in London," Reuters UK, March 2, 2018.

175 Aaron Williams, Kaeit Hinck, Laris Karklis, Kevin Schaul, and Stephanie Stamm, "How Two Brussels Neighborhoods Became a 'Breeding Ground' for Terror," *Washington Post*, April 1, 2016.

176 Paul Cruickshank, "The Inside Story of the Paris and Brussels Attacks," CNN.com, October 30, 2017.

177 Pieter Van Ostaeyen, "Belgian Radical Networks and the Road to the Brussels Attacks," CTC Sentinel, 9·6, June 2016.

178 By some accounts, Zerkani was responsible for convincing more than 60 young men to go to fight in Iraq and Syria; see Guy Van Vlierden, "Molenbeek and Beyond. The Brussels–Antwerp Axis as Hotbed of Belgian Jihad," in Arturo Varvelli, ed., *Jihadist Hotbeds: Understanding Local Radicalization Processes*, Milan: Italian Institute for International Political Studies (ISPI), 2016.

179 Rik Coolsaet, "Facing the Fourth Foreign Fighters Wave: What Drives Europeans to Syria, and to Islamic State? Insights from the Belgian Case," Egmont Institute, Egmont Paper 81, March 2016, p. 8: www.egmontinstitute.be/facing-the-fourth-foreign-fighters-wave.

180 Teun Voeten, "Molenbeek Broke My Heart," *Politico*, March 23, 2016.

181 Matthew Levitt, "My Journey to Brussels' Terrorist Safe Haven," *Politico*, March 27, 2016.

182 Cynthia Kroet, "Belgium's Molenbeek Home to 51 Groups with Terror Link: Report," *Politico*, March 20, 2017.

183 Thomas Renard and Rik Coolsaet, "Reassessing Belgium's 'Failed' Counterterrorism Policy," *Lawfare*, March 22, 2018. See also Rik Coolsaet and Thomas Renard, "Returnees: Who Are They, Why Are They (Not) Coming Back and How Should We Deal with Them? Assessing Policies on Returning Foreign Terrorist Fighters in Belgium, Germany, and The Netherlands," Egmont Institute, February 6, 2018.

4 From "Remain and Expand" to Survive and Persist

1 Jonathan Spyer, "Welcome to Syria 2.0," *Foreign Policy*, January 25, 2018.

2 Colin P. Clarke, "How ISIS is Transforming," *Foreign Affairs*, September 25, 2017.

3 "Experts: ISIS Still Capable of Recapturing Iraqi Areas," *Ahsarq Al-Awsat*, January 19, 2018.

4 Jones et al., *Rolling Back the Islamic State.*

5 Sune Engel Rasmussen, Nour Alakraa, and Nancy A. Youssef, "ISIS Remnants Fight On, Despite U.S. Campaign," *Wall Street Journal*, July 9, 2018.

6 Rhys Dubin, "ISIS 2.0 is Really Just the Original ISIS," *Foreign Policy*, April 3, 2018.

7 Johnston et al., *Foundations of the Islamic State.*

8 Raja Abdulrahim, "Islamic State Returns to Guerrilla Warfare in Iraq and Syria," *Wall Street Journal*, January 2, 2018. See also Eric Schmitt, "The Hunt for ISIS Pivots to Remaining Pockets of Syria," *New York Times*, December 24, 2017.

9 Hassan Hassan, "Insurgents Again: The Islamic State's Calculated Reversion to Attrition in the Syria–Iraq Border Region and Beyond," *CTC Sentinel*, 10:11, December 2017.

10 Hassan Hassan, "Down but Not Out: ISIL Will Regroup and Rise Again," *The National*, December 25, 2017.

11 Benjamin Bahney and Patrick B. Johnston, "ISIS Could Rise Again," *Foreign Affairs*, December 15, 2017.

12 Borzou Daraghi, "After the Black Flags of ISIS, Iraq Now Faces the White Flags," Buzzfeed, April 1, 2018.

13 Qassim Abdul-Zahra and Susannah George, "Islamic State Haunts Northern Iraq Months After Its Defeat," Associated Press, March 28, 2018. See also "Islamic State Regrouping in Iraqi, Disputed Kurdish Territories," *VOA News*, March 26, 2018.

14 Hassan Hassan, "ISIL Sleeper Cells in Iraq Are a Warning Sign the Extremist Group is Already Reforming," *The National*, March 28, 2018.

15 Vera Bergengruen, "Trump Keeps Saying ISIS Has Been Defeated. But the U.S. Military Says It's Gaining Ground," Buzzfeed, April 17, 2018. See also Hassan Hassan, "ISIS is Ready for a Resurgence," *The Atlantic*, August 26, 2018.

16 Shiraz Maher, "Islamic State is Not Beaten and Will Return," *New Statesmen*, October 17, 2017. See also Sune Engel Rasmussen,

"Online Propaganda Builds Islamic State Brand in the Face of Military Losses," *Wall Street Journal*, August 26, 2018.

17 Sune Engel Rasmussen, "Islamic State Leader Emerges in Audio Message," *Wall Street Journal*, August 22, 2018. See also Hassan, "ISIS is Ready for a Resurgence."

18 Hassan Hassan, "Zawahiri's Statements Reveal Plenty About Syria's Fractured Jihadi Scene," *The National*, November 29, 2017.

19 Charles Lister, "New Opportunities for ISIS and Al Qaeda," in Paul Salem, Bilal Y. Saab, Alex Vatanka, et al., "2018 Middle East Preview: What to Expect," Middle East Institute, January 8, 2018.

20 Gareth Browne, "Al Qaeda's 'Re-Radicalisation' Schools Lure ISIL Fighters in Syria," *The National*, January 20, 2018.

21 Daniel L. Byman, "The Middle East After the Defeat of the Islamic State," Brookings Institution, March 28, 2018: https://www.brookings.edu/blog/order-from-chaos/2018/03/28/the-middle-east-after-the-defeat-of-the-islamic-state.

22 Jones, *Waging Insurgent Warfare*, pp. 18–19.

23 Assaf Moghadam, *Nexus of Global Jihad: Understanding Cooperation Among Terrorist Actors*, New York: Columbia University Press, 2017, p. 168.

24 Christoph Reuter, "'Liberated Areas' of Iraq Still Terrorized By Violence," *Der Spiegel*, March 21, 2018.

25 Sirwan Kajjo, "ISIS: Surging in Syria Again," Gatestone Institute International Policy Council, March 27, 2018: https://www.gatestoneinstitute.org/12097/isis-surging-syria.

26 Rhys Dubin, "Coalition Analysis Warns of Potential Islamic State Resurgence," *Foreign Policy*, January 10, 2018.

27 Michael R. Gordon, "Areas Newly Seized from ISIS Seen at Risk of Backsliding," *Wall Street Journal*, December 12, 2017.

28 Erika Solomon and Asser Khattab, "ISIS 'Far from Finished' as Jihadi Fighters Regroup in Syria," *Financial Times*, February 3, 2018.

29 Jeff Seldin, "IS Fighters Fleeing to Assad-controlled Parts of Syria," *VOA News*, December 27, 2017.

30 Shelly Culbertson and Linda Robinson, *Making Victory Count*

After Defeating ISIS: Stabilization Challenges in Mosul and Beyond, Santa Monica, CA: RAND Corp., 2017.

31 Tamer El-Ghobashy, Mustafa Salim, and Louisa Loveluck, "Islamic State's 'Caliphate' Has Been Toppled in Iraq and Syria. Why Isn't Anyone Celebrating?" *Washington Post*, December 5, 2017.

32 Hassan Hassan and William McCants, "Is ISIS Good at Governing?" Brookings Institution, April 18, 2016: https://www.brookings.edu/blog/markaz/2016/04/18/experts-weigh-in-part-7-is-isis-good-at-governing.

33 Joby Warrick, Will McCants, and Aaron Y. Zelin, "The Rise of ISIS: 'Remaining and Expanding,'" The Washington Institute for Near East Policy, PolicyWatch 2522, November 12, 2015.

34 Email exchange with Haroro Ingram, August 2018.

35 Daniel L. Byman, "Comparing Al Qaeda and ISIS: Different Goals, Different Targets," prepared testimony before the Subcommittee on Counterterrorism and Intelligence of the House Committee on Homeland Security, House of Representatives, April 29, 2015.

36 Clarke and Ingram, "Defeating the ISIS Nostalgia Narrative."

37 Email exchange with Craig Whiteside, August 2018.

38 Colin Clarke and Daveed Gartenstein-Ross, "How Will Jihadist Strategy Evolve as the Islamic State Declines?" *War on the Rocks*, November 10, 2016.

39 Daniel Byman, "Divisions Within the Global Jihad," *Lawfare*, September 29, 2017.

40 Robin Wright, "After the Islamic State," *New Yorker*, December 12, 2016.

41 Tore Refslund Hamming, "Jihadi Competition and Political Preferences," *Perspectives on Terrorism*, 11:6, 2017.

42 Moghadam, "How Al Qaeda Innovates," pp. 466-97.

43 Daveed Gartenstein-Ross, "The Manchester Attack Shows How Terrorists Learn," *The Atlantic*, May 23, 2017.

44 Bridget Moreng, "ISIS' Virtual Puppeteers," *Foreign Affairs*, September 21, 2016; see also Clint Watts, "Inspired, Networked &

Directed – The Muddled Jihad of IS & Al Qaeda Post Hebdo," *War on the Rocks*, January 12, 2015.

45 Daveed Gartenstein-Ross and Madeline Blackman, "ISIL's Virtual Planners: A Critical Terrorist Innovation," *War on the Rocks*, January 4, 2017.

46 Rukmini Callimachi, "Not 'Lone Wolves' After All: How ISIS Guides World's Terror Plots from Afar," *New York Times*, February 4, 2017.

47 R. Kim Cragin and Ari Weil, "'Virtual Planners' in the Arsenal of Islamic State External Operations," *Orbis*, 62:2, 2018, pp. 294–312.

48 R. Kim Cragin, "The November 2015 Paris Attacks: The Impact of Foreign Fighter Returnees," *Orbis*, 61:2, 2017, pp. 212–26. See also R. Kim Cragin, "The Challenge of Foreign Fighter Returnees," *Journal of Contemporary Criminal Justice*, 33:3, 2017, pp. 292–312.

49 Seth G. Jones, "Will Al Qaeda Make a Comeback?" *Foreign Affairs*, August 7, 2017.

50 Clarke, "The Moderate Face of Al Qaeda."

51 Tore Refslund Hamming, "The Al Qaeda – Islamic State Rivalry: Competition Yes, but No Competitive Escalation," *Terrorism and Political Violence*, 2017, p. 3. Salafi characterizes an adherent of an ideological strain in Sunni Islam that seeks to emulate, as purer, the thinking and practices of Muhammad and the earliest generations of Muslims. Jihadists believe that violent struggle against non-Muslims and Muslims they judge as apostate is an important religious duty (Bahney et al., *An Economic Analysis of the Financial Records of al-Qa'ida in Iraq*).

52 Cole Bunzel, "Jihadism on Its Own Terms," Hoover Institution, May 17, 2017: https://www.hoover.org/research/jihadism-its-own-terms.

53 Rik Coolsaet, "Anticipating the Post-Daesh Landscape," Egmont Paper 97, October 2017, p. 9: http://www.egmontinstitute.be/anticipating-post-daesh-landscape.

54 Hassan, "The Sectarianism of the Islamic State."

55 Thomas Joscelyn, "Islamic State Rescinds One of Its Most

Problematic Religious Rulings," *FDD's Long War Journal*, September 20, 2017.

56 Cole Bunzel, "A House Divided: Origins and Persistence of the Islamic State's Ideological Divide," *Jihadica*, June 5, 2018.

57 R. Green, "Dispute Over Takfir Rocks Islamic State," *MEMRI*, August 4, 2017.

58 Tore Hamming, "The Extremist Wing of the Islamic State," *Jihadica*, June 9, 2016.

59 Byman, "Divisions Within the Global Jihad."

60 Daveed Gartenstein-Ross, Jason Fritz, Bridget Moreng, and Nathaniel Barr, "Islamic State vs. Al Qaeda," New America Foundation, December 1, 2015: https://static.newamerica.org/attachments/12103-islamic-state-vs-al-qaeda/ISISvAQ_Final.e68 fdd22a90e49c4af1d4cd0dc9e3651.pdf.

61 Hamming, "The Al Qaeda – Islamic State Rivalry: Competition Yes, but No Competitive Escalation," fn. 65.

62 Daveed Gartenstein-Ross and Nathaniel Barr, "How Al Qaeda Survived the Islamic State Challenge," Hudson Institute, March 1, 2017: https://www.hudson.org/research/12788-how-al-qaeda-survived-the-islamic-state-challenge.

63 Matthew Phillips and Matthew Valasik, "The Islamic State is More Like a Street Gang Than Like Other Terrorist Groups," *Washington Post* Monkey Cage Blog, November 15, 2017.

64 Colin P. Clarke, "Al Qaeda in Syria Can Change Its Name, But Not Its Stripes," *The Cipher Brief*, March 23, 2017.

65 Charles Lister, "US Officials Just Mislabeled a Syrian Terror Group as al Qaeda. Worse, They're Missing a Far Bigger Threat," *Defense One*, June 1, 2018.

66 Email exchange with Hassan Hassan, August 2018.

67 Clarke, "The Moderate Face of Al Qaeda."

68 Colin P. Clarke, "Expanding the ISIS Brand," *The National Interest*, February 17, 2018.

69 Rukmini Callimachi, "Protest of U.S. Terror Listing Offers a Glimpse of Qaeda Strategy," *New York Times*, November 17, 2016; see also Daveed Gartenstein-Ross and Thomas Joscelyn,

"Rebranding Terror," *Foreign Affairs*, August 20, 2016; and Daveed Gartenstein-Ross and Nathaniel Barr, "Extreme Makeover, Jihadist Edition. Al Qaeda's Rebranding Campaign," *War on the Rocks*, September 3, 2015.

70 Colin P. Clarke and Barak Mendelsohn, "Al Qaeda's Ruthless Pragmatism Makes It More Dangerous Than the Islamic State," Reuters, October 27, 2016.

71 The author is thankful to Bruce Hoffman for this observation.

72 Colin P. Clarke and Chad C. Serena, "Why Syria's War May Be About to Get Even Worse," Reuters, August 25, 2016.

73 Bruce Hoffman, "Al Qaeda's Master Plan," *The Cipher Brief*, November 18, 2015.

74 Eric Schmitt and David E. Sanger, "As U.S. Focuses on ISIS and the Taliban, Al Qaeda Re-emerges," *New York Times*, December 29, 2015.

75 Bruce Hoffman, "Al Qaeda: Quietly and Patiently Rebuilding," *The Cipher Brief*, December 30, 2016.

76 Gartenstein-Ross and Barr, "How Al Qaeda Survived the Islamic State Challenge."

77 The Soufan Center, "The Forgotten War: The Ongoing Disaster in Yemen," June 2018: http://thesoufancenter.org/research/the-forgotten-war-the-ongoing-disaster-in-yemen.

78 Bruce Hoffman, "The Global Terror Threat and Counterterrorism Challenges Facing the Next Administration," *CTC Sentinel*, 9:11, December 2016.

79 Andrew H. Kydd and Barbara F. Walter, "The Strategies of Terrorism," *International Security*, 31:1, Summer 2006, pp. 49–80.

80 Bruce Hoffman, "The Coming ISIS–Al Qaeda Merger: It's Time to Take the Threat Seriously," *Foreign Affairs*, March 29, 2016.

81 Bruce Hoffman, "A Growing Terrorist Threat on Another 9/11," *Wall Street Journal*, September 8, 2017.

82 Assaf Moghadam, "Marriage of Convenience: The Evolution of Iran and al Qaeda's Tactical Cooperation," *CTC Sentinel*, 10:4, April 2017. See also Adrian Levy and Cathy Scott-Clark, "Al Qaeda

Has Rebuilt Itself – With Iran's Help," *The Atlantic*, November 11, 2017.

83 Email exchange with Hassan Hassan, August 2018.
84 Email exchange with Seth G. Jones, July 2018.
85 Email exchange with Bruce Hoffman, July 2018.
86 Tore Refslund Hamming, "With Islamic State in Decline, What's Al Qaeda's Next Move?" *War on the Rocks*, April 27, 2018.
87 Bruce Hoffman, "Al Qaeda's Resurrection," Council on Foreign Relations, March 6, 2018: https://www.cfr.org/expert-brief/al-qaedas-resurrection.

5 After the Caliphate: Preventing the Islamic State's Return

1 Seth G. Jones, Charles Vallee, Nicholas Harrington, and Hannah Byrne, "The Evolving Terrorist Threat: The Changing Nature of the Islamic State, Al-Qaeda, and Other Salafi-Jihadist Groups," Center for Strategic and International Studies: https://www.isis.org/analysis/evolution-salafi-jihadist-threat.
2 Rukmini Callimachi, "ISIS Leader Baghdadi Resurfaces in Recording," *New York Times*, August 22, 2018.
3 Lorne L. Dawson, "The Demise of the Islamic State and the Fate of Its Western Foreign Fighters: Six Things to Consider," International Centre for Counter-Terrorism – The Hague (ICCT), ICCT Policy Brief, June 2018, p. 4.
4 R. Kim Cragin has argued that, contrary to popular belief, most foreign fighters do not die on battlefields or travel from conflict to conflict, but return home. See Cragin, "The Challenge of Foreign Fighter Returnees."
5 Alastair Reed and Johanna Pohl, "Disentangling the EU Foreign Fighter Threat: The Case for a Comprehensive Approach," *RUSI*, February 10, 2017.
6 Simon Cottee, "Pilgrims to the Islamic State," *The Atlantic*, July 24, 2015.
7 Jessica Stern and J. M. Berger, "ISIS and the Foreign Fighter Phenomenon," *The Atlantic*, March 8, 2015.

8 See Callimachi, "Not 'Lone Wolves' After All"; see also Gartenstein-Ross and Blackman, "ISIL's Virtual Planners"; and Alexander Meleagrou-Hitchens and Seamus Hughes, "The Threat to the United States from the Islamic State's Virtual Entrepreneurs," *CTC Sentinel*, 10: 3, March 2017, pp. 1–8.

9 Thomas Hegghammer, "Should I Stay or Should I Go? Explaining Variation in Western Jihadists' Choice between Domestic and Foreign Fighting," *American Political Science Review*, 107:1, February 2013, pp. 1–15.

10 Cragin, "The November 2015 Paris Attacks," pp. 212–26.

11 Callimachi, "How a Secretive Branch of ISIS Built a Global Network of Killers"; see also Hoffman, "The Global Terror Threat and Counterterrorism Challenges Facing the Next Administration."

12 Daniel Byman, "Where Will the Islamic State Go Next?" *Lawfare*, June 22, 2018.

13 United Nations Security Council Counter-Terrorism Committee Executive Directorate (CTED), "The Challenge of Returning and Relocating Foreign Terrorist Fighters: Research Perspectives," April 2018.

14 Radicalisation Awareness Network (RAN) Manual, "Responses to Returnees: Foreign Terrorist Fighters and Their Families," July 2017.

15 "Belgian Investigators Shed Light on Liège Gunman as IS Group Claims Attack," *France 24*, May 30, 2018.

16 Robin Wright, "ISIS Jihadis Have Returned Home by the Thousands," *New Yorker*, October 23, 2017.

17 Yolande Knell, "Inside the Iraqi Courts Sentencing IS Suspects to Death," *BBC News*, September 2, 2017.

18 Will Worley, "At Least 100 European ISIS Fighters 'To Be Prosecuted in Iraq, With Most Facing Death Penalty,'" *Independent*, October 7, 2017.

19 Tanya Mehra, "Bringing (Foreign) Terrorist Fighters to Justice in a Post-ISIS Landscape Part I: Prosecution by Iraqi and Syrian Courts," International Centre for Counter-Terrorism – The Hague (ICCT), December 22, 2017.

20 Hollie McKay, "Syrian Opposition, Out of Jail Space, Fears Threat of Released ISIS Prisoners," *Fox News*, May 29, 2018.

21 Eric Schmitt, "Battle to Stamp Out ISIS in Syria Gains New Momentum, but Threats Remain," *New York Times*, May 30, 2018.

22 Tanya Mehra, "Bringing (Foreign) Terrorist Fighters to Justice in a Post-ISIS Landscape Part II: Prosecution by National Courts," International Centre for Counter-Terrorism – The Hague, January 12, 2018.

23 Jenna Consigli, "Prosecuting the Islamic State Fighters Left Behind," *Lawfare*, August 1, 2018.

24 Margaret Coker and Falih Hassan, "A 10-Minute Trial, a Death Sentence: Iraqi Justice for Iraqi Suspects," *New York Times*, April 17, 2018.

25 Alissa J. Rubin, "She Left France to Fight in Syria. Now She Wants to Return. But Can She?" *New York Times*, January 11, 2018.

26 Ben Hubbard, "Wives and Children of ISIS: Warehoused in Syria, Unwanted Back Home," *New York Times*, July 4, 2018.

27 Jamie Grierson and Caelainn Barr, "Police Facing Surge in Extremists Released from Jail, Analysis Finds," *Guardian*, June 3, 2018.

28 Anthony Loyd, "A Close Encounter with British ISIS Jihadis," *New Statesman*, June 20, 2018.

29 Paul Sonne, Devlin Barrett, and Ellen Nakashima, "U.S. and Britain Are Divided Over What to Do with Captured IS Fighters," *Washington Post*, February 14, 2018.

30 Kevin Baron, "US-Backed Syrian Force Holding 'Hundreds' of Foreign Fighters," *Defense One*, February 1, 2018.

31 Tanya Mehra, "Bringing (Foreign) Terrorist Fighters to Justice in a Post-ISIS Landscape Part III: Collecting Evidence from Conflict Situations," International Centre for Counter-Terrorism – The Hague, June 12, 2018.

32 Christophe Paulussen and Kate Pitcher, "Prosecuting (Potential) Foreign Fighters: Legislative and Practical Challenges," International Centre for Counter-Terrorism – The Hague (ICCT), ICCT Research Paper, January 2018.

33 Department of Justice, Office of Public Affairs, "Former Iraqi Terrorists Living in Kentucky Sentenced for Terrorist Activities," Press Release, January 29, 2013.

34 Georgia Holmer and Adrian Shtuni, "Returning Foreign Fighters and the Reintegration Imperative," United States Institute for Peace (USIP), Special Report 402, March 2017.

35 Georgia Holmer, "What to Do When Foreign Fighters Come Home," *Foreign Policy*, June 1, 2015.

36 Arsla Jawaid, "From Foreign Fighters to Returnees: The Challenges of Rehabilitation and Reintegration Policies," *Journal of Peacebuilding and Development*, 12:2, 2017, pp. 102–7; see also Andrew Higgins, "For Jihadists, Denmark Tries Rehabilitation," *New York Times*, December 13, 2014.

37 Lucy Williamson, "How France Hopes to Help Radicals Escape Jihadist Net," *BBC News*, February 28, 2018.

38 Fabian Merz, "Dealing with Jihadist Returnees: A Tough Challenge," Center for Security Studies (CSS), Report no. 210, June 2018.

39 "How Belgium Copes with Returning Islamic State Fighters," *The Economist*, December 19, 2017.

40 Charles Lister, "Returning Foreign Fighters: Criminalization or Reintegration?" Brookings Institution Policy Briefing, August 2015.

41 Jessica Trisko Darden, "Compounding Violent Extremism? When Efforts to Prevent Violence Fail," *War on the Rocks*, June 6, 2018.

42 Humera Khan, "Why Countering Extremism Fails," *Foreign Affairs*, February 18, 2015.

43 Walle Bos et al., "Capacity-Building Challenges: Identifying Progress and Remaining Gaps in Dealing with Foreign (Terrorist) Fighters," International Centre for Counter-Terrorism – The Hague (ICCT), ICCT Policy Brief, May 2018.

44 Dipesh Gadher, "Generation Jihad: The British Children Brutalised by Terror," *The Times*, March 25, 2018.

45 Kinana Qaddour, "ISIS's War on Families Never Ended," *Foreign Policy*, February 1, 2018.

46 Jacob Olidort, "Inside the Caliphate's Classroom: Textbooks, Guidance Literature, and Indoctrination Methods of the Islamic State," The Washington Institute for Near East Policy, Policy Focus 147, August 2016.

47 Clarke and Ingram, "Defeating the ISIS Nostalgia Narrative."

48 Robin Simcox, "Children of the Caliphate: Victims or Threat?" *Lawfare*, December 10, 2017.

49 Joana Cook and Gina Vale, "From Daesh to 'Diaspora': Tracing the Women and Minors of Islamic State," International Centre for the Study of Radicalisation (ISCR), 2018.

50 Liesbeth van der Heide and Jip Geenen, "Children of the Caliphate: Young IS Returnees and the Reintegration Challenge," International Centre for Counter-Terrorism – The Hague (ICCT), ICCT Research Paper, August 2017.

51 Patrick B. Johnston, "Does Decapitation Work? Assessing the Effectiveness of Leadership Targeting in Counterinsurgency Campaigns," *International Security*, 36:4, Spring 2012, pp. 47–79.

52 Ben Connable and Martin C. Libicki, *How Insurgencies End*, Santa Monica, CA: RAND Corp., 2010.

53 Eric Schmitt, "ISIS May Be Waning, But Global Threats of Terrorism Continue to Spread," *New York Times*, July 6, 2018.

54 Anne Gearan and Dan Lamothe, "From Iraq to Syria, Splinter Groups Now Larger Worry Than Al Qaeda," *Washington Post*, June 10, 2014.

55 Audrey Kurth Cronin, "How al Qaeda Ends: The Decline and Demise of Terrorist Groups," *International Security*, 31:1, Summer 2006, pp. 7–48.

56 Jonathan Powell, "Negotiate with ISIS," *The Atlantic*, December 7, 2015.

57 Brian Michael Jenkins and Colin P. Clarke, "In the Event of the Islamic State's Untimely Demise . . .," *Foreign Policy*, May 11, 2016.

58 Email exchange with Daveed Gartenstein-Ross, August 2018.

59 Coolsaet, "Anticipating the Post-Daesh Landscape," p. 22.

60 Berenice Boutin, "Administrative Measures against Foreign

Fighters: In Search of Limits and Safeguards," International Centre for Counter-Terrorism – The Hague (ICCT), December 16, 2016.

61 Daniel Byman, "Frustrated Foreign Fighters," Brookings Institution, July 13, 2017.

62 Andrew Liepman and Colin P. Clarke, "Demystifying the Islamic State," *U.S. News & World Report*, August 19, 2016.

Index